Hollywood's High Noon

THE AMERICAN MOMENT

Stanley I. Kutler

Series Editor

THOMAS CRIPPS

Hollywood's
High Noon

Moviemaking & Society
before Television

The Johns Hopkins University Press

Baltimore & London

© 1997
The Johns Hopkins University Press

Printed in the United States of America
on acid-free paper

06 05 04 03 02 01 00 99 98 97
5 4 3 2 1

The Johns Hopkins University Press
2715 North Charles Street
Baltimore, Maryland 21218-4319
The Johns Hopkins Press Ltd., London

Library of Congress Cataloging-
in-Publication Data will be found
at the end of this book.

A catalog record for this book is
available from the British Library.

ISBN 0-8018-5315-X
ISBN 0-8018-5316-8 (pbk.)

To the memory of Alma and

to a renewal of life with Lynn

Contents

Editor's Foreword

From World War I to the decade following World War II, Americans found their lives, their fantasies, and their hopes in great measure bound up with the movies. During the grim years of the Great Depression, Americans went to the movies nearly three times a week per household and spent more than one percent of their annual income on movie tickets. What better way to escape their ravaged, precarious lives than viewing a Busby Berkeley musical, complete with geometrically designed choruses of beautiful people, "screwball" comedies, bedroom farces (as long as there were twin beds), or an occasional exploration of the underside of life with thinly veiled portraits of famed gangsters? For several generations of Americans, going to the movies was a weekly ritual. After all, what other form of passive recreation could they find?

The dominant, nearly monopolistic, grip that movies had on Americans' use of their leisure time is unimaginable in today's diverse, rich world of recreation and entertainment. Until the advent of television, movies were the most available and utilized popular art form in history. Television broke that grip in the early 1950s. The Hollywood "dream factory" eventually was reinvented—virtually making television its very own subsidiary—but the totality of its power abruptly ended. Movies killed vaudeville and burlesque to acquire their dominance; today, however, Americans have endless choices for their leisure and pleasure. The house itself is a pleasure palace and not simply a place for eating and resting. Television, the care of the house and the land, and the consumption of consumer goods, ranging from furniture to basketball hoops, keep people happy and busy in their homes. Exercise, sports, and easy access to travel also preoccupy Americans today.

Thomas Cripps, a distinguished historian and critic of films who has written the authoritative history of African Americans in films, here offers a rich narrative and analysis of that so-called Golden Age. He understands and considers moviemaking as an art form on its own terms, but he also is keenly aware of the economic significance of what the social philosopher Erich Kahler derisively called the entertainment "industry"—as if to underline the tenuousness of any artistic or aesthetic considerations. Cripps's portrayal of the links between "art" and capitalism are especially thoughtful, devoid of any dull determinism. Movies are business—big business—and always have been. Economically, movies are more important than ever, both as a powerful force in the domestic economy and by contributing substantial credit to the United States' balance of payments. Even more, films from Hollywood have been a dominant force in creating a global culture—with, some sadly note, dubious results.

The history of twentieth-century America cannot be understood without serious attention to the movies and to Americans' preoccupation with them. For the large immigrant and second-generation American population of the twenties and thirties, movies offered their own history and explanation of the nation. The movies tied people to both American dreams and myths, be they westerns, the savagery of the aborigines, the bloody struggle for occupation of the land, or the romanticism of the Civil War. Movies offered blatant propaganda during World War II, but also inspiration and unity. Alas, television in a well-lit living room has been a puny substitute for the transforming magic of the movie palace of yesterday. There, moviegoers seemed to form a special bond from their shared hopes, dreams, and even fears. Those feelings and moments sometimes are in danger of being swallowed in sentimental nostalgia; however, they form a vital, important element of the social history of the twentieth century.

Stanley I. Kutler

THE UNIVERSITY OF WISCONSIN

Acknowledgments

Writing this book has been a humbling experience in that its subject had always been a compelling interest of mine and yet one I viewed from outside the centers of its power. My attention had almost always been given not so much to Hollywood itself as to its historic treatment of African Americans' images. Thus this book on what is called "classical Hollywood" obliged me to enter the capital of, in a way, a foreign culture. And in so doing to reread and rethink a massive literature that would be my guide down a historical path that was, as they say in Hollywood, "the same, only different" from the one I had previously traveled.

It was Henry Y. K. Tom of the Johns Hopkins University Press who suggested that I try to write something about Hollywood's history in this broader context. I owe him a debt of gratitude for encouraging me at every point along the way into this new yet old field. I am grateful, too, for the persistent faith in the project shown by the general editor of The American Moment series, Professor Stanley I. Kutler of the University of Wisconsin. My copyeditor, Deborah Klenotic, taught me to write for a broader audience than students of film history, an audience who might not know the arcana of the movie industry or the argot of the current crop of theoretical historians. Her sense of what a general readership might know or "get" or "see" seemed unerring throughout. And her love of the English language and its rigors did much to clarify the work at hand. Of course, neither she nor the others can be held responsible for my failure to make good use of their suggestions.

Much to their credit, they respected my need to work slowly and deliberately through the saddest time of my life—the last awful, yet enriching year that Alma Taliaferro Cripps, my wife of thirty-nine years, and I were able to share before she died. Parallel to this time of despair, I spent more than a year as Visiting Professor in the Departments of Visual Environment Studies and Afro-American Studies at Harvard University, a rich, stimulating interlude that contributed to this book in many ways. For their boundless hospitality, I extend thanks to the chairs, Alfred Guzzetti and Henry Louis Gates Jr.; Leonie Gordon of the Carpenter Center; and their colleagues who made my time there a productive delight.

Elsewhere I have praised the research libraries and archives of Europe and America that have contributed to my lifetime's research into movie history. They continue to have my abiding gratitude. Here I should like again to cite the Enoch Pratt Free Library of the city of Baltimore. In the face of fiscal adversity and dauntingly changing times, the library has for me remained an ever-flowing spring. The nameless voices of the telephone reference service have made me, as H. L. Mencken said of his own ties to the Pratt in his *Heathen Days* (1943), "one of the most assiduous customers . . . in its whole history." I wish particularly to thank for their seemingly endless favors Faye Houston of the Humanities Department and Marc Sober of the Audio-Visual Department.

Finally, during the course of an otherwise dismal time during which my children, neighbors, and friends together shored up my, and their own, failed spirits, I met and eventually married Lynn Ann Cripps. Together she and her sons, Brian and Jason Ransdell, have restored my spirits in ways that I could not have imagined. The finishing of this book rests both on the memory of almost half a century of one delightful life and on the beginning of a new life with them.

Hollywood's High Noon

Looking at Hollywood's
Classical Era

Why should we be interested in looking again at the movies made in the thirty years between the onset of World War I and the dying embers of World War II? Pauline Kael, perhaps the most influential movie critic alive in the United States today, has recalled that when she was growing up in the 1920s her father found the time and money to go see a western almost every night of the week. During the Great Depression, some Americans admitted to being willing to give up any other amenity in their lives, rather than allow poverty to take away their weekly movie, as much a nourishment as bread. I recall having similar feelings when I began my own moviegoing habit in the late 1930s. My weekly routine started on Wednesday evening, when the split-week change of features occurred. I was back at the theater on Saturday morning for the B western, a "chapter" of a serial, a two-reel comedy, and perhaps a "short subject" (often a didactic film on an "unusual occupation" or a travelogue) or an animated cartoon. Seemingly a full plate for any youngster; nonetheless, the menu seemed scant to the cadre of regulars, myself among them. On Sundays, a major (often Technicolor) motion picture opened, and when a kid reached a certain age there would come a Sunday afternoon that was almost a rite of passage into adolescence: attendance at this "adult" movie. The kid who on Saturday morning made rude noises by blowing through an empty Jujube box found himself the next day scrubbed and in clean linens, watching, say, the *The Ox-Bow Incident* without emitting so much as a cheer for Gil, the good-guy saddletramp. Adulthood dawned when a kid learned the etiquette of moviegoing.

Movies in the classical era of Hollywood, then, formed a nutrient broth of dramatized versions of emotions and ideas—ideas that, far from being handed down unbidden from a ruling authority, were already half-formed in the audience through their prior knowledge and experiences. Surely these movies warrant our attention, for their value to moviegoers in times past as well as for the window they offer on the social, emotional, and political life of our century. And yet, as we shall see, only recently have historians, literary critics, and students of cultural studies taken them up with any intellectual rigor.

Certainly in their own day, these movies were regarded with contempt by both their makers and the high end of the consumers' scale. Many newspaper critics of the day joined with James Agee, the American novelist and film critic, in finding them at best "superb trash." Hollywood itself, the company town where the movies were made, suffered the slings and arrows of its own denizens. "Bonbon town," the radical playwright Clifford Odets called it, as he pocketed his lightly taxed weekly paycheck. "A putty knife factory," the wit H. Allen Smith called it. "A nice place to live," quipped the comedian Fred Allen, "—if you're an orange." In an equally oft-quoted colloquy, three Hollywoodians vied with each other to explain what movies were: "An art form," insisted one. "An industry," said another. "Not so," asserted the third. "Movies are a racket."

To be sure, there were movie men (men, almost always) who were less cynical, but even they regarded their work as nothing more than harmless entertainment. And almost no one in Hollywood concurred with the Communists that Hollywood was tantamount to a state apparatus handing down the ideology of the dominant classes. Even if they did hold strong convictions, few moviemakers would have thought to slather them onto a movie. "If you want to send a message," Sam Goldwyn reputedly said, "call Western Union."

Clearly, moviemaking between the two world wars was all of these things: an entertainment medium that was both art and industry and, in the excesses of its profits, a racket. And yet the audiences seated in the receptive darknesses of their fantastically named and decorated Palaces, Bijous, Hippodromes, Royals, Ritzes, and Grands gave their loyalty largely to movies that pleased them and rarely to movies that argued a political point. Indeed, so loyal were some Americans to the beauties of their Hollywood movies that during the worst of the Depression, they attended as often as three times a week per household and spent more than 1 percent of their annual income on movie tickets.

Ironically, the winsome productions of Hollywood's classical age emerged each week not from ateliers but as though from a bread factory: artfully made, similar enough to last week's batch to entice the regulars, varied enough to seem new and fresh, seemingly unique but made from an oft-used recipe, sold off on the cheap like day-old bread, and as regulated by codes as those loaves sitting in wrappers waiting for the delivery trucks surely were.

Comparing a Hollywood studio to a bread factory is a more flippant formulation than I intended, but let it pass. The point is that Hollywood was a system. It produced commodities for consumption by a variegated audience who formed a sort of movie culture and with whom it had a relationship not unlike the contentious one between painters and patrons in the art world Peter Burke describes in *The Italian Renaissance* (1987). In both cases, buyers were offered—weekly, in Hollywood's case—creations that played to a set of refined expectations. The sources of these expectations in moviegoers were many. The studios, of course, turned out weekly previews of "coming attractions," loaded the newspapers with artful advertising, and helped underwrite the publication of fan magazines. However, word of mouth among moviegoers, some of its aesthetic standards drawn from the broader culture of which they were part, also gave rise to certain expectations. Thus, movie culture was a syncretism of the beliefs of buyer and seller that helped define the product so precisely that many movies came to be designed according to a formula. In turn, the formula allowed studio managers to impose a rational order on production, much as Henry Ford did in Detroit.

The individual studios differed with respect to how they played the game, however. From its ads a reader could guess something of the style of each studio's movies. Warner Bros. represented itself in print with bold, graffiti-like script. Metro-Goldwyn-Mayer's (MGM's) weekly ads took the form of a chatty column headed by a cartoon lion and signed "Leo." RKO's ads imitated the tabloid style of a Hearst newspaper. David O. Selznick affected a quiet dignity befitting his status as an independent who made movies from literary classics. Paramount seemed breezy and flippant, as though its two contract players, Bob Hope and Bing Crosby, appeared in every movie the studio made. Columbia seemed somber in its ads, doing little to rebut the wits' jest that its stinginess made it "the port of missing stars."

In any event, the movies that emerged from the system and were offered to their "world" were entertainments that aroused the fears of only a few groups, such as the clergy, social reformers, and social psychologists, all of whom were concerned mainly for the well-being of children, rather than the body politic.

If it is true that movies in the classical era were no more than "superb trash," why have generations of commentators wrestled with the problem of the meaning of movies and their place in the society that made them? Perhaps it was the challenge to traditional culture implied in the oxymoron "superb trash." Here, a brief word should be said about the history of History. Historians, social scientists, linguists, and litterateurs have only just recently formulated strategies for "interrogating" movies in the name of a broad new discipline called "cultural studies."

Early movie historians typically were retired Hollywoodians, speaking as inside dopesters, or trade paper journalists or reviewers. The most famous of the first generation of this type of movie historian was Terry Ramsaye, who wrote *A Million and One Nights* (1926); the most widely read of the second generation of insiders was Arthur Knight, who contributed *The Liveliest Art* (1957). Both of these writers, and a few others, dominated the literature until the 1970s, when a run of survey histories by scholars of literature or history, among them Garth Jowett and Robert Sklar, began to ask more systematic questions and answer them with tabular data. They strove for a shimmering ideal of objectivity, which they meant to obtain by means of testing primary documents for their credibility, reliability, and authenticity. Only then would the documents reveal the past as it had actually been.

Contributing to this rise of a scholarly literature was the importation of the work of a generation of first German and then French critics who began to ask questions rooted in the fragility, rather than reliability, of surviving documents and in the social, rather than aesthetic, importance of movies. In 1947, Siegfried Kracauer's *From Caligari to Hitler: A Psychological History of German Film* introduced American academics to the notion that societies had psyches to which movies spoke. Thereafter, the study of movies' social significance not only grew, but also was augmented by the work of French critics who borrowed analytical tools from anthropology, linguistics, psychoanalysis, Marxism, and feminism. The link between popular art and society would be decoded!

And yet, these imported theories scarcely would have affected the study of movies had it not been for several parallel lines of development in these and other fields of social and intellectual engagement. First, soon after the end of

World War II, several urban movie men challenged the studios' dominance of the marketplace by booking foreign films into independent houses and playing to an urbane market that had grown cosmopolitan during the war. Second, critics in several weekly newspapers, particularly papers on the political left, began to review the foreign films and contrast them with the Hollywood product. In turn, these critics—Dwight Macdonald, James Agee, Otis Ferguson, and soon, in San Francisco, Pauline Kael—whetted their readers' appetites for foreign reviews, the most accessible of which, appearing in *Films and Filming* and *Sight and Sound,* were blessedly in English. Third, the old Marxist left began to lose credibility and stature. In France, the legend of the Communist-led Resistance against Nazi occupiers could not mask the fact that many intellectuals had a comfortable life under the regime of the *Wehrmacht.* In America, the Marxist left was never able to break free of its Soviet masters and therefore never carved out a specifically Americanist radicalism, a circumstance that went largely unnoticed by several congressional "investigating" committees in their frenzy of unconstitutional prosecution of suspected Communists. However, as a result of opposition to America's presence in Vietnam, a new left that stood apart from both Moscow and the barrenness of the old American left took the field, embraced popular culture as a mode of expression, and carried movies into the universities. With this new constituency of the young left sitting in its classrooms, the academy needed a theoretical base for film study that broke with the early narrativist historians such as Ramsaye and provided a link between movies and society. Finally, drawing on concepts from other fields, a number of French critics, some of them connected to the serials *Cahiers du Cinema* and *Tel Quel,* found their way into English through the writings of the British academics Stephen Heath and Colin McCabe, contributors to the journal *Screen.* Through the semiology branch of linguistics, Jacques Lacan's extensions of Freud's psychoanalysis, Louis Althusser's extensions of Marx, the structuralism created by the anthropologist Claude Lévi-Strauss, Jacques Derrida's deconstruction of language and literature, and Christian Metz's deconstructionist forays into film (to cite but a few workers in the vineyard), movie criticism entered what has come to be known as the postmodern era. Postmodern inquiry's main contribution to scholarship has been to destabilize older forms of formal inquiry into art and challenge their authority.

This book is informed by these new (though now a quarter of a century old) authorities but is not pervaded by them. This is so because I believe the narrative form provides access to analysis and understanding that has been denied by recent critics who argue that narrative, by virtue of its seamless flow of argument, daunts the reader who wishes to challenge it. In the diction of the political left, the narrative is a "bourgeois trick" intended to obfuscate, rather than inform. In *Making Movies Black* (1993), I gently make the case for narrative by invoking Steven Runciman, the Byzantinist who once wrote that the duty of the historian was "to write history," not "reduce history to a series of economic or sociological laws."

By invoking Runciman I do not mean to argue that the documents speak for themselves and that, therefore, no theory at all is necessary. Rather, it seems to me that history has often been guided by circumstance, wambling, tentativeness, chance, and error and to suppose that it has been guided by some inexorable ideology is to miss the point that policies, much like war aims, are contested by "countervailing forces" (as the economist John Kenneth Galbraith writes in *American Capitalism*, 1972). Similarly, in the making of American movies, the adversarial lines were drawn at every stage, from script to screen. Banks withheld lines of credit from moviemakers who wished to take up radical themes; state and local censors ransacked movies in search of deviations from regional mores (and politics); creators of movies struggled for power over the final cut; distributors wheedled theater owners into putting their inventories, and not their rivals', onto downtown screens; and audiences let it be known with their feet and wallets when a movie offended them or amused them. Thus the attention to contest and conflict that so animates Galbraith's analysis of capitalism commends itself to the study of Hollywood, its movies, and its audiences.

So as not to leave the matter entirely in the hands of an analyst of capitalism, it seems noteworthy to point out that the founder of the Italian Communist Party, Antonio Gramsci, arrived at a similar conceptualization of conflict in his analysis of classic Marxism. If his advocates in English are to be trusted—I do not read Italian very well—Gramsci abandoned the notion of a classical Marxist/Leninist proletarian revolution occurring in some future working-class Eden. Rather, he expected conflict to take place in a fluid, contentious arena in which no one adversary would exercise dominance over another. He envisioned a shifting hegemony, with the weak overturning the status quo in times of crisis under the guidance of able organic leaders (rather than Lenin's revolutionary corps waiting in the wings).

By means of this conceptualization of conflict as abrasive, fragmented contentiousness, we might come to understand something of the politics of the popular that made Hollywood from 1920 to 1948 what it was: the producer of apparently trivial entertainments set in a classical form determined in part by the social and political forces at work among its clientele.

Thus the history of a marvelous entertainment machine is what this book is about. It is not about great men ("moguls," as they liked to be called) heroically making great movies. The story is too ironic. And how could it be otherwise, when it is the story of a machine that, although it made a few great movies, was seemingly more concerned with making a sow's ear out of every silk purse it could lay its hands on; that celebrated folkish populism on the screen while busting every union that picketed its gates; that was wedded to an advertising rhetoric that promised new ideas, even as it turned out decades of movies that were merely "the same, only different"; that proclaimed that each new movie "boldly" exposed social problems, only to hedge its reformist bets in the last reel; that trumpeted the freedom of America while knuckling under to censorship.

In short, the history of Hollywood is the story of a crass, pandering, hypocritical, derivative, capitalist moviemaking machine, a machine whose products were *ours,* and we bought at least once a week during its classical era.

CHAPTER ONE

The Incunabula
of Movies

Movies as Americans have come to know them could have resulted only from the clash of the contentious social and technological forces that composed American culture around the turn of the century, when moving-image technology was being developed. This encounter was necessarily preceded by, as the critic Brooks Adams characterizes it in *The Degradation of the Democratic Dogma* (1919), the age of the dynamo, the electromagnetic energizer (better known to us as a generator) that drove everything urban, from the lights of Broadway to the streetcars shuttling masses of people to theaters, baseball parks, and department stores. Had there been no dynamo, there would have been no Roxy, Fenway Park, or Macy's.

The social forces that joined this technological development in defining the American movie started with the individualism that Jefferson learned while he studied the works of the English philosopher John Locke at the College of William and Mary and that he encapsulated in the Declaration of Independence as the unalienable rights of "life, liberty, and the pursuit of happiness" (not "lives, liberties, and . . . property," as Locke had written). The Gilded Age that followed the Civil War saw American business take individual self-interest to its extreme, embracing the social Darwinism that justified both immense wealth and abject poverty. Waves of immigrants soon reached America's shores in search of their own forms of Jeffersonian "happiness."

Amid the ensuing struggles for social justice and equitable wages and the Progressive era's drive to improve urban life, movies were born. That movies might have turned out differently in a different social setting becomes evident when we examine the incunabula of the moving image, the optical toys made to amuse aristocrats in a time before electrical energy, massive industrialism, the heaping together of crowds of fractious adversaries, and the growth of leisured workers in search of diversion and recreation.

Thirty years ago, Kurt W. Marek, author of such popular books on archaeology as *Gods, Graves, and Scholars* and *The Secret of the Hittites*, turned his attention to the history of preindustrial moving images. He adopted an appropriately romantic style in portraying the long line of tinkerers working alone in their labs, dreaming of inventing the magic lantern. Even the book itself, *The Archaeology of the Cinema* (1965), had a romantic look, with its sepia-toned, roughly textured, deckled paper; its marvelous photographs of antique optical curiosa and their inventors; and Marek's own cryptically reversed pseudonym, *C. W. Ceram*, on the cover. No other mode of writing could have better captured the cloistered cleverness of these pioneers of optical theory. Their motives and accomplishments form a startling contrast to the brassy, acquisitive modus operandi of the capitalist *machers* of the age of Hollywood. This age dawned when the enterprise of making moving images passed from the hands of often aristocratic seekers of knowledge into the hands of men in gray suits who transformed movies from quaint artifice into a commercial commodity that dominated a worldwide marketplace.

Unlike the incunabula of print—the handful of extant books that have come down to us from the age of Gutenberg and Caxton—the surviving optical artifacts, often regarded as mere visual toys, have a provenance that stretches over centuries and bear little similarity to the eventual artifact that we call movies. Thus the magic lanterns of yore and today's movies are linked only in the sense that they share a pedigree rooted in optical physics, whereas Gutenberg's Bible is clearly of the same sewn and bound species as the *Random House Bible*.

Therefore, the evolution of magic lanterns is instructive for the light it sheds on the process through which some discoveries and inventions enter into marketplaces and others do not. Although the creators of magic lanterns had the same goal as the creators of electrically powered movie projectors—to create the illusion of motion—their inventions made little impression on the culture of the social elites whom they were meant to amuse, whereas the movies have profoundly altered the psyches of their twentieth-century audiences; indeed, as the philosopher Marshall McLuhan observed in *The Mechanical Bride* (1951), movies have become the vehicle for "the folklore of industrial man."

Not that the entrepreneurs of the classical era of Hollywood would not in their own minds have regarded themselves as romantics. Certainly at the outset of this era of motion pictures, the principal actors in the drama enjoyed portraying themselves as possessing the loner streak that Ceram found so attractive in their forebears. However, their heroic achievements unfolded not under the smoke of their lab lamps, but on the big stage of the public arena. They liked to see themselves as speculators, risk takers, outsiders, even outlaws, in pursuit of their prizes in countinghouses, courtrooms, and copyright offices. It was in these places that they would be rewarded for their labors. The American tinkerer was nothing unless also a salesman and an entrepreneur.

Seldom do movie historians begin their narratives of this age of capitalist buccaneering in southern California. More often, like Ceram, they begin with prehistoric cave paintings of horses in apparent motion, as though these anticipated Eadweard Muybridge's 1877 legendary sequentially shot stills of horses, by means of which he hoped to demonstrate that all four hooves of a galloping horse at some moment simultaneously left the turf. From cave paintings, the histories traverse the ages like Muybridge's horses, invoking Aristotle's account of the play of sunlight on a wall as an anticipation of the modern camera's aperture, the study of optics by the Arabs during the Middle Ages, the Italian Renaissance painters' use of perspective, and the intersection of the culture of the lab with the rage to popularize learning that occurred during the Enlightenment.

In addition to the histories of the development of optical theories and the attempts by artists to incorporate them into aesthetic theory and practice, another history had a bearing on making classical Hollywood what it was. This was the popularization of knowledge that began during the Enlightenment of the seventeenth and eighteenth centuries. From the publication of Comenius's *Didactica Magna* (1628-1632) in Moravia and Locke's *Essay Concerning Human Understanding* (1690)in England, in which he offered his famous metaphor of the mind as tabula rasa, a trend was born that brought about the sharing of the fund of adult knowledge through "news" papers; the *Encyclopaedia Britannica* (1771); the 28-volume *Encyclopédie ou Dictionnaire Raisonné des Sciences, des Arts, et des Métiers* (1772), written by Diderot, d'Alembert, and Condorcet; the nineteenth-century rage for the "common school" (free public school) of Pestalozzi in Switzerland and Horace Mann in Massachusetts; as well as the proliferation among middle-class homes of a little museum nook called a *Kunstkammer* or *chinoiserie*.

This broadening of knowledge into classes formerly denied access to it created the prospective sophisticated audience for technological wonders. These classes, open as they were to the delights of change and innovation, would form the audiences for the new media made possible by the eventual linkage of optics and electricity.

Over time, various light boxes, such as the camera lucida and camera obscura, tantalized students of optics, until, in 1666 the Germans Athanasius Kircher and Johannes Zahn stood on the verge of projecting animated figures by means of painted glass slides mounted on a rotating, slotted cylinder. Here, at last, write Thomas Bohn and Richard Stromgren in *Light and Shadows* (1975), was the germ of the idea of motion pictures, the idea of communicating "with the help of machines in a format that opened up the moving images to the masses."

The leap from inspired innovation to the exploitation of new devices in a marketplace awaited only the aforementioned social and technical developments. To this mixture we should add the factor of urbanization itself, without which the assemblage of audiences into "crowd containers" (the term is Lewis Mumford's) could not have taken place. Like professional baseball, the exhibition of movies to masses of spectators awaited the ancillary technology of people-moving in the form of the coal-burning locomotive that brought players (and film cans) to the cities, where dynamo-driven trams brought spectators downtown to the "rialtos," or theater districts. By way of contrast, Kircher and Zahn enjoyed no such networks; their market, if they had used the term, would have been a handful of aristocrats and favored merchants who would have been amused at dinner.

At the turn of the century, then, the United States possessed electrical power, mass transportation, and the infancy of moviemaking technology; its society believed that social change was not just good but necessary; and its corporate culture teemed with an unbridled sense of individualism. The time was ripe for movie entrepreneurs.

Enterprisers such as W.K.L. Dickson; Thomas Edison; and, abroad, Cecil Hepworth, Max Skladanowsky, and the Lumiere brothers needed no invitation. They refined inventions, filed patents, heaped up capital, sought partners, and otherwise set themselves afloat in the sea of commerce. Indeed, movies in America rewarded not so much their inventors as the geniuses of the marketplace and patent office—the Edisons more than the Armats of this energized capitalist cockpit. Not to put too fine a point on it, Alexander Graham Bell's telephone might have become a mere aid for teachers of the deaf had it not been for J. P. Morgan's interest in the device, without which the corporate family of American Telephone and Telegraph, Western Electric, and, eventually, the Radio Corporation of America might never have been born.

Here we might reckon that as long as the moving image remained a creature of the lab, patent office, and investment house, it would attract only practitioners, such as Edison, from old-line ethnic stock. But that, too, would change. Later, when the shrewd intelligence bred of climbing alternative ladders of success was called for, when achievement depended on challenging the established practice of boardrooms, new immigrants to America found in moviemaking the sort of alternative path to the top that, as outsiders, they needed. Thus in what be might be called a hyperamerican style, as immigration peaked during this first decade of the movie era, a new crop of Americans joined the oligopoly of mainly old-stock Americans that the movie business had thus far drawn, that is, the entrepreneurial scientists such as Edison and Dickson and the first crop of creators, Edwin S. Porter, Thomas Ince, J. Stuart Blackton, and D. W. Griffith. Many of the new speculators were Jews who had emigrated from Eastern Europe. They emerged from the shabby margins of business, the junk dealerships and seasonal fur businesses to which they had been consigned by the closed doors of the prim halls of banking and brokering, to break into the raffish setting of early moviemaking and exhibiting. With their sharpened skills, they were just right for the part.

The rush from tinkering to research to investment to exploitation of a moving image presented on a screen to audiences that changed daily took only a quarter of a century of fevered activity on the part of the interlocking, competitive, antagonistically cooperative system that American capitalism had become by the opening of the new century.

The shift from one set of motives to another, from what Bohn and Stromgren call the "driving need to discover" and "show off" the results of long, lone hours in the lab to capitalist adventurism, was startling in its speed. Spanning the last half of the nineteenth century were Simon Ritter von Stampfer's stroboscope and other lightboxes; Baron Franz von Uchatius's grafting of the magic lantern onto a form of sequential projector; George Eastman's (patented) printing of images on pliable strips of "celluloid"; Etienne-Jules Marey's replication of Muybridge's horse-photographing experiment with a single camera (rather than the twelve cameras that Muybridge used); Edison's Kinetoscope peepshows; and, finally, the projection of images, first at the Cotton States Exposition in Atlanta in 1895 and then in Koster and Bial's Music Hall in Manhattan.

Though the game was under way, no one seemed able to pass Go. Only Edison, who had one foot in the lab and the other in the bank, seemed capable of playing the whole game. Indeed, he saw both endeavors as quintessentially American and himself as their icon. He played both the tinkerer at the kitchen table, slouching over his breadboard of solenoids and alligator clips, chin in hands and white hair awry, and also shrewd confidante of men of power. For such men, the patent office, the countinghouse, and the lab shared sectors of their souls. Indeed, in Edison's case, life in the marketplace was so compelling that he merely "assigned" W.K.L. Dickson to work on the moving image and then, as an addendum to his first love, recorded sound.

This was the stuff of Edison's legend. However, it was Dickson who synthesized the work of Marey and Eastman, making it possible to project moving images to the large audiences that warranted investment, and it was the patent lawyers who bought patents such as that for the "Latham loop," which lessened both the flicker of the moving image and the strain on the rolling strip of film. These realities notwithstanding, Edison loved his legend. In a typical example, presented by Garth Jowett in *Film: The Democratic Art*, a reviewer for the *New York Herald* wrote of a stage production of *Ben Hur* in which the chariot race was conducted on a hidden treadmill that "the only way to secure the exact sense of action for this incident in a theater *is to represent it by Mr. Edison's invention.*"

At the height of his powers at the turn of the century, his firm seemed to drive the entire industry. From the moment he first displayed his Kinetoscope at the Chicago Columbian Exposition of 1893, the trend of the future seemed chained to some form of exhibition of 50-foot reels of topical trivia that viewers paid a penny to view through an eyepiece that opened onto the innards of the box that contained the endlessly looped film. Anything that was celebrated, newsy, or merely curious warranted shooting a minute's worth of moving images for the nation's penny arcades: Annie Oakley firing her rifle, the hurly-burly of a Chinese laundry, and sight gags at the expense of African Americans who clowned for the camera in such fare as water-melon-eating contests. There was even footage from Caribbean locales that showed West Indians in their daily rounds of life; footage of the arrival of the U.S. Army to fight the Spanish-American War; and, of course, the famous few seconds of the vaudevillian Fred Ott kissing a woman. In addition to these glimpses of the world's curiosa, Edison brought performers from Manhattan to New Jersey to his famous Black Maria Kinetoscope production studio, which rotated on wheels as a means of catching the sun for a full day's shooting. Yet, as the Kinetoscope peepshows caught on, the only improvement that Edison's firm thought to make was to primly call their venues "parlors."

Thus although he bridged the years from invention to enterprise, Edison misread the prospects of movies and soon lost the lead with which he had entered the twentieth century. He even failed to file for European patents for those devices that would become essential components of classical moviemaking. How should Edison have played his hand? To answer this question, we might reexamine what we mean by "Hollywood movies" in order to define what was most Americanly classical. After all, filmmaking at the fin de siècle stood on the verge of becoming . . . Becoming what? Movies were formed by forces outside themselves and thus were affected even as they effected change.

American life began to take the shape that it was to hold for at least half of the coming century. It would grow urban, corporate, polyethnic, reformist, and contested for by what the economist John Kenneth Galbraith called "countervailing forces." Obsessed with notions of individual liberty, yet half persuaded of the need for regulation of the extreme forms of corporate buccaneering, American politicians were more pragmatic than ideological.

A certain boosterism celebrated America's need to achieve. A round of world's fairs reached America with the Philadelphia Centennial Exposition in 1876, the Columbian Exposition in Chicago in 1893, and the Cotton States Exposition in Atlanta in 1895. The growth of a national marketplace was aided by other things as well: the debut of the Sears Roebuck catalogue; the founding of the N. W. Ayer advertising agency; the southern railways' adoption of the nation's standard gauge and thus "reunification" with the union in 1886; and the nationalization of time with the establishment of four time zones across the country. Symbolizing the fusion of the drive for a national market, the growth of cities, and the technology of transport capable of carrying people to "crowd containers" was the founding of the National League of Baseball Clubs in 1876. The movie business was poised to rush through the door right behind baseball.

In fact, audiences at the Cotton States Exposition in the summer of 1895 saw movies projected on a screen by means of a machine patented by C. Francis Jenkins and Thomas Armat. The event signaled the impending readiness of a national audience for the debut of movies. Indeed, when Norman Raff and Frank Gammon, Thomas Edison's marketeers, learned of the machine (and of the Lumiere brothers' cinematographe in Paris) they quickly bought the rights to build it, with a view to selling "state rights" licenses. They debuted its use in New York, referring to it as "Edison's vitascope."

In classic American fashion, Edison had set out to corner the American market, while his rivals contested his claims to exclusivity, offered their own machines, and imported tons of foreign movies after Edison had tried to block them from producing movies domestically by claiming patent infringements. Despite a first round of adjudication that found for Edison, he eventually lost his hoped-for monopoly, even as movies became a staple of the vaudeville houses that provided an instantaneous national marketplace for the wares of movie men.

Vaudeville, usually a series of eight acts of music, performance, and recitation, reached audiences everywhere by means of "wheels" (what we call "chains" today) of theaters that helped minimize the complexity of booking on a national scale. This "variety" art reached a broader spectrum of the national audience than any other performance art. An emerging middle class, more clerkish than entrepreneurial, found in it an eclectic, genteel fun that ranged over ten-minute bits of Shakespeare; fast-paced feats of animal training; magic acts; and songs, dance, and patter (in various dialects). So varied was it that Albert McLean in *American Vaudeville as Ritual* (1965) asserts that at the same time it provided its white-collar fans what they considered good clean fun, new immigrants found it an assimilationist medium, a sort of crucible of Americanness.

Thus when movies arrived on the scene they spoke to an already existing clientele composed of aggregations of audiences gathered into "crowd containers" whose offerings were standardized by virtue of being links in a chain of similar venues in cities. The shows the audiences attended, whether vaudeville, burlesque, Wild West shows, road show melodramas, or operettas, were narrative forms of performance distributed from a central source outward through the theater chains. Only the details of the adaptation of this system for the movies remained.

All classes of people, even new immigrants, had grown to expect action and motion and innovation as part of their entertainments. Not only had they been products of two centuries of broadening access to education, but, in America at least, their lives seemed swept along by a drive for newness and movement. They had begun "going out" for amusement, whether to baseball games or to melodramas at the local "opera house." The dynamo had arrived and was transporting them in electric cars through electrically lighted streets. Indeed, everything seemed on the move. Even Buffalo Bill Cody's "Wild West" shows wowed their audiences with spectacles such as real cowboys and Indians mounted on real horses and chasing each other around a sprawling tent.

The entertainments of the late Gilded Age were also driven by a rage for the real. Much as Cody brought real Indians to eastern cities, in dozens of road show productions of *Uncle Tom's Cabin* Eliza crossed over real ice floes in her escape to freedom, and in traveling productions of *Mazeppa*, it was a real white horse that leapt over the footlights and up the aisle. Touring companies staging Shakespeare's bloody history plays grew ever more vivid in their mayhem.

In the realm of photography, the authentic was being tampered with in the name of aesthetics. This trend had started with the Civil War photographers Matthew Brady and Alexander Gardner, who had "sat" dead soldiers in evocative poses, and would continue through Jacob Riis, the Progressive-era "muckraking" photographer who chose his subjects for their photogeneity as well as to expose "the shame of the cities," and Dorothea Lange and other photographers of the Depression era.

Coincident with the arrival of movies was the appearance of mass-produced photography in "rotogravure" sections of Sunday newspapers. For these sections, layout artists enhanced reality by cropping, retouching, and even combining photographs, adding yet more artifice to the photographers' contrivances in the service of visual beauty. Allowing the quick development of pictures in a sequence, the rotogravure process also extended photography's ability to convey a narrative. We might reckon that with the rotogravures presenting visual stories, moviemakers felt free to make their products visual novels. In any case, movies in the age of the rotogravure quickly shifted from mere spectacle into narrative fiction. The first decade of movies, beginning in 1895, featured snippets of reality: a New York garbage scow being towed into the Atlantic for dumping, Boers trekking to Pretoria, the U.S. Army in combat against Filipino insurgents, Theodore Roosevelt on safari (this included a bit of faked footage), championship boxing matches, the ruins of the Baltimore fire of 1904, and so on. It ended with the rudiments of narrative fiction in place, as well as the emerging use of the close-up, which allowed the portrayal of inner states through the expression of emotion, leading to the rich excesses of popular melodrama. Together with the emerging aesthetic of photographic beauty—"they had *faces* then," says Norma Desmond of the silents in *Sunset Boulevard* (1950)—and a growing urbane audience, the narrative formed a blueprint for Hollywood movies and their distribution.

Until around 1906, movies had merely augmented vaudeville shows. After that time, movie men felt sure enough of success that they built houses especially for showing movies—"nickelodeons" they called them. Within another decade, huge "picture palaces" appeared that, depending on which historian one reads, either melded moviegoers into a national clientele or, by drawing moviegoers away from their class- and ethnicity-based neighborhoods, helped homogenize Americans into a false consciousness that subverted the true interests of their groups. Whichever view is subscribed to, the reader should know that movies arrived coincident with Theodore Roosevelt's presidential assault on "malefactors of great wealth" even as corporations used the Fourteenth Amendment as a defense against government litigation against corporate privilege.

We might also view moviemakers and their audiences as Galbraith's "countervailing forces." That is, volatile, unpredictable audiences voted with their wallets for or against the movies released by the studios and their theaters. The growing movie culture knew what it wanted; the movie men guessed what it would accept.

What were the resulting movies like? Almost as a matter of course, they became narrative in form. The movie studios knew that through folktales, novels, histories, Wild West shows, road show melodramas, and even vaudeville skits their audiences had become familiar with this form, and they discovered early on that it was the familiar that sold tickets. Also, as one might guess, the movies became as realistic in style as American drama was rapidly becoming and adopted an urbane, wise guy mode of address. Thus the soul of movies took the route to Biograph's *The Black Hand* (1908), a melodrama about a band of mafioso kidnappers; the road not taken was the one that led to D. W. Griffith's *Lines of White on a Sullen Sea* (1909), a poetically visual meditation on the misty gray lives of women left ashore by sailors. Few such merely atmospheric films followed Griffith's momentary departure from narrative.

Indeed, the narrative construction was used by movie pioneers even before they had the technical capacity to assimilate it. For example, in the Lumiere brothers' brief shot of workers leaving their factory, narrative derived from action within the frame of a single shot; the women walked in a foreshortened angle across the frame but toward the camera (and went home), unaided by editing. The origin of the technique of cutting the exposed film for narrative effect has been traced to Edwin S. Porter, whose work has been singled out as the seminal creative moment, a credit warranted despite recent revelations that Porter retroactively augmented his work by means of additional crosscutting. In the first version of his *The Life of an American Fireman* (1902–13), the exposed film was cut to tell the story of a heroic firefighter and his rescue of a woman from a burning building from the point of view of the woman. But Tom Gunning's demonstration in John O'Connor's *Image as Artifact* (1990) reveals a story later modernized by crosscutting with reverse-angled shots from the firemen's point of view. Another famous pioneering tale that Porter told by means of editing came only weeks after *Fireman* first opened. His *Uncle Tom's Cabin* (1903), perhaps because it was an antique melodrama that might have seemed spoiled by tampering, was edited as though it was nothing more than scene changes in a cheap road show heralded by cards mounted on an easel. Thus Porter's *Uncle Tom's Cabin* unfolded in fourteen scenes drawn from decades of road show *Uncle Tom's Cabins*, rather than from an urge for cinematic narrative.

Along with the narrative form, editing, the aesthetic of the pretty, and the close-up formed the blueprint of what eventually came to be known as the "Hollywood movie." Thus in this visual medium, narrative, far from being simply the preferred form of a leisured bourgeoisie, as is discussed shortly, served as a nutrient broth in much the same way it had in other arts, for example, in Vernet's narrative painting *Papal Troops Surprising Italian Brigands*.

Almost any tale rooted in American popular culture was a suitable source for moviemakers. Touting the 1905 movie *The Night before Christmas*, based on the Clement Clarke Moore poem that had been published to wide circulation only sixty years earlier, Edison's catalogue said it "closely follows time honored Christmas legend" and was "sure to appeal to everyone." Other movies echoed or borrowed from artifacts of popular culture: *Huckleberry Finn*, *The Katzenjammer Kids*, and "human interest" angles on the news, such as a movie of Theodore Roosevelt's refusal to cheapen a Mississippi bear hunt by shooting a bearcub—a "teddy bear"—tethered to provide him an easy target.

Of course, from here movies would eventually grow more urbane, employing devices that anticipated later Hollywood conventions. Much in the manner of a vaudevillian who spent a career endlessly polishing a favored skit, so the studios shaped the movie formula, giving it a dramatic "build" toward a climax or a laugh that topped all before it and constructing hot pursuits that ended in last-minute rescues. Each new device further refined the narrative form.

This is not to suggest an evolutionary model of change. Change came in fits and starts, as the movie men discovered new uses for old conventions and ransacked other media, such as stage and spectacle, for gimmicks. For example, in *Before the Nickelodeon* (1991), Charles Musser argues that Edwin Porter's *The Life of a Cowboy* (1906), a "western" shot on rustic Staten Island, originated in a stage drama. He infers that it may have been meant as a coattail to David Belasco's *The Girl of the Golden West*, then on Broadway, while at the same time he sees in it incipient conventions that anticipated the future western genre.

Early on, surely by 1907, genre movies drove from the screen the early topical forms that Tom Gunning (in Thomas Elsaesser's *Early Cinema* [1990]) called "the cinema of attractions." When we consider films such as the Lumiere brothers' *Voyage dans la Lune* (1902), with its melange of "science" and "fiction"; *Hale's Tours*, with their mock observation cars that "visited" filmed tourist attractions; and topical footage such as William McKinley's inauguration, we see that the impulse to show and tell, in the manner of a schoolchild, at first seemed more compelling than the urge to tell a story. But by the end of the first decade of the new century, the "cinema of attractions" had given way to a cinema of storytelling.

Without doubt, the movies' transformation from the presentation of spectacle to the performance of stories had its genesis in the fertile mind of the early Porter and the enterprise of the early Edison. However, as we shall see in Chapter 2, the future was to fall into other hands. For decades, movie historians have awarded to the young David Wark Griffith a godlike role as creator of the classical Hollywood movie—and with good reason, one might add. Yet circumstance added to Griffith's reputation, just as it subtracted from Porter's. Like Porter, Griffith had one foot in the sentimental pieties of the Gilded Age and the other in the reform-minded Progressive era. As the historian Henry May notes in his 1959 book of the same title, "the end of American innocence" had arrived and, with it, the demise of the certainties of the Victorian age. But, unlike Porter's, Griffith's active life extended far into the era of silent Hollywood and beyond it into the age of soundfilm. This lengthy, if ever declining, career, together with a genius for self-advertisement that the circumspect Porter could not match, eventually assured Griffith, not Porter, lionization as "the father of movies." The title was clinched also because their career trajectories crossed while Griffith's was ascending and Porter's was descending.

Otherwise, the two men's careers followed similar courses. In addition to sharing a paradoxical ethos that mingled Victorian with Progressive sentiments, they shared a belief in vigilantism as a form of social control over the "criminal element" (African Americans, in Griffith's view). For example, both Porter's *The Ex-Convict* (1905) and Griffith's *In Little Italy* (1909) took up the social goal of assimilating convicts and criminals, as Progressives might have done, but in the last reel each left the solution to individual sentiment and charity, as the Victorians might have done. At the same time, in dealing with unrepentant criminals both men preferred vigilantism to charity and forbearance. In *The White Caps* (1905), which appeared as Thomas Dixon's *The Clansman* went into Broadway rehearsal, Porter offered hooded nightriders as an instrument of social control. This same play was one of the sources for Griffith's masterpiece, *The Birth of a Nation* (1915), which also included a lynching.

In any event, Porter's Edison films reached early heights of artistry and technical competence combined with the organizational skills that anticipated Hollywood's eventual attention to preproduction detail. This flair for both art and industry not only allowed the firm to charge a premium for its output, but also set a standard for Griffith and his firm, Biograph, to emulate. Porter's attention to social themes, increasingly polished narrative devices, and borrowings from both folk and popular culture all foreshadowed the age of Biograph and Griffith. Coupled with the effect of the "rich man's panic" of 1907, they also ushered out the nickelodeon era.

But more than anything it was the fiftieth anniversary of the Civil War and the Reconstruction, Griffith's personal *Iliad*, that brought Griffith to the fore. The half decade from around 1910 through 1915 began with Porter at the top of his form. His *The Blue and the Gray* (1908) had received uncommonly effusive praise. It was said that no film could be classed with this tale of brothers fighting in opposing armies. But for Griffith the war not only meant using such well-worn contrivances as putting one brother in blue and the other in grey, but was the defining myth of his life. In making *His Trust* and *His Trust Fulfilled* (1910) and *The Birth of a Nation* (1915), Griffith deployed his outsized sense of the intersection of myth and history, his synthesis of all the film techniques (including some of Porter's) that had come before, and his flair for publicity to such effect that he easily vaulted himself into the catbird seat ahead of the fading Porter.

Yet Porter left a lasting legacy of filmmaking techniques. Whereas most historians have cast Porter in the role of wistful veteran who had come to be seen as old hat in the glare of Griffith's rising star, Musser in *Before the Nickelodeon* documents a Porter who played the fox who knew many wiles as against the hedgehog who knew only one. After he was fired by Edison in 1909, he opened his own studio, where he designed and built his facilities; wrote, shot, and cut his own movies; and tinkered with Edison's machines until the Kinetoscope became a first-rate projector for its time. Moreover, when he moved West and worked for Adolph Zukor's Famous Players in its early days, he contributed to the eventual Hollywood convention of drawing on presold stars from other media, such as Sarah Bernhardt and Minnie Maddern Fiske, and presold works such as *Queen Elizabeth*, *The Count of Monte Cristo*, and *The Prisoner of Zenda*.

As for Porter's own moviemaking approach, it fell between the dominant-director mode that Griffith pursued and the eventual Hollywood mode of producer-units dominated by an overseer of everything from script to screen. According to Musser, Porter "worked collaboratively in a nonhierarchical fashion" that stood somewhere between the one-man show and the studio system. Perhaps his atelier was akin to Elizabeth Mills's *Life on a Medieval Manor* in its shared division of labor that had not yet fallen victim to F. W. Taylor's "time and motion study" of efficiency.

In a way, Porter became a sort of twentieth-century Ned Ludd, the legendary leader of rural English textile workers who in 1811 destroyed their spinning machines and looms, imagining that a return to handicraft might arrest the descent of their wages. But caught as he was between life as it had been and life as it would become, the settled and even-tempered Porter felt comfortable with neither Ludd's nor Taylor's perspective and therefore spent the last years of his life gradually lapsing into retirement. Yet, together with Griffith and other innovators of their age, he bridged the gap between the volatile, hypercompetitive nickelodeon years and the Hollywood that was a stable oligopoly of studios and their theaters.

CHAPTER TWO

Hollywood Becomes
HOLLYWOOD

Early in the new century, after Porter and Edison and other stars of their generation reached their zenith and faded, moviemaking became institutionalized. Just how institutionalized is indicated by the fact that in writing her fine history, *The Transformation of Cinema, 1907-1915* (1990), Eileen Bowser relied heavily on trade papers, the appearance of which is a sure sign of the stabilization of an industry.

Porter and Edison's volatile age of moviemaking, which began in the 1880s, was at first the very model of Adam Smith's classic free market, comprising many buyers and sellers whose atomized acts of self-interest set prices and quality. It stabilized with Edison at the top of a diminishing number of sellers and a swelling mass of eager buyers (that is, ticket buyers), having arrived there through unrelenting courthouse pressure against those he supposed to be infringing on his patents.

In moving toward oligopoly, Edison was doing in the movie business what was being done in other industries. In the building and selling of motor cars, for example, Charles Durant's General Motors and Walter Chrysler's family of cars were swallowing Ransome Olds, Gaston Chevrolet, and other manufacturers. Henry Ford organized his automobile manufacturing system into, as Europeans called it, *Fordissmus*, along the lines first formulated by F. W. Taylor in his "time and motion studies" in the 1880s. The story was the same in many other industries; the ranks of competitive rivals were gradually shrinking into a few survivors. The survivors would eventually compete in more pampered settings, forming trade associations through which they took stands against their unorganized workers; refining both their products and their advertising, so that the range of products they offered narrowed and their advertising exaggerated ever smaller nuances of difference; and adopting more nationally angled names. Marmon became Ford, Gate City became Metro, Dixie Stores became A&P, and so on.

This was the system Edison entered in the 1880s and as moviemaker in the twentieth century should have thrived in, linked to it as he was by a wide circle of capitalist friends in other industries. However, his focus on protecting his capital rather than taking up bold new adventures eventually sealed him off in the penny arcades in West Orange, New Jersey, rather than ushering him into the era of picture palaces. He remained tied to the ways that had brought him early success: the arcades full of Kinetoscope machines showing their penny-a-minute peepshows and a jerry-built litigious system of "state right" sales, leases, and patent licenses for both his film and equipment.

Edison meant to grind out indefinitely his vignettes of vaudeville gigs, skyscrapers going up (or burning down), and exotic subjects such as life in the Caribbean islands, with the intention of distributing them to a network of exhibitors who were contractually bound to use his Kinetoscope and later his projectors. The idea was akin to any vertically integrated business, such as a steel mill that mined its own ore, converted its own coal to coke, and then smelted, rolled, and sold its own steel. Edison, too, would integrate his rivals into a trust that, with the blessings of a friendly Republican Congress and complaisant Supreme Court, attempted to license every step of movie production, from camera to projection.

What he left out of his scheme was any vision of advancing the medium beyond mere novelty into movies; as chance would have it, among the many infringers on his patents were newly arrived Jewish immigrants, who were accustomed to using antiestablishment business practices and who *did* have a vision of motion pictures as more than arcade entertainment.

Throughout the first decade of the new century, Edison felt various pressures buffeting his system. The "rich man's panic," a brief recession in 1907, did not affect the public's moviegoing, but it did serve to tighten venture capital. In addition, Edison's rivals began forming film "exchanges," or wholesale organizations, and transforming nickelodeons into picture palaces to suit the movies' potential to be classy entertainment and to keep up with the public's appetite for moviegoing. Among these rivals were the savvy Jewish business men from Europe (the "outlaws" Edison called them), who were arriving in a tide of Jewish immigration to the United States that peaked at almost one million in 1906. As mentioned in Chapter 1, old-line enterprises had managed to freeze out these newcomers. Accustomed to this role of out-cast by virtue of their Jewish history, their exile from the old country, and the prevailing rules of the game, which more often than not were used to ex-clude them, they found livelihoods in the various marginal businesses to which they were consigned—junk dealing, seasonal businesses such as fur selling, small haberdasheries, and the like. For them, the raffish world of motion picture making, which drew its lifeblood from the tradition of Wild West shows, road shows, vaudeville, burlesque, penny arcades and itinerant Bible thumpers, was merely the newest form of slightly déclassé enterprise that might hold its door ajar to newcomers and contained no hard-and-fast rules. As befit men whose families had just survived the Tsar's pogroms and Otto von Bismarck's nativist-German Kulturkampf of the 1870s, they quickly learned some of the rules of the old-line game, made up some rules of their own, and became more American than the Americans. As storefront ex-hibitors, nickelodeon men (with emphasis on the nickel), buyers and sellers of state rights, exchange men who bought film like so much yard goods, wildcatters carrying their reels around under their arms, and patent in-fringers, they practiced the movie business *only* as a form of sharp practice and raffishness. In short, the movie business behaved like any form of young capitalism, ill-bred and ill-mannered.

Still, Edison had great hopes of teaching them who was boss. In 1907 he successfully appealed challenges to his camera patents, and thereafter the challengers, many too poor to afford patent attorneys, grudgingly paid up for their licenses. Seeking still more dominance, in 1908 he invited a group of major patent holders and producers to his lab in West Orange, New Jer-sey. Attending were the Englishmen Alfred Smith and J. Stuart Blackton; George Kleine, the eventual importer of Italian epics; Sigmund Lubin and William N. Selig; the men of Edison's own house, Edwin Porter and W.K.L. Dickson; and delegates from Biograph, Essannay, Vitagraph, Kalem, and even the French firms Melies and Pathe. From this arose the Motion Picture Patents Trust, which attempted to be the exclusive supplier of films to dis-tributors and to regulate the entire filmmaking process.

However, movies were evolving into a linear structure that, as Charles Musser writes in *Before the Nickelodeon* (1991), "was readily executed by filmmakers and accepted by spectators," thereby anticipating what came to be known as the "Hollywood movie." The linear structure allowed all sorts of complexities of morality, values, ideologies, and politics to be explored on the screen. Jesse Lasky was among the first to see that this warranted elevating the quality of movies and with Adolph Zukor created Famous Players–Lasky, through which they brought literary classics to the screen. Exchanges and their clienteles of exhibitors began to cater to diverse audiences who had begun to learn the codes and conventions that were beginning to convey ever more sophisticated meaning. Off screen, the moviemaking process was quickly breaking down into tasks, leading to the development of craft guilds and specialties.

As discussed in Chapter 1, rather than adapt to these new conditions Edison began to live with one foot in the past, protecting his assets and reputation and preferring to go down in the manner to which he had grown accustomed. His enemies nibbled at his empire with increasing impunity, paying their license fees late, renting film from "outlaws," seeking out unlicensed machines, baiting Edison into additional risky court actions by refusing to pay fees, and allying with angry theater men who themselves balked at paying up. By 1909, many movie men had boldly torn up their agreements and aligned with distribution exchanges and exhibitors who also wished to break with the cartel and form their own networks.

Carl Laemmle, an exchange man in the Midwest, had already done so, in 1909 forming his own deliciously named Independent Motion Picture Company, or IMP. In 1913, Laemmle moved to California, pioneer in what was to be an exodus of moviemakers to the West Coast. There he gave his company the grandiloquent name of Universal Pictures and played a new game made possible by the cheapness of western land—real estate speculation.

Porter had already gone west, in 1910, but his career trajectory was descending and he was there mostly as a tribal elder who knew all the old war stories. He worked for Famous Players–Lasky during its early days of bringing to the screen *Queen Elizabeth*, *The Prisoner of Zenda*, and Hardy's *Tess*, all the while regarded as little more than an expendable mechanic. Remaining on the East Coast, Edison played, as Talleyrand said of Louis XVIII, the man "who had learned nothing and forgot nothing" since the days of the Revolution. He was still making one-reelers while the opposition moved toward feature-length movies. In 1915, he would oversee the dismantling of his oligopoly at the hands of a federal court.

The movies' drive to maturity would thus be led by D. W. Griffith. When one considers that other men brought the same strengths to the cinema that Griffith brought—a life in the theater and ideological roots in Victorian sentiment—and still others possessed a broader range of experiences than Griffith, such as success on the New York stage, a cosmopolite's sophistication, an eye for the erotic, or a grounding in electronic technology, one may wonder why it was Griffith who wore the mantle of spiritual and aesthetic leader of the movies' advance into maturation. One reason may have been that Griffith early on possessed a strong sense of himself as a director, and he clung to this identity long after others had become lost in the thrall of corporate production. In addition, he had a gift for synthesizing each new technique into an expression of his own Victorian voice. Finally, a flair for self-advertisement that led him to claim credit for every innovation since the magic lantern and a knack for softening bankers' hearts were not unhelpful. These factors combined to give Griffith twenty years of grace in which to make scores of movies that often soared above the pioneering standards set by Porter and his cohort.

Griffith directed *The Birth of a Nation* (1915) and *Intolerance* (1916) when the Hollywood that was the unremarkable suburb of Los Angeles was on the cusp of becoming HOLLYWOOD the movie mecca, and these two films provided the basis for his lionization as second-generation pioneer. These movies, like their maker, straddled two sociopolitical ages as well as rode a wave of technical and artistic accomplishment. Griffith was what Porter or, for that matter, Thomas Ince, J. Stuart Blackton, and others might have become had they not exhausted their powers early.

Like many another early moviemaker, Griffith marked his work with the signs of the social flux of the time. As Progressive Americans hit their stride in the decade and a half before World War I, electing reformist congresses, cheering the rhetoric of their Progressive president, Theodore Roosevelt, campaigning for change in a dozen national muckraking magazines, such as *McClure's*, *Survey Graphic*, and *The Independent*, Griffith's movies marched with them—until their final sentimental endings, that is. Even as his early Biograph one- and two-reelers grew more sophisticated in their narrative devices, their reformist politics were given an ever brighter gloss of sentimentalism. Thus could the *New York Dramatic Mirror* say of Griffith's *The Red Man's View* (1909), "[It is about] the helpless Indian race as it has been forced to recede before the advancing white, and as such it is full of poetic sentiment." That is, a Griffith movie, like the scores of "message movies" that followed his example, usually took a social problem, coated it with saccharin, solved it in a singular dramatic incident, and then dropped it. Sometimes Griffith used the social issue merely as background. In *The Musketeers of Pig Alley* (1912), for example, he shot a romantic story in the actual gangster-ridden slums of the Lower East Side that had inspired a public crusade against urban crime.

It was also Griffith's knack for synthesis that led him to making the large-scale movies that ushered in the watershed phase of his career and his departure from Biograph. In *D. W. Griffith* (1984), Richard Schickel writes that upon viewing the Italian epic *Quo Vadis?* in 1913, Griffith may have been seized with envy, not only because of the grand scale of the import (he remained hobbled by the two-reel format) but also because of the splash it made. "The most ambitious photo drama that has yet been seen here," the *New York Times* called it.

At this point, Griffith began to behave startlingly like the directors of Hollywood's coming classical age. He continued to grind out for Biograph the two-reelers that were due almost every week. But 1913 marked a veering away from Biograph and its East Coast–style social melodramas. In December 1912 and throughout the following year, Griffith took production units to California, where he shot brief melodramas in the varied western landscape—adventures in the gold fields, conflicts between European settlers and Indians, and the like. In addition, in midsummer he shot *Judith of Bethulia*, a six-reel biblical epic drawn from a story by Thomas Bailey Aldrich, a major figure in genteel American letters and an editor of the prestigious *Atlantic*. As Schickel reports, the nearly hour-long movie caught the attention of the poet Vachel Lindsay, who praised its "balanced alternation" (Griffith's crosscutting among four discrete scenes). Much later, the critic Edward Wagenknecht, in *The Movies in the Age of Innocence* (1962), called it "the greatest achievement of early American film."

Whatever the merits of *Judith*, Biograph was appalled at the cost of its extravagant length; its heroically scaled sets, done in the manner of Italian epics; and, most of all, Griffith's distance from the restraining hand of the accountants. He was removed from active directing and reassigned to supervise other directors' work while he finished editing the last of his own work at the studio.

Chafing at these constraints, Griffith left Biograph in October 1913 and sought ways of clinging to directorial independence while releasing through Harry and Roy Aitken, brothers who imported films as Western Imports, shot movies in New York at their Reliance studio and in Los Angeles at their

Majestic studio, and released movies as Mutual Film Corporation.

The path was cleared for Griffith to make *The Birth of a Nation*. A rival director, Thomas Ince, had already made the five-reel *Gettysburg* in 1913, and in 1915 the nation was in the midst of a rage for reunion on the occasion of the fiftieth anniversary of the Civil War. The times were propitious, and Griffith, having essayed a few Civil War sketches of his own (nine, in fact, since 1909) was ready for a treatment of the subject on a grand scale.

As legend, racist bugbear, and profoundly affecting work of cinema art, *The Birth of a Nation* is well known. Equally well known are its production history and angry black activists' protest of its opening. But we might also take up the movie as a key document in the history of Hollywood's becoming HOLLYWOOD. Along with *Judith of Bethulia*, the movie signaled the end of the two-reeler as the standard fare of movie houses. It called attention to the movie moguls' migration to California that had begun five years earlier. And it revealed the possibilities of making a massive epic and preserving some artistic independence. Throughout the late teens, Griffith would make movies not only through the Aitken brothers' Reliance and Majestic studios, but also through Epoch and Wark Producing Corporation and under his own full name, while releasing through Mutual, Zukor's Paramount–Artcraft, and First National.

With the making of this signal event in movie history, Griffith showed that he foresaw the glitzy side of the emerging Hollywood. Through his lawyer Griffith took out an ad in the *New York Dramatic Mirror* on December 3, 1913, in which he announced his departure from Biograph and claimed credit for inventing almost every convention that governed what would eventually be called the classical Hollywood style: the close-up, the crosscut, the fade, and the wide-angle shot (or, as he called it, the "distant view"); he even claimed credit for "raising motion picture acting to a higher plane" by encouraging restraint in his actors. Further assuring the movie a place in history were the outsized billboards and sleek three-sheets that accompanied its opening, its musical enhancement in the form of a traveling orchestra and ambitious score, and strident word-of-mouth publicity that included an eventually withdrawn but nonetheless priceless endorsement from the president of the United States.

Its topicality is not to be dismissed as a factor in the success of the film. Being based on the novels of Thomas Dixon, the movie was assured the clangor of interracial controversy. Not that Dixon's racist views were extreme; on the contrary, they were widely embraced by many white Americans, northerners and southerners alike. Indeed, Dixon in his preaching days had pastored the largest church in New York City. This while possessed of a vision of African Americans as a species that ranked a notch below the European on the evolutionary scale, a genetic circumstance, he asserted, that had been the basis for their victimization during the Reconstruction by unscrupulous white carpetbaggers, who had cozened them into voting into power a corrupt "black and tan" wing of the Republican Party. Hollywood had been half-formed by forces that it had helped half-form.

Accompanying *The Birth of a Nation* was a comet's tail of unaccustomed national black protest. Indeed, the movie's release brought into being the first coherently organized national black movement, and one that effectively introduced pressure groups into the politics of American moviemaking. Black viewers bristled particularly at the movie's sharp, simplistic division of blacks into two Manichean social types: those virtuously faithful to kindly white masters and those straining furiously against the tethers that held mulatto ambition in check. Thus in this single episode, both Hollywood and African Americans announced their arrival in American political culture as forces to be reckoned with.

In the decade that followed, Griffith's career anticipated the course taken by later American moviemakers: the clinging to tried-and-true two-reelers, the assertion of independence to make what one wished (in Griffith's case, to refine his curious melding of Victorian morality and the social changes of the age of urban Progressivism), the attempt at a compromise in the combination of personal moviemaking and corporate releasing, and, finally, the succumbing to the vertical hierarchy of the Hollywood studio.

Griffith stuck with his relationship with the Aitkens through *The Birth of a Nation*, after which he struck out entirely on his own under the aegis of Wark Producing Corporation. Completely lacking the safety net of corporate cash, he plunged into the making of *Intolerance* (1916), a fourteen-reeler that intercut four tales of the awful consequences of intolerance. He lost his shirt.

He lost his freedom as well. Unavoidably, he entered the Hollywood system, at which point he ran off a string of movies meant to be his major period, such as *Hearts of the World* (1918) and *The Greatest Thing in Life* (1918), all of them commentaries on World War I that have not survived intact. He also indulged in a bit of autobiographical nostalgia in *A Romance of Happy*

Valley (1919). The significance of these movies lies less in their merits, which are difficult to rate, than in the fact that they were backed and distributed by Zukor's Paramount–Artcraft, which was on its way to becoming one of the eventual half-dozen "majors." These films therefore opened at Clune's in Los Angeles and the Strand in New York, as any major Hollywood movie would thenceforth do.

Making another attempt to keep from being yoked to the Hollywood system, Griffith joined forces with Charles Chaplin, Mary Pickford, and Douglas Fairbanks to form United Artists, a backer and distributor of films more personal than those possible in the maturing studio system. Apart from a couple of 1919–20 films released through First National (which would eventually become an arm of Warner Bros.), Griffith at the height of his powers released through United Artists. As though confirming the belief that Hollywood had no room for the singleminded artist in his or her atelier, Griffith's most Griffithlike work emerged from the loose alliance of friends that was United Artists. The best of these films—*Broken Blossoms* (1919), *The Greatest Question* (1919), *Way Down East* (1919), and *Orphans of the Storm* (1920) —revealed his capacity for sentiment in the context of modern issues. In a tribute to Griffith's struggle for independence, Schickel judges *Broken Blossoms* "the first memorable European film made by an American."

However, in addition to these successes there were other films that turned fans away, and his sentimentality gave critics an easy target. Eventually, in order to continue making movies, he was forced to sell his property in the East, break off from United Artists, and come in from the cold winds of freelancing. He returned to Zukor's Paramount–Artcraft for a few years, after which he joined Joseph M. Schenck's Art Cinema and eventually retired.

World War I's ruination of Europe's economy provided yet more fuel for the Hollywood engine, which shifted into high gear after the war. Perhaps the only European country that did not have its movie industry made prostrate by the war was Germany. It was not until Germany's economy collapsed in the 1920s that its Universum Film Aktiengesellschaft (UFA) needed bailing out and saved itself by means of an arrangement with MGM and Paramount that obliged UFA houses to play American products on half their play dates. In 1927, the British, facing even worse enervation of their movie industry in the face of an invasion by American movies, passed an act that limited imports by insisting on the exhibition of a minimum quota of British-made products. Even before the war and its resulting American cultural hegemony, European intellectuals had mourned the arrival of strident American voices and images. In their edited volume *Hollywood in Europe* (1994), David Ellwood and Rob Kroes quote Menno ter Braak, a cofounder of the Amsterdam Film League, as saying, "Mind bestows life. Americanism kills." In the same book, Richard Maltby and Ruth Vasey document that Erich Schlaikjer found American culture "barbarian" and driven by a traditionless "nervous energy." American film clearly had its attractions, though. As early as 1911, when Germany was already importing 30 percent of its movies from America, American film was described by Karl Hans Strobl in *Kein Tag ohne Kino* (*No Day without Movies*) as "a theater in top speed" that "opened choices as though it were an automat restaurant of visual pleasure."

Thus with the onset of World War I in the summer of 1914, the American cultural hegemony that had already begun stealing over Europe mushroomed. The war quickly gave birth to a diplomacy that calculatedly entwined American ideology with Hollywood profiteering. *Spreading the American Dream*, the title of Emily Rosenberg's 1982 book, captures the intent of the propaganda through which George Creel, chair of the wartime Committee on Public Information (CPI), intended to present "the wholesome life of America."

The gain for Hollywood was incalculable. Early in the war, Europeans faced shortages of the nitrate that was used to make gunpowder and, coincidentally, film stock. With Europe's industry and Edison's Motion Picture Patents Trust both in ruins, Hollywood achieved "commercial supremacy" by, as Gerald Mast puts it in *A Short History of the Movies* (1971), being "lucky enough to be in the right place at the right time." Indeed, in the single season of 1915–16, the year of the slaughter on the Somme, American exports rose 400 percent.

As though answering the nation's call, the moguls embraced the war. So strident were their movies, argues Garth Jowett in *Film: The Democratic Art* (1976), they tipped America toward the British side long before Woodrow Wilson's foreign policy did. J. Stuart Blackton's *The Battle Cry for Peace* (1915) played on Americans' rage at the sinking of the Lusitania and the fear raised by Hiram Maxim's alarmist book, *Defenceless America*. Anti-German polemics such as *The Beast of Berlin*, *To Hell with the Kaiser*, and *My Four Years in Germany* served, as Cecil B. DeMille said, "to bring the great war home to the people."

Even a "race movie" made for African American audiences broke with its original theme of racial tolerance. *The Birth of a Race* (1918) had begun as an antidote to *The Birth of a Nation* drawn from Booker T. Washington's autobiography *Up from Slavery*. As the war raged in Europe, however, the focus of the movie subtly shifted to a pious plea for world peace. When Germany's submarine warfare in the North Atlantic brought the war home, the movie was further reworked into an apologia for Wilson's entry into the war. By then it focused not on black America, but on two German families, one loyal to America and the other sadly duped into fighting for the Kaiser.

Thanks to the Export Division of its trade guild, the National Association of the Motion Picture Industry, Hollywood ended the war a winner. Both the CPI and the Export Division shipped thousands of movies overseas, institutionalizing the habit of export. Moreover, in a gesture of goodwill, the CPI agreed to count as educational, and therefore particularly exportable, almost any Hollywood movie that proffered "some idea of American life and purpose." In contrast, the German film industry slowly suffered a decline in exports, mainly as a result of an American campaign to keep German films off neutral screens. Everywhere, movie fans saw glamourous signs of the symbiosis of war and movies, such as the appearances of Fairbanks, Chaplin, and Pickford at public rallies on behalf of federal liberty bonds.

Even apart from the windfall of the war, the movie industry persisted in its growth. Coincident with the war years, Sigmund Lubin's firm, one of the last with eastern ties, went under; Vitagraph absorbed VLSE; Samuel Goldwyn formed his own independent studio; and Famous Players–Lasky, headed by the hard-driving Adolph Zukor, began to buy theaters, notably, the Publix chain. Briefly luminous firms such as Triangle expired and their veteran staffs hooked on with the gradually emerging major players; as was typical of these transfers, the Triangle lot in Culver City, which had been founded by Thomas Ince, ended up in the hands of MGM.

Thus by 1920 or so Hollywood had become both powerful and respectable, an outcome that was reflected in both the movies and the countries in which they dominated marquees. During the war, movies followed the course set by the Italians and Griffith. They grew to feature lengths of ten or more reels. They took on a formerly unthinkable psychological complexity. The promoting of anonymous actors such "the Biograph girl" (Florence Lawrence) led to the first crop of movie stars. The public's desire for ever larger movie palaces continued to rage. Business in ancillary services, such as air cooling, graphic advertising, and even popcorn, grew with equal vigor.

All of these developments were reported by a new chorus of trade papers and fan magazines: *Motion Picture World, Motion Picture Herald, Wid's,* and *Film Daily,* along with *Photoplay, Motion Picture,* and other fan publications. Joining them in reporting Hollywood news were the broader-focused show-business papers such as *Variety,* as well as mainstream magazines such as *Ladies' Home Journal* and *Collier's* and metropolitan dailies ranging from the *New York Times* to the *New Orleans Picayune.*

Much as William Caxton and Johannes Gutenberg and their printing presses had inadvertently contributed to the standardization of languages in an earlier age, the printed word helped define the postwar movies. Behind the studio gates, scripts, memoranda, account books, and shooting schedules formalized everything into an institutional order—a sort of hybrid of factory and atelier. Outside the gates, not only did aspiring producers and their clientele learn their roles from printed periodicals, but every studio guild, as it matured into the emerging system, taught its members shop practice and innovations through a corpus of technical newsletters and manuals.

These publications codified every stage of production and distribution. Writers learned plot, character, atmosphere—all the ingredients of classical drama—and formalized them into movie conventions. "I have studied the subject of the photoplay from every angle," wrote Louella Parsons in *How To Write for the Movies* (1915), "and . . . I have evolved these lessons for the help of those who have photoplay ambitions." Eustace Hale Ball loaded his *Photoplay Scenarios* (1917) with sample comedy and drama scripts, the reading of which would lead to "practical authorship." In *How To Write Photoplays* (1921), John Emerson and his wife, Anita Loos, told readers what to write and how to sell it; they also provided a glossary of movie lot lingo, presumably in case the selling required using it. In *The Art of Photoplay Making* (1918), Victor Freeburg went a step further, providing a note on "the psychology of the cinema audience." Other publications, such as the serial *Exhibitor's Herald* and handbooks such as E. G. Lutz's *The Motion Picture Cameraman* (1927) and Arthur Meloy's *Theaters and Picture Houses* (1916), took up the process from the script on, all the way to the designing and building of theaters.

On the movie lots, technical sophistication progressed by leaps and bounds. As photography improved, film became capable of recording faster motion in less light and lighting became more subtle. Directors became ever surer in blocking scenes and framing shots for the camera's eye, rather than the theatergoer's. They blocked for perspective by placing actors in different planes at varying distances from the lens. They blocked for subsequent cutting from, say, a group shot to a person within the group, and they learned to move the action by means of cutting conventions such as the shot–reverse shot sequence.

As such tactics became conventional and more refined, lighting grew sophisticated to the point of setting mood and texture, almost as though it were a character in the movie. In this way, movies might "quote" a currently favored painter—for example, Sir Lawrence Alma-Tadema, Sir Edward Coley Burne-Jones, or Maxfield Parrish—much as scenarists drew or adapted their work from novels. In William Fox's *A Fool There Was* (1914), the style of Theda Bara, the "vamp" who bled men white, was drawn from a painting Burne-Jones did based on a scene in a Kipling poem.

The studio system itself grew to accommodate the increasing complexity of the technology and imagery on the screen. Various midlevel managers learned to dissect their materials into the shooting script; the costing script; the casting-call script; and, finally, from the legal department, the as-released script (providing protection against future legal wrangles). No longer was there any of Griffith's fabled practice of shooting off the cuff or from the back of an envelope. Each new task required a new craft and shop practice manual. The assistant director served as sergeant-at-arms, calling the unit to order, calling the cast to their marks, and calling the camera crew up to speed. The art director used the cash flowing in from Europe's wartime rentals of American movies to dress their sets in ever greater detail to evoke the French Revolution, the trenches at Verdun, or what have you. The unit manager oversaw the daily operations, the casting calls, dress extras, box lunches, busses, and so on. "Script girls" recorded things like the time on the prop clocks, how many unfired rounds remained in the Prussian's Luger, and the direction of the posse's horses during the last take before lunch. Story editors combed piles of proofs of upcoming novels in search of likely material. Script doctors wrote and rewrote even as daily shooting ground onward.

As though surrounding the resulting institutional oligopoly with a protective wall of legal stratagems, the survivors of the bloody days of the patent wars defended their fiefs in the federal courts. In 1915 the federal judiciary had given its blessing to the drift of things by finding against Edison's patents trust. The result was an incremental increase in the size of the majors, with a corresponding diminution in the number of rivals. The age was fought out and won by "combination and litigation," Janet Staiger writes in Thomas Elsaesser's *Early Cinema* (1990). The majors' accretion of chains of movie houses in the provinces, where the tickets were sold (never constituting a monopoly, but large enough to dominate the market) and use of marketing strategies designed to keep exhibitors in line pressed against the limits of the antitrust law.

Following Zukor's lead, the other majors sought exclusive runs in their own or affiliated houses and obliged bookers to grant "clearances" of days or weeks before beginning second runs in the "nabes" (*Variety*'s coinage for the theaters in average residential neighborhoods, as opposed to the picture palaces). The practice not only whetted the appetites of their prospective second-run audiences, but also averted competition with their own incoming products. Theater men were also compelled to "blockbook" (rent mediocre movies as a precondition of renting Class A movies), "blindbook" (book movies before they were released), pay premiums for access to lushly mounted star vehicles, and accept other limits on the freedom of the marketplace.

Thus by the end of World War I and the onset of "the Republican Ascendancy" (the term is John D. Hicks's) of the 1920s, Hollywood had become HOLLYWOOD and stood astride the world. No more seedy arcades; a single movie such as Douglas Fairbanks's *The Thief of Baghdad* (1922) might gross $2 million. In the glow of Republican hegemony, the men who made the system—Zukor, Lasky, Fox, Laemmle, Loew, and the Warners—counted a gate of $750 million in their fifteen thousand theaters in the single season of 1919-20. By then, they were collectively making six hundred, sometimes eight hundred, movies a year, with an average "nut" (the cost of a completed movie) of $200,000. In only ten years' time these figures would seem quaint in the light of an audience of 100 million, capital totaling $2 billion, a share of Europe's market that reached 95 percent of the French and 70 percent of the British take. Governments responded to the "assault" on their "national lives" by enacting quota laws, to which Secretary of Commerce Herbert Hoover responded in 1926 by creating a movie desk in the U.S. Department of Commerce. In 1925 the *London Post* warned the world, "By its means, Uncle Sam may hope someday to Americanize the world."

By the time the writer for the *Post* penned this worried line, the movie business had been in Hollywood for fifteen years, the last five of which had seen the moguls' small, steady migration west turn into an exodus. The stereotyped tale is that of the Jewish furrier turned nickelodeon boss during the dog days of summer. But the real story is about a cadre of Jews in the postwar boom abandoning the East in favor of westering to what had become HOLLYWOOD and making it in the movie business.

The migration of Jews to California and the transference of corporate power to them soon became one of the defining characteristics of the moviemaking business—and for the rest of the century gave anti-Semites a sitting target. One by one, the sons of the old Celtic and Anglo-Saxon stock—the Edisons, Porters, Smiths, Griffiths, and Inces—were replaced by Zukor and Lasky of Paramount; the brothers Warner; William Fox; and of course their trailblazer, Carl Laemmle, who had his Universal Pictures studio up and running by 1913.

Any one of the new men might have stood in for another. Laemmle, for instance, a German Jew, went from being a sometime storekeeper in Oshkosh, Wisconsin, to owner of several exchanges in the Midwest; to adversary of the Trust as both licensee and litigant in more than three hundred suits; to the tactician who imported the Lumiere brothers' films from France; to the innovator who wooed the nameless Biograph girl from her New York studio and gave her star billing; to the founder of IMP; and finally to "Uncle Carl," the boss of a vast new movie lot and real estate venture, Universal City. The careers of Zukor, Lasky, the Warner brothers, and others were similarly fantastic.

It would fall to Laemmle and men like him to fulfill the promise shown by the best movies of the East Coast studios Biograph and Vitagraph—that movies could be lifted from the ranks of nickelodeon to the realm of classy entertainment for the carriage trade. No longer would trade papers rail against "the morbid and vulgar" stuff that the "inferior elements" (Jews, they seemed to say) had brought to the screen. Instead, the sprawling movie lots of southern California would become the ateliers of the new industry (although the countinghouses remained in the East). Griffith had shot his first California movie on a sojourn there in 1909, but it was thanks to Laemmle's move west that by 1919, four out of five of the world's motion pictures were created in this western desert.

Edendale was the suburb of Los Angeles where Chaplin's first studio sat. And indeed, California seemed to be Eden. The appreciating realty and the sanguine climate provided a dual bonanza for the movie men. A glance at surviving photographs of Los Angeles and its northern suburb, Hollywood, reveals the extent to which land and sunny days contributed to this new social order. The Mediterranean climate, coupled with the variety of the landscape, with its parched hills, neighborly mountain ranges, seashores broken by outcroppings and crags, offshore islands with their resident seals, and fertile and lushly irrigated valleys, formed an attractive hinterland to the city of Los Angeles.

As for Los Angeles, it had begun life as a Spanish mission in the sixteenth century and soon filled up with Yankee traders and adventurers, who gradually came to outnumber the Indians, Mexicans, and aristocratic Californios (the Hispanics who traced their ancestry back to Spain through royal patents that had given them title to vast haciendas). By the time the movie men arrived, the city had grown in appearance to mimic eastern cities, with streetcar lines, busy intersections, caverns formed of skyscrapers, and dense traffic jams. At first, no distinctive California style marked the city. The residences lining the boulevards named for presidents were bungalows that echoed the architecture of the New Jersey shore, rather than Spanish America. This was so until the mid-1920s, by which time the University of California, Los Angeles, and its surrounding neighborhoods had come to look like stereotypes of Spanish mission architecture. By then the "movie people"—as distinct from the "old settlers" who joined the Sons and Daughters of the Golden West—sprawled across the Los Angeles basin, southward to Culver City and northward across the Santa Monica Mountains to Laemmle's Universal City. Like most eastern urban centers, Los Angeles was linked to its suburbs by trams, specifically the "red cars" of the Pacific Electric lines.

The movie people did not define Los Angeles, however. Far from it, at least in the view of the old settlers. The city and its hinterland acted out its own brand of the boosterism that colored American urbanization in the nineteenth century when great, if unrealized, ambitions were trumpeted in the names towns gave themselves—Metropolis, Illinois; Troy, New York; Rome, Georgia; and Athens, Ohio, to name a few. The local version of this civic pride centered in Harrison Gray Otis's *Los Angeles Times* and its campaign to bring eastern railroads to the city. The most famous action the city government took on this behalf was to annex the harbor town of San Pedro by linking it to the city by means of a "shoestring district," a narrow strip that appeared as only a line on a map. In this way, the city conformed to a law that allowed annexation of only contiguous communities. Thenceforth, Southern Pacific and other railroad lines provided access to the East, while local communities reached out by means of both the red streetcars and the Peerless Stages (the parent company of Greyhound). So famous was the resulting wheeled cityscape that one of the second bananas on Jack Benny's radio show used to end the show by calling out red-car stations: "Anaheim, Azusa, and Cucamonga."

The combination of this cultural uniqueness in isolation from the East and the social distance, not to say apartheid, between the movie people and old settlers heightened Hollywoodians' clannishness. "The movie colony" journalists dubbed Hollywood. Although not as socially remote from their old lives as, say, serving in the Anglo-Indian Army had been for British colonial officers, the insular life of the Jewish moguls helped give them a particular mentality, a sense of remoteness from America while embracing its values. Neither pristinely Jewish nor Middle American, they prevailed. They worked in blessed isolation from their masters in the home offices in New York; they seemed immune from the labor strife that countervailed against the more savage impulses of capitalists in other industries; they enjoyed the perspective of aliens, which gave them a vision of America that was at once hazy and stylized and politically pointed; they lived in splendid Jewish isolation apart from the old settlers.

Their social distance from the old settlers of Los Angeles derived not only from their Jewishness, but also from the raffishness of life in the early movie "camps," as some movie lots were at first called. This distance eventually contributed to some of Hollywood's most enduring traits. First, the moguls were able to generalize and "type" audiences. Moreover, in *The Classical Hollywood Cinema* (1985), David Bordwell, Janet Staiger, and Kristin Thompson make a convincing case that the itinerant, tentative aspect of moviemaking life contributed to the forming of the director-unit system of organizing work, a system that encouraged artistic freedom from the remote masters in New York, if not from their audiences' presumed tastes. They also freed themselves from older American business practice in everything from inventing the star system to elaborating and extending the narrative form into the only form movies would take.

Socially, the moguls responded to the old settlers' coolness by adopting a mentality of assimilationism that buffed off the burrs of Jewishness that set them apart from their Gentile neighbors. As Neal Gabler illustrates on the basis of hundreds of sources in *An Empire of Their Own* (1988), although traces of these men's pasts as junkdealers and storefront arcade owners could be gleaned in their mangled grammar, outsized arrogance, and garish tastes, some of them shed their Jewish names, wives, and religious practices and hoped to polish their children by sending them to Ivy League schools.

Perhaps asserting Jewishness as a central factor in the evolution of the Hollywood system is to make too much of one ingredient among many. But it is an ingredient that compels attention. Jewishness no more drove Laemmle to Universal City than Anglo-Gaelicism rooted Edison to West Orange, but it helped. No Jew whose history included enduring Prussian May Laws, tsarist pogroms, and the restrictive charters of American country clubs could ever feel as lionized, accepted, and *settled* as Edison had felt. Thus, all other things being equal, Jewish history predisposed Jews to migration, indeed flight at times. Moreover, having experienced deprivation, they may have preferred the feel of power in retailing genteel palatial venues, as opposed to the slum tradition on which the Gentiles had founded movies. Yet, like Nathan Rothschild hiding his resources below the stairs rather than in Frankfurter banks, the moguls liked to hide their acumen behind a facade of vulgarity and malapropisms. Samuel Goldwyn's legendary flubs "Include me *out*" and "In two words, *im* possible," his expressed wish to have "a bust" made of his wife's graceful hands, and other "Goldwynisms" served him well as a disarming mask behind which the real Goldwyn operated.

It was behind the studio gates that the moguls displayed their mettle. A merchant-furrier who owned arcades lined with Edison's machines, Zukor entered into the theater end with Marcus Loew (later the central figure at MGM through his Loew's theaters). Through his Famous Players partnerships, first with Edwin Porter and then with Jesse Lasky, Zukor bought into both production (Paramount) and exhibition (Publix Theaters) and, for a while, even broadcasting (the young CBS). To Gabler, the biographer of Jewish Hollywood, Zukor seems the perfect mogul, deriving his powers from walking the line between two cultures: "the Hungarian Jew transformed into the American gentleman, the ideal facilitator for the movies, . . . [a] synthesis between the new and the old, between the working class and the middle class." Minus the theater chains, the German immigrant Laemmle attained the same vast success at Universal, albeit by playing "Uncle Carl" the sage, rather than Zukor's mediator between two cultures. Fox followed a similar course, which led him from Hungary to theaters in Brooklyn to his own Hollywood studio. Unlike some of the others, Fox took pride in not giving up the grammar of the streets and the white socks of the workingman. Louis B. Mayer's life was the same, only different. Like the others, he was born overseas (Russia), fled formal schooling, and learned of life in jobs unwanted by any but the lumpen working class; then he transformed a burlesque house into the bourgeois Orpheum, parlayed it into a New England chain, and finally moved west to form a lachrymose patriarchate called (long after Goldwyn left it) MGM in Culver City. "Carnivorous," said an associate in describing Mayer's demiurge. As to the Warner brothers, two had been born in the East and remained there; Jack had been born in Canada and, after accompanying his brothers to Baltimore and Youngstown, eventually headed for Hollywood, learning to revel in the glory that seemed his due. Still other moguls, such as Harry and Jack Cohn, the New York scions of immigrants and founders of Columbia, relished their life as bottom feeders, delighting in their crudeness, their shrewdness in borrowing stars from others, and the joy of tweaking lions' tails by winning Oscars.

Did these men succeed because they were Jewish? Probably not. But they had entered the marginal movie business because it not only gave free play to their immigrants' drive to make it, but also was the sort of declassé arena into which they were assured admission, unlike the gray circles of corporate banking that seemed a preserve of the old line. Indeed, they quickly learned to deal only with the banks that would have them, such as the Italian A. P. Giannini's San Francisco fief, the Bank of America. As Gabler observes in *An Empire of Their Own,* "Giannini and the Jews were equally marginal to the cultural establishment, and both were equally suspicious of the country's powerful economic forces." In much the same way, the moguls, acting out their roles as "others," eventually accepted lines of credit extended by emerging Jewish banks in the East: Zukor through Otto Kahn of Kuhn, Loeb; Laemmle through S. W. Strauss; and the Warners through Goldman, Sachs. Only the merged 20th Century-Fox (the "goy" studio after Fox's death) linked its credit line to the more ethnically neutral Halsey, Stuart.

Not that this network was exclusively tribalist. After all, Giannini was "Jewish" only in that he too felt the pinch of otherness, and the Warners' man at Goldman, Sachs was in fact Waddill Catchings, a banker who had been at Morgan Guarantee and Trust before his move to Goldman, Sachs. The basis for the professional relationship between Catchings and the Warners was pragmatic and focused eventually on helping turn the Warners into major players by exploiting soundfilm technology. Catchings helped by seeking out practicable sound systems at Western Electric or Bell Labs and promoting a mentality of readiness to exploit the new.

Largely, though, the movie moguls banked with other Jews, and, similarly, their studios were rife with nepotism. Even as F. W. Taylor's "time and motion studies" were permeating many American industries, including the movies, in the 1920s, spurring a drive for efficiency and rationality, there always seemed to be a place for a n'er-do-well uncle. As each studio took up the crusade toward budgeting, cost accounting, tightly managed producer-units, and soundstages, little cells of relatives— "glacier watchers" they were called in some studios—clung to their offices.

By the 1920s, production had stratified into producer-driven units. In fact, Bordwell and his coauthors characterize the system by then as a "central producer period," a moment of evolving efficiency when the units began to trim for productive action and when the favored relatives were shunted out of the way. To take only one instance, for the brief time that Irving Thalberg was production boss at MGM, the position of director, which had dominated production in Griffith's era, became akin to that of simply a master mechanic in a systemwide scheme of things. Thalberg, a slight, almost frail, Dartmouth graduate, was himself at first no more than the boss's pet son-in-law and an exemplar of nepotism. However, over the span of his brief career before his early death, he achieved notoriety for hobbling and finally silencing the extravagant Erich von Stroheim, who had become famous for his unrestrained attention to detail, particularly details of his various costume fetishes. Under Thalberg's command, Buster Keaton, famous in the early days of silent movies for his beautiful choreographing of chase sequences, was reduced to a consultant.

The other studios pursued their own versions of Taylorism. Supervisors and accountants oversaw the producers' units and in turn were monitored by the executives in New York, who analyzed everything from budgets to marketing. Each department in the system generated its own script: one for costing, one for costuming, yet another for casting calls, and finally a shooting script of three or four completed pages per day. More millwrights in a system than artists shaping their scenes, the departments managed to turn out movies that became "classical" in style. Only the odd maverick or tyro in from the East might occasionally slip the harness.

Within Thalberg's system a surprising range of personal styles was to be found among directors. For example, at MGM W. S. Van Dyke, a craftsman who had learned at the shoulder of Griffith, marched through every assignment with astonishing alacrity, earning the title of "One Take Woody." The moguls trusted him with everything, particularly odd, problematic details of movies that might have cost a fortune in retakes and insurance shots or even lost days or weeks. Van Dyke did epics of the wild, such as *White Shadows of the South Seas* (1928), *Trader Horn* (1931), and *Rose Marie* (1936), shot in the South Pacific, East Africa, and a backlot in Canada, respectively. He did big movies with all-star casts and elaborate historical settings and costumes, such as *San Francisco* (1936), which came complete with a special effects earthquake; *Marie Antoinette* (1938); and a string of Nelson Eddy/Jeannette MacDonald costumed romances. He did the studio's programmers that earned a steady profit each week, such as *Andy Hardy Gets Spring Fever* (1939), *Another Thin Man* (1939), and *Dr. Kildare's Victory* (1942). And he did them all on budget and on time.

Another director who managed to be both good soldier and savvy stylist was Sidney Franklin, who gave MGM the polished, urbane style that became Mayer's pride. And yet, Franklin accomplished his work by means of a self-effacement that preserved for the moviegoer the style of the novel or drama that was the movie's source. Like most contract directors, he had range too, as seen in such chestnuts from him as *Smilin' Through* (1932) and *Beverly of Graustark* (1926); Broadway fare such as *Private Lives* (1932) and *The Guardsman* (1931); and popular novels such as *The Good Earth* (1937). Together with Jack Conway, Clarence Brown, King Vidor, Frank Lloyd, and the others, they formed the center of MGM's identity as a stylish leader in the system.

Along with von Stroheim, Clarence Brown and King Vidor were among the few mutineers at MGM. Von Stroheim managed to slip his stylistic and erotic excesses into only one MGM film, *The Merry Widow* (1925), before Thalberg edged him out. Brown, however, enjoyed a reputation as a man with integrity rather than mere excess and a willingness to fight the front office, including Mayer himself, all the way up to 1949, when he and Dore Schary were able to bring William Faulkner's racial novel *Intruder in the Dust* to the screen over Mayer's objections.

Much as Brown enjoyed a long career with a studio of which he once said "they do everything in Christ's own world to stop you," so Vidor thought of himself as the maverick who forced Mayer to bend and allow him to do the risky, all-black, first truly soundfilm feature, *Hallelujah!*, in 1929. And not only was he allowed to do it, but he was able to do it as a rare location-shot movie.

At any rate, from the time Van Dyke began his apprenticeship with Griffith in the teens to Thalberg's heyday in the mid-1930s, the power gradually shifted from the director to either a producer at large, like Thalberg, or a production supervisor who guided teams assembled by producers, who in turn gingerly governed the unit's director, much like the hierarchy of workers, foremen, and "suits" who ruled any shop floor. Bordwell and his coauthors write that as early as 1916 the accounting firm of Price, Waterhouse had codified the business of moviemaking by means of their bookkeeping manual.

Hollywood did not become an institution simply because a few tough moguls cowed some authorial directors, however. And it was not just the publication of some handbooks on fiscal and manufacturing conduct, the solidification of the early free-market movie technology business into an oligopoly, the opportunities that the economic and industrial wreckage of World War I provided, or the new Jewish immigrants' victories in their dogfights with the patent-happy Edison and their migration to the cheap land in California that turned Hollywood, California, into HOLLYWOOD the movie mecca.

Rather, the tactics of both Hollywood and Washington in promoting overseas movie markets and maintaining a lax policy toward oligopoly arose out of a national business culture of managed laissez faire, which rewarded corporate buccaneering and conglomeration as never before. Finally, as we shall see in Chapter 3, HOLLYWOOD was also brought into being by the rows of people sitting in the darkened theaters, who had plans of their own for the movies.

CHAPTER THREE

Moviegoers

During Hollywood's classical era, the studios plied their movies through first, second, and even third and fourth runs, much like the "A-rabs" who hawked soft-shelled crabs in the alleys of Baltimore, working the best alleys early in the day when the crabs were lively and hitting the worst alleys on their way home late in the day, when the crabs were near death. As befit the uniformed ushers, fans, ice water, palmed grottos and genteel decorum of the first-run theaters, such as B. F. Keith's in Union Square, the moviemakers left vaudeville fare behind and increasingly put on the screen the tony ambience and uplifting fulfillment that brought in the people with the wallets. From its first run at a picture palace, and after a clearance of a couple weeks, a movie headed for its second run to the nabes, where (particularly during matinees) viewers were free to raise up the voices of conviviality, ethnic chauvinism, and dissent. Finally, scratched and spliced and as much as ten or fifteen minutes shorter than it started out, the movie reached the grind houses, where it was often played all day and all night.

This class-based approach to selling movies allowed the coexistence of mainstream bourgeois moviegoing on the Broadways and an alternative form of moviegoing in the nabes. In America, however, class was not caste (as the steelworkers knew, preferring the word *workingman* over *working class*), and every workingman had it within his power to save up a few pennies to take his family to a downtown theater to see an uplifting feature in exotically gilded and, more important, clean and decorous surroundings. African Americans (albeit in the balcony), immigrants, steelworkers—anyone with a yen for a posh night out and the cash to splurge on it could head for the picture palace. Thus exhibitors early on noticed the fractionate nature of movie audiences. In the working-class nabes and the cheap seats of the downtown palaces, the crowds were noisy, shabby, often fresh off the boat or off the train from Tuscaloosa. In the middle-class nabes and the loges in the palaces, the moviegoers were more genteel and expected amenities, especially after Adolph Zukor began to retail his "famous players in famous plays" in the teens. Adding still further to the multifaceted nature of movie audiences, as we shall see, was the "twoness" that ethnic and working-class audiences brought with them to either venue.

Who went to the movies, and why? Were movies informative and therefore appealed to an audience of the intellectually inquisitive? Or were movies mere exhibitions, attracting only curiosity seekers? In the early days were they mere chasers, signaling the ends of vaudeville shows, or had they quickly become attractive elements of vaudeville? Was it really so true, as some historians contend, that movies, by their silence, drew immigrants into their accessible orbits? Did women find in them a private space in which to act out their melodramatic fantasies, much as the nineteenth-century novel had spoken to their inner selves? What did movies provide to children to make some parents view movies as threatening the links between them and their children? Was it true that the movies, unreeling in the dark as they did, provided a deep-seated emotional experience akin to that attainable only in the circle of a primary group such as the family? Or were movies truly a universal medium that spoke to all peoples as one, as Carl Laemmle surely must have thought when he named his firm Universal Pictures. Surely the answer to these queries must be a slippery, tentative "both/and," a reckoning that allows for many readings of movies by many audiences.

This apparently evasive depiction of the movie audience arises in part from what every historian of the medium must confess is true: that the current state of "reception theory," as its practitioners call it, allows only light sketches of the audience to be drawn. Moreover, the image of the audience is often derived not so much from the historian's search for documents and his or her faith in their openness to analysis as from techniques and theories—rather than data—borrowed from other disciplines, particularly those grounded in Freudian, feminist, and Marxist formulations. Still, together with the vivid anecdotal accounts of audience behavior found in the bound volumes of old trade papers these analyses throw light on the "great audience" (as Gilbert Seldes titled his 1950 book) seated in the darkness, revealing its prismatic nature.

That is, unavoidably, the self of the moviegoer was composed of at least a "twoness," to borrow W.E.B. Du Bois's term for the mentality of African Americans as being, more than the mentalities of other Americans, both ethnic and American. More about this theoretical mode of inquiry later; for the moment, suffice it to say that Americans walked into movie theaters as embodiments of more than one psyche. They walked in as American, ethnic, gendered, colored, and classed.

If the primarily black section of Lexington, Kentucky, is any indication, African American audiences reflected this drive for both the American gentility at the palaces (though they often lacked the means to act on this desire) and the values of the "race movie" playing in their nabe. In general, theater men were baffled by blacks' attitudes toward moviegoing. Either they stayed away because, as one trade paper correspondent wrote, "no pictures are made with Senegambian faces," or their movie viewing was marked by "lots of singing and dancing and horseplay" and seemingly little actual viewing. Yet in Lexington, as early as 1907 a black theater man aimed for the black version of the same churched, literate, socially well affiliated, and employed middle class at whom Zukor aimed his "famous plays"—and he succeeded in finding it. "Come where you are welcome and meet your friends," encouraged his ads, with a nod to Jim Crow Lexington. The moviegoers he sought were "cultured and aristocratic," and he played to them in his "elegantly fixed up" Frolic Theatre. Gregory Waller, the historian who used the local press to pry into black Lexington, found that a similar black bourgeois taste-culture ranged over middle America from Lake Charles, Louisiana, to Evansville, Indiana. Some more urbane black moviegoers followed the example of Lester Walton, late ambassador to Liberia, and expressed their tastes by actively protesting against racist advertising such as lobby cards (posters) that luridly portrayed a lynching.

David Gordon Nielson reports in *Black Ethos* (1977) that the black bourgeoisie, churched, affiliated, and employed, constituted a small elite of old settlers, civil servants, preachers, and teachers, the "respectables" sitting at the head of a vast army of "riffraff." Short and shaky compared with the white social ladder, theirs was nonetheless a ladder of achievement and the respectables were on its top rung.

As Mary Carbine argues in "'The Finest Outside the Loop': Motion Picture Exhibition in Chicago's black Metropolis, 1905–1928" in *Camera Obscura* (1990), this black bourgeoisie, far from merely aping white culture, set about forging "a new, urban black culture" to replace the suddenly less usable one they had brought from the South. They felt a duty to aspire to "the finer things," as a character in the race movie *The Scar of Shame* put it, and this ideology of "uplift" accompanied them on their trips to the movie houses. Well aware of this, the ghetto theater men often advertised, along with their feature films, the toniness of their surroundings and the decorum of the clientele thereby attracted. "The Finest Outside the Loop," said one ad; "The Home of the Colored Race," boasted another. In such a setting, the black audience might view the general run of Hollywood fare, along with the occasional race movie that passed through, but the movie was so often accompanied by a black stage show that, according to Carbine, the totality of the experience "mitigated against the hegemony of mass [white] culture."

This urge for elegance within black circles was echoed in the printed record in Lexington. It was not so much the movies as the setting that was the draw. Waller writes that a clean establishment "run exclusively for colored people" meant more than a mere movie to "colored professional people of intelligence." If blacks' behavior differed from whites', it was in their noisy responses to "the serious places of great tragedies," said the black *Indianapolis Freeman*. Such irreverence in white circles seemed limited to the impish behavior at the Saturday children's matinees or, as Roy Rosenzweig (*Eight Hours for What We Will* [1983]) reports of working-class Worcester, Massachusetts, a "sociability, conviviality, communality, and informality" that clashed with the primness of bourgeois etiquette.

As Hollywood matured into HOLLYWOOD, the various sectors of the national audience, such as African American circles, often held their tongues and grudgingly went to see mainstream movies. However, they also sometimes challenged the hegemony of the studios and sometimes opposed it with products of their own. For example, when *The Birth of a Nation* appeared in 1915, Ambassador Walton attacked it as "vicious, untrue, and unjust" and declared that it had been "produced to cause race friction." The *Amsterdam News*, a black newspaper based in New York, cried, "Organize! Organize! Organize!" And indeed, after a season of blacks' taking to the streets and demanding that the movie be censored, *Crisis*, the mouthpiece of the fledgling National Association for the Advancement of Colored People (NAACP) was able to crow, "The latter half has been so cut . . . that it is . . . sometimes *ridiculous* in its inability to tell a coherent story." Simultaneously, Emmett J. Scott, secretary to Booker T. Washington, called for a new kind of movie with "that indefatigable something which I shall call *the colored man's viewpoint*." A quarter of a century later, on the eve of World War II, blacks still managed to embrace two modes of reception of movies, turning out for the all-black western *Bronze Buckaroo* (1940), while also celebrating signs of Hollywood's slow accommodation to black spectatorship, such as in 1938 when the *Amsterdam News* promoted a "Greater Negro Movie Month."

Thus to sectors of the black audience, movies served variously to rebut racism, to convey moral values, and simply to entertain. Perhaps it was the riffraff who bought more tickets, but it was the respectables' ideology of uplift, despite their fundamentalist prejudice against moviegoing, that dominated the press. The white press took a similar line. *Variety*, for example, reckoned that the racist tract *Free and Equal* (1925) had "no chance . . . to get a nickel anywhere." Black reviewers often took the point of view of the black critic Calvin Floyd, who urged *Uncle Tom's Cabin* (1927) on black moviegoers because "all through it the Negro is shown to splendid advantage." Even makers of race movies pressed the case for uplift. Their brochures insisted on such a goal; for example, in its handouts the Douglass company promised "to show the better side of Negro life" and thereby "to inspire in the Negro a desire to climb higher." And when a black filmmaker fell short, some black critic stood ready to shout, "No, Mr. Micheaux, society wants a real story of high moral aim."

In times of crisis in America's history, black ideals and white goals intersected, much as the Marxist theorist Antonio Gramsci might have predicted. According to Gramsci, at such moments indigenous leaders might arise from the ranks of the aggrieved and bargain for new political arrangements through which the group might advance its cause. In 1929, the Great Crash resulted in such an intersection, and it and the coincidental arrival of sound movies led to a considerable cultural event: black musical culture's move into white movies. King Vidor's *Hallelujah!*; a sister project from the Fox lot, *Hearts in Dixie*; and a string of musical shorts that tinkered with the uses of sound, among them Dudley Murphy's *St. Louis Blues*, with Bessie Smith, and *Black and Tan*, with Duke Ellington, were all released in that year. Oscar DePriest, the nation's only black member of Congress (and thus a delegate from all of African America), certainly saw it as a significant cultural event. "We are standing on the threshold of civic and cultural emancipation in America," he announced at the "colored" premiere of *Hallelujah!* at Harlem's fabled Lafayette Theatre, and he congratulated MGM for having "opened a new field" of Negro expression. Not only did DePriest and other public figures keep before the movie moguls this black agenda of emancipation, but several black letter writers nagged the moguls whenever they lapsed into the worst of the old images.

As I discuss in more detail in Chapter 9, during World War II this black activism merged with the efforts of like-minded federal agencies, for whom "Hitler had given racism a bad name." For the first time since the Reconstruction, the government seemed the likely agency for reforming historically oppressive racial arrangements. As though with a nod to Gramsci, this coalition—for indeed it became one—of black organic leaders and their white allies among the Marxists; the non-Marxist left who embraced a "liberalism of the heart," as one of them put it; and the staff of the Office of War Information and the Pentagon not only spoke for an audience, but also sought to convert a broader audience to their racial politics.

Although this frail alliance did not transform Americans' or even Hollywood's racial attitudes, it did heighten alertness to racism and taught audiences that they had a capacity to act in concert and were not restricted to sitting passively in the darkened theater. In the vanguard of this movement was Walter White of the NAACP, who held his group's 1942 annual convention in Los Angeles, where he could reach the moguls in their lairs. As a champion he chose Wendell Willkie, the defeated Republican presidential candidate of 1940, special counsel to the NAACP, chair of the board of 20th Century-Fox, and a figure in the liberal wing of his party. As though pointing out to the moguls the link between the war and racism, in a memo David O. Selznick instructed his writer on *Gone with the Wind* to see that "the Negro comes out on the right side of the ledger . . . in these fascist-ridden times." Conveying these ideas and actions to the audience itself was William G. Nunn of the black *Pittsburgh Courier*. For weeks on page 1 of the *Courier*, Nunn called for a "Double Victory" over foreign fascism and domestic racism.

In this way, the African American movie audience more than any other showed that it was possible for a dedicated group to countervail against an oppressive status quo. It not only voted for a changed cinema with its purchase of tickets, but also actively shared in the creation of a new cinema from the shards of the older cinema that once had treated African Americans either as a "structured absence" or, worse, as incidental servants and entertainers.

To find a similar vein of activism regarding movies among other ethnic groups is a tantalizing ambition, yet proves more difficult. The sheer number of immigrant taste-cultures, not to mention stark differences in numbers, recency of arrival, and old-country values, obligates the student to exercise more caution. Perhaps the main trait that blacks and immigrants shared was their sense of neighborhood, with its warm embrace that conveyed a "members only" exclusivity. Blurring of the lines between classes was the result in the immigrant groups, and therefore the distinction between respectables and riffraff that characterized black circles was less clear. Perhaps it is for this reason that movie historians have often merged class and group in their treatment of audiences, particularly in the early years of movies.

Immigrants, women, and members of the working class often shared the "twoness" that characterized African American cultural affiliations or identities, but because they were seldom segregated according to their group, they more readily shifted between ethnicity and Americanness, gender-determined and general behavior, and class-based and classless activity. Of course, like African Americans, they knew where to go to feel like members of a club when they wanted to. Children knew their rude behavior and their whistling through candy boxes were tolerated during Saturday matinees. Teens might catch a Saturday matinee in corduroy knickers and cloth caps, only to come home and change into their Easter suits and porkpie hats in time to join their parents in a Saturday evening viewing of *The President Vanishes* (1934). Women knew that afternoon "shoppers' delights" were meant for them, featuring "women's movies." Immigrants knew that they might just as well go see *Love Finds Andy Hardy* (1939) at Loew's Valencia (with its glistening stars set in its cerulean ceiling) as see *Der Kongress Tanzt* (1931) at the neighborhood Cameo. Leftists similarly might relish *We from Kronstadt* (1936) at the World, yet go see *Navy Blue and Gold* (1935) at the Paramount. However, unlike black audiences, the white working-class audiences did lack a specific alternative cinema to Hollywood's paeans to individualism, which celebrated work while ignoring the corporate barriers to earning its rewards (much as evil in *Black Fury* [1937] is attributed not to corporate greed but to trade union greed). Still, come Saturday night, they knew they could just as well stay in the neighborhood, sharing two hotdogs at the Greek's and settling down in the worn seats of the Grand, as splurge on a movie at a Stanley-Warner house downtown. If they opted for the nabe, they might take in the second run of Hollywood product, giving it a spin, an alternative meaning, that being in a darkened auditorium among neighbors invited them to do. However, they might be back at the nabe on Sunday, seeking "the finer things" in a second-run Technicolor feature. Wednesday night might find them once again at the same nabe, this time embracing ethnicity in a foreign-language film or race movie that was starting its split-week run.

In other words, ethnic and working-class moviegoers experienced a duality of selves, one normative and the other alternative. Only African Americans found this twoness to be represented in the laws, in which were embedded many weightier discriminations and disabilities that were based specifically on a group trait—skin color. So for many Americans (even African Americans), it was possible to embrace two identities and therefore two strands of moviegoing, the one centrist and the other not. Whether they viewed a movie from a centrist perspective or the perspective of "other" and, if they took the latter perspective, to what degree they gave the movie an alternative spin depended what the movie was, what time of day they were viewing it (a matinee showing or evening showing), what venue they were in (was the rustling of ushers' uniforms or the grinding of the projector in the air?) and in what proportions ethnicity and assimilationism contributed to their identity. To understand this is to understand the prismatic quality of movie audiences.

We might account for the sensibility of moviegoers experiencing American life as a twoness—Americanness along with a doppelganger rooted in gender, ethnicity, race, class, and even region—by briefly considering the work of Jürgen Habermas. Habermas argued that certain "crowd containers" —arenas, theaters, all sorts of public places—constitute a *bürgerliche Öffentlichkeit*, a space in which, for example, workers can be themselves, free from the eyes of their bosses. Some movie historians, such as Miriam Hansen, have applied Habermas's notion to the theater, arguing that in its darkness minorities are free to read mainstream or alternative meanings into movies, each in his or her own style.

Now that we have seen how multiform the audience was, let us take a look at the forces that were at work to homogenize it and whether they succeeded. We must proceed with caution in this inquiry, bearing in mind that the idea of a homogeneous audience is "an abstraction generated by the researcher," write Robert Allen and Douglas Gomery in *Film History: Theory and Practice* (1985). Still, it is possible to take a measure of the extent to which the myriad psyches, each itself a prism, were sculpted into one inside the darkened theater.

The attempt to homogenize occurred primarily in the picture palaces. As we know from Chapter 2, movies, arrived on the American scene at a time when capitalists had free rein to make of them whatever the market would bear, and this situation invited moviemakers to cultivate the audience with the most disposable income and the biggest slice of leisure time. This was the ever increasing, ever more professional, ever more urbane middle class of trained white-collar workers. Exemplifying the newly forming class, architects in America earned many times over the wages of factory hands, yet worked on average under 40 hours per week and expected generous vacations and liberal sick leave. Thus they had the means to obtain, the leisure to enjoy, and a collective wish for "the finer things." It was this class who most buffed off their ethnic group traits and most valued conformity to the larger group.

This new class of managers and professionals readily embraced the emerging gentility of movies, abandoning other forms of entertainment to the working class. In "The Leg Business" in *Camera Obscura* (1990), Robert Allen writes that in the Gilded Age, the time of prosperity that ensued after the Civil War, burlesque became "that arena of culture evacuated by the bourgeoisie in the process of its consolidation." The middle class was culturally trading up. At the end of the century, movies arrived, and within a decade, thanks to the vision of producer Adolph Zukor and his followers, who chose "to kill the slum tradition in the movies," the medium was opened to the prospect of dominance by middle-class taste-culture. Movies would be "art," wrote the scriptwriter Frank Woods, "instead of merchandise"; indeed, said the *New York Dramatic Mirror*, they would be "democratic art."

In the palaces that both echoed and fantasized on their lives, the new professional class sat back in their seats with plenty of time to enjoy the movies in the story form they were coming to expect and the signs of the capital the moviemakers poured into this class-based market: air cooling (not yet air conditioning), popped corn and other nourishments, and acres of gilded plaster that made the Aztec Theater in San Antonio, the Alhambra Theater in Manhattan, the Valencia Theater in Baltimore, and the Roxys everywhere reminiscent of romantic locales. Thus venue and product worked together to create the darkened world said by culture critics such as Jacques Lacan to convey the politics of the status quo so effectively as to render onlookers powerless to resist.

The movie fare reflected society's drive for a higher political ground, at once reformist and capitalist, Progressive and yet acquisitive. Much as vaudeville had been two-edged in the way it addressed its audience, movies spoke to their viewers' wish for inclusion even as they spoke to their otherness, thereby simultaneously, Albert McLean writes in *American Vaudeville as Ritual* (1965), "creating a community of city dweller, by establishing norms of taste and behavior" while allowing the "others" in the audience—surely not the middle-class folks—to laugh at the immigrant humor of the comedy duo Weber and Fields, the black humor of Dusty Fletcher, or the smirking feminism of Mae West. Thus, almost every ethnic group, save for Asians and Mexicans, appeared with a winsome softheartedness that promised that any "other" might enter the charmed circle of Americanness.

At the same time, Lary May points out in *Screening out the Past* (1980), the century also marked a break with many constraints of middle-class decorum, a drift that movies both trailed after and served. After the bohemianism of Greenwich Village and the famous avant-garde Armory Show of 1913 revealed a fissure in the primness of American culture, movies celebrated this liberation in the forms of Douglas Fairbanks and Mary Pickford—their on-screen personas, their off-screen exuberance, and the open-faced philosophies expressed in his advice books and her daily column. That is, even the universal movies ploughed new ground.

Expressed as an American ideal, the emerging culture seemed to be rooted in both the puritan virtues of work and moderation and openness to the new. By extension, the new class of managers and professionals offered a visible lesson of openness to upward mobility, in that their accomplishments were made to seem an outcome of education rather than of venture capital. This ideal embraced immigrant icons of success such as the publisher Edward Bok, the scientist Nicola Tesla, the broadcasting entrepreneur David Sarnoff, and the novelist Anzia Yezierska. Unlike their forebears, they embraced the ideals of both work and pleasure. Even the aristocracies of the industrialists—German tool-and-die manufacturers, machinists, and master mechanics—joined in, as subscribers to the newly formed Baltimore Symphony. All told, the result was nothing less than what Garth Jowett calls a "recreation revolution" (*Film*) that followed from a national "shift from the

Protestant ethos toward a therapeutic ethos stressing self-realization" (T. J. Jackson Lears in "From Salvation to Self-Realization," in his and R. W. Fox's *The Culture of Consumption* [1983]).

In the cities, as we have seen, these sophisticates were served by networks of electrified trams, elevated and underground trains, and other public transport that brought them to movies, sporting events, and other amusements staged in crowd containers. As never before, this middle class not only was served a swelling inventory of amenities, but also shared some of them with the lower classes through their advocates among the Progressive social workers. They read socially conscious magazines such as *Collier's, Harper's,* and *Outlook.* Their cities rivaled each other in a civic spirit reflected in the "City Beautiful" campaign, which led to the creation of parks and public spaces open to strollers, skaters, players, and cyclists. Every city either engaged the services of Frederick Law Olmsted, the designer of rustic, yet urban dells, or wished it had. When social dysfunction marred the civic order, reformers and social workers called it "juvenile delinquency" and set out to remedy it.

Consumption of commodities began to be driven by advertising. The pioneering N. W. Ayer agency as well as the Sears Roebuck catalogues proclaimed the new economic order. And order it was. Remote from "the anarchic competitiveness of laissez faire capitalism," reports David Cook in *History of Narrative Film* (1990), it seemed on the cusp of "a more orderly pursuit of profit." By the end of World War I, with its national distribution system firmly in place and Hollywood having become HOLLYWOOD, the moviemakers must have shared similar feelings of unity with a corporate system. As a child of this bold new world—small town version—the critic Henry Seidel Canby remembered himself as "by easy and natural experience part of a conscious, an organized, a unified society" (quoted by May in *Screening out the Past*). Similarly, in the palaces, the classical Hollywood A movie enjoyed access to its bourgeois audiences in what Rosenzweig calls in *Eight Hours for What We Will* "a national market insulated from local pressures."

During the age of classical Hollywood, how did ethnic and working-class moviegoers negotiate the contested ground between the palaces and the nabes, Hollywood's A and B movies and the alternative cinema that made war on "the stuffiest white convention"? Could they find and enjoy "this ideal [and] democratic" cinema, as Hansen calls it, or were they mere dupes being fed images of "legitimation for capitalist practices and ideology"?

Although a quasihomogeneous audience of the middle class emerged, the marketplace of alternative cinemas for politically active blacks, feminists, radicals, class cohorts, and regional chauvinists (such as southerners) persisted in parallel to the bourgeois main market.

Clash of cultures or coexistence? Which trope best explains the dual existence of the crowd who took the streetcar to the downtown theater and those who walked or took the bus to the second run in the nabe? Perhaps it was a little of both, clash and coexistence. If we view the setting in the light of John Kenneth Galbraith's "countervailing forces," we see that no one group could entirely win the game. The studios' pursuit of a national market and homogenization intruded on the working-class neighborhood in the form of the second-run Hollywood feature, but the intrusion was on the neighborhood's terms—if Hollywood wanted their 25 cents, it usually had to come to their nabe, where they sat in the psychic comfort of a "club" composed of others like themselves. In the nabe, too, alternative movies persisted in the form of foreign-language films and "ghetto films," often double-billed with an American product. In "dark towns," that is, neighborhoods in which the majority of the population was African American, audiences were kept apart by race either by law or by such practices as having simultaneous black and white premieres and first runs, one in the black neighborhood and one in the white neighborhood. MGM did this for the opening of *Hallelujah!* (1929) in New York City, showing it simultaneously in Harlem and in Midtown. Blacks, too, brought with them to the theaters a pluralistic etiquette and class culture, as indicated by theaters that advertised their gentility and those that catered to the riffraff.

When the working class journeyed to the downtown theater, they did a little intruding on Hollywood's homogenization, taking their boisterousness with them, albeit dampened slightly by the moms who required man and boy alike to wear ties and the man to stay awake through the weepy parts and the boy to sit still.

And so it was that in the years between the two world wars, even though the bourgeois national marketplace was growing, bringing with it A&P supermarkets, McCrory's and Woolworth's five-and-dimes, and the chains of movie houses owned either by studio affiliates, such as Loew's, or by regional chains, such as Wilby-Kincey and Saenger in the South and Balaban and Katz in the Midwest, working-class audiences clung to cultural and ethnic pluralism, refusing to allow the trend toward homogeneity to pass unchallenged.

The pioneering chroniclers Maurice Bardèche and Robert Brasillach wrote in *The History of Motion Pictures* (1938) that the movies taught "Babbitt how to kiss a countess' hand, how to peel a peach, [and how to] use finger bowls and keep his hands out of his pockets"; however, this was only as Babbitt read these through the prism of class and group.

That said, the contest between the universal "American" and the particularistic "other" was an uneven one, in that in both arenas, the picture palace and the nabe, assimilationism held the high ground. This was particularly so after the coming of sound and thus the spoken word. In "Making America Home" in the *Journal of American History* (1992), Michael Rogin argues that talkies provided a platform for Jewish performance that offered a sentimental assimilationism without actually surrendering identity. Furthermore, he argued, Jewish performers such as Al Jolson and Eddie Cantor came to the nuances of their Americanism under the mask of blackface, an American show business convention derived from minstrelsy that gave them access to the feelings of marginality felt by both blacks and Jews. Blacks saw this, marveled at it, and, in a grudging way, sometimes even credited Jewish performers with a unique racial prescience. "Every colored performer is proud of [Jolson]," wrote a critic in the *Amsterdam News* in 1930.

Another way that talkies furthered assimilation was the fact that they obliged moviegoers to listen silently, imitating middle-class decorum in a way that unavoidably challenged the hegemony of working-class conviviality. In contrast, in the silent era the main threat to the "other" had been the images themselves and the implicit theses they enacted. As Kay Sloane reports in *The Loud Silents* (1988), silent movies may have seemed "threatening to society," but they were also an effective and "uplifting . . . vehicle for middle class reforms." Sloane documents, moreover, that interest groups ranging from the reformist Russell Sage Foundation to the National Association of Manufacturers served as "angels," or financial backers, for Edison movies that exposed loan-sharking and advocated safety on the job, among the sort of paternalistic messages that might help shape the ethnic audience into the tractable toilers whose diet of happily ending movies fed them what Lenin called a "false consciousness."

However, neither moviemakers nor moviegoers were conscious of their roles, the former as purveyors of ideology and the latter as sponges absorbing it. The moviemakers made what sold; moviegoers bought tickets to what pleased them. Considering that women made up a large proportion of moviegoers, let us examine the variety of images offered to women during the 1920s, what we might think of as the High Middle Ages of Hollywood's classical era. Of course, at that time the studios had no measure of their audiences other than ticket sales. Still, these revenues served as at least a crude form of, as a 1940s poll put it, a "want-to-see index." And women, whether housewives, "career girls," mothers, shoppers, or workers between shifts, bought tickets.

When one thinks of women in the United States in the 1920s, one thinks of flappers, but in fact portrayals of women acquired uncommon breadth, a spectrum in which the flapper merely took her place. However, because of her coyly flippant sexuality, the flapper became the icon of the era. Such directors as Ernst Lubitsch and Cecil B. DeMille treated her with a fragile irony or a slyly pornographic eye, and writers such as Anita Loos and Bess Meredyth fed her her lines. Mary Pickford and Clara Bow, each in her own way, cashed in on the androgyny that had held a place in American popular culture ever since the legend of Molly Pitcher, the artillerist at the battle of Monmouth. This ambiguous sexuality also appeared in movies in the form of Tom Sawyer's cross-dressing and Julian Eltinge's drag act, which had come to the screen from vaudeville. Pickford's boy-girl roles earned her the title of "America's sweetheart." Bow's bouncy innocents possessed "it," a sort of unselfconscious sexuality. Helen Kane's Betty Boop provided an animated cartoon version of Bow's boyish sexiness. In the serial *The Perils of Pauline*, each Saturday morning brought new dangers for Pearl White to contend with, her slight frame conveying a feminine agility rather than frailty.

In 1914, William Fox brought to the screen the most disturbing "new woman" in the person of Theda Bara (an anagram, it was said, for "Arab Death"), the exotic stage name given Theodosia Goodman of Cincinnati. In that year she appeared as a "vamp," a female vampire who fed off men. Written of by Kipling, given a visual image by the painter Burne-Jones, the vamp was finally rendered on film in Fox's *A Fool There Was*. Bara's movies caught the rakish spirit of the moral outlaws of the times who, like the bohemians of Greenwich Village and the persona Edna St. Vincent Millay presented in her poems, burned their candles at both ends and "loved the lovely light." These melodramatic movies about women at the end of their rope became known as "women's movies" and reached across the lines of class and group by applauding women's breaking with their constricted past, embracing sexuality, and challenging men's dominance. The movies carried the message from bohemia to Dubuque.

Although strong women characters gained entry to the movies as the exotic heroines of romantic melodrama, they soon appeared as quite conventional women who decide to rebel. How quickly Hollywood learned to exploit the successes of other popular media may be seen in the movie made from Zona Gale's 1920 novel *Miss Lulu Bett*. Gale, a rare female graduate of the University of Wisconsin, told the story of a drudge who spends her young adulthood in servitude to a family of ungrateful, even contemptuous, relatives, and for whom marriage is not a ticket out but only more of the same. Her husband, who turns out to be a witless clod and apparent bigamist, manages to reduce her life to an indentured toil easily as oppressive as her former life. Only a last-minute reprieve in the form of a decent man offers her an improbable path toward fulfillment.

Gale's book became an immediate best-seller and in October 1920 the theatrical producer Brock Pemberton invited Gale to write an adaptation for the stage (a feat she accomplished in a single weekend). The play opened in December 1920 and in May of the following year won a Pulitzer prize for drama. The director William C. DeMille, acting on behalf of Paramount, made an offer for the movie rights, and he and his wife, Clara Berenger, a scenarist of note, wrote the script from which a fine movie was produced.

No telling how Gale's stage drama actually played, but the movie version is a marvel for the way in which it offers a feminist rebellion as the political choice of a commonplace woman. DeMille and Berenger gave Lulu a triumphant kitchen-vandalizing scene in which she literally and symbolically ends her current mode of living and opens up the prospect of a new one with a rustically handsome schoolteacher who is uncommonly understanding about her forlorn past. More dramatically conclusive than the novel, and perhaps a bit heavy on the Hollywood ending, the movie nevertheless kept enough of its realistic edge that Edith Wharton called it "a hard little picture."

The movies presented these new women—the vamp and the rebel—to a waiting audience of not only women, but also men recently returned from the war in Europe, where they had encountered women who seemed more multidimensional than either the drudge or the vamp. Certainly, Cecil B. DeMille's women seemed so, be they the wisecracking, androgynous

Calamity Jane in *The Plainsman* (1937) or the rueful women in *Manslaughter* (1922) and *Male and Female* (1919). The cosmopolitan women of Erich von Stroheim's *Foolish Wives* (1921) and *Blind Husbands* (1919) reached beyond convention and carried American female audiences with them. King Vidor similarly extended the range for African American women in *Hallelujah!* (1929). From 1930 to 1934, Josef von Sternberg gave Marlene Dietrich the same sort of reach in the exotic settings of *Morocco, Blonde Venus, The Shanghai Express*, and *The Scarlet Empress*.

To fill the void left by the loss of innocence that Henry F. May identified on the eve of World War I, Americans turned not to Protestant salvationism, but to a religion of secular fulfillment. Enjoyment of the moment replaced the hope for heaven; the diversions of the new took precedence over the substance of tradition. A surface slickness hardened all things, including dress and manners; games and sports leavened lives flattened by the daily round; the wisecrack and the deadpan left no room for sincere expression of feelings.

This new mentality was fueled by, even defined by, the movies. As Lary May argues in *Screening out the Past*, not only did movies prod the rush toward play and consumption, but actors and their ghostwriters served as a secular priesthood who celebrated the decline of puritanism. Almost all the big movie stars wrote autobiographies that testified to both their demiurge for success and their zest for the materialism that was their due. Popularizations of Freud loosened the hold of old conventions as surely as Emily Post freed the bourgeoisie from the stuffiness of outworn manners. As for people's regard for the movies, a woman interviewed by Robert S. Lynd and Helen M. Lynd *(Middletown,* 1929) said that in the twenties she had routinely sent her kid to the movies "to learn the ways of the world."

What of the size of this ever growing spectatorship? Garth Jowett in *Film: The Democratic Art* (1976) and Robert Sklar in *Movie-Made America* (1975) present data culled from trade papers and federal agencies that reveal a startling transformation of American behavior. In the 1920s, as many as one-third of urban youth attended movies twice each week. By 1923, *Film Daily* reckoned that in America alone 50 million tickets were sold each week, for a $500 million annual gross. To this imposing figure was added the revenues from overseas theaters, where nine out of ten movies were American movies. American households were seeing an average of three movies a week by the end of the decade, when the Great Depression hit. Surprisingly, despite the moviemakers' striving for the carriage trade, the lower class had the stronger predilection for spending their leisure time in the movies. Boy Scouts and Girl Scouts contented themselves with one or two movies a week; it was the delinquent kids who went to the movies three times a week, according to Alice Miller Mitchell in *Children and Movies* (1929).

The fearful watchdogs of ominous shifts in American moral behavior and observers of trends in real estate prices were equally riveted by the consumption boom between the wars. The watchdogs wished for a movie culture that was proper recreation and would dampen adolescents' bent upon a life that, as moralists, they saw as out of control. The real estate speculators, as one of Jowett's sources reports, looked with favor on clearing the land where fading nickelodeons stood and erecting movie palaces where property and land values were high. Their interests intersected at the grind houses in the urban tenderloin districts, where delinquent kids went as often as five times a week to lounge in the dark, smoke Sweet Caporals unnoticed by bluenoses, and gaze at grainy chronicles of "expeditions" to darkest Africa, which seemed overpopulated by brown-skinned, bare-breasted women. Here realtors envisioned new generations of Roxys and Bijous growing amid the decay.

But such scenes were only sidebars to the larger story of Hollywood's creation of new markets among the comfortable, genteel, and well-off—and those who wished to be so. Rudolph Valentino, for example, was made into the same sort of object for the female audience that advertising culture had made of women for men. Quite apart from his glittering place among the stars, the complexity of his persona made him a marketing strategist's dream come true. In *Babel & Babylon* (1985), Miriam Hansen writes that while watching the movie version of Blasco Ibanez's novel of the bullring, *Blood and Sand* (1922), one woman might have fantasized that she aroused the erotic glances from Valentino, playing the role of vamp in her mind, whereas another, more conventionally passive woman may have merely received Valentino's suggestive looks. The point is, both women went to the movie, as did many others, who found Valentino a complex figure, part athlete, part gigolo, part lounge lizard, part man on the make—a menu, it must be said, that might have appealed to men as well, either homosexual or straight.

Such goings on were unnerving to the defenders of the American home and hearth, particularly when these exotic stars—not only Valentino but Theda Bara, Nita Naldi, Vilma Banky, or Pola Negri, Ramon Navarro,

Ricardo Cortez, and the other "continental" stars—were offered up in the fan magazines and gossip columns as vaguely foreign and therefore creatures free from American conventions. The clergy and other guardians of morality felt assailed. To them, the magnetism of the movies for the young seemed overpowering. Their fears were grounded both in the nature of Hollywood as vaguely foreign and remote from church halls and service clubs and in the weak nature of moviegoers, who were perceived to have, as the critic Walter B. Pitkin wrote, "poor minds." Unavoidably, genteel culture struggled to gain control of this erotic curiosa in order to render it wholesome enough to play Peoria.

Other genres of movies, particularly those whose formulas began at the birth of the movies, such as the various action movies, including the slapstick comedies of Charles Chaplin and Buster Keaton; the westerns of Bronco Billy Anderson, William Surrey Hart, and later Tom Mix; and the adventure yarns that carried their audiences to the outbacks of the world, evaded the attention of reformers and sociologists, who had turned a wary eye upon women's movies. Apparently, because these genres owed their lives to forebears in the preelectronic culture of traveling performance, vaudeville circuits, superreal road-show melodrama, and the "real" cowboys and Indians of Buffalo Bill Cody's Wild West shows, they escaped the reformers' attention.

Without them and the women's movies, what was eventually to become the classical Hollywood movie might not have emerged. For without these inherited forms, movie culture might have taken a more cerebral, refined form, perhaps along the lines of the metaphysical poetry of Gerard Manley Hopkins or D. W. Griffith's *Lines of White on a Sullen Sea* (1909) or *Pippa Passes* (1909), a moving tableau illustration of Browning's poem that Griffith shot in what he called "Rembrandt light." Effete rather than energetic. Elevating rather than elating. Enigmatic rather than exciting.

In any case, on the verge of the Great Depression, the movies, at least some of them, carried a scarifying onus as purveyors of values that clashed with those of the nation's preachers and divines. Despite this and despite the stock market crash in October 1929 that plunged the nation into an economic slough from which an entire decade was not time enough to recover, the vertically integrated system of moviemaking somehow survived—perhaps *because* of its hierarchical division of labor that drove production from script to screen. In fact, in the months after the crash, attendance at movies shot up, and the nut of a typical Hollywood movie reached about a quarter of a million dollars, compared with a few thousand in 1920. True, as the Depression settled over the land, attendance slumped from some 90 million in 1930 to a low of 60 million in 1934, before an incremental recovery began. But this relatively brief period on the bottom gave rise to the legend that Hollywood had been immune from the economic forces that had wracked other industries, a fable that was probably true of those studios that had not overinvested in theatrical realty. To be sure, five thousand theaters closed, but many of them had been marginal anyway. More important was the fact that through the worst of economic despair the percentage of the average American family's income that was spent on moviegoing actually rose.

Indeed, amusement seemed such an urgent matter that Americans were ready to give up anything else, rather than stint on simple pleasures. Even poor families preferred to do without an icebox or even a bed, rather than give up their radios, Erik Barnouw reports in *History of Broadcasting* (1966–70). In *Film: The Democratic Art*, Jowett reports that people he interviewed said that moviegoing was "a comparative necessity" during hard times. So firm was the weekly habit that Gerald Mast (*A Short History of Movies*, 1971) reckons that a "circle of dependence" forged production, exhibition, and moviegoing into a well-oiled apparatus as never before seen.

As for those studios burdened by disused theaters, most of them retrenched, sold off holdings, and resorted to double features and bingolike games. Thus only one of them, Paramount, which had spread its resources too thinly over its Publix theaters and its rash purchase of a share of CBS, reached the verge of bankruptcy. As for the rest, their audiences fed on the midweek double features; went to B-movie matinees; and were drawn by programs augmented by animated cartoons, "short subjects" (topical one-reelers about an exotic place, an unusual profession, and so on), and serials, the one- and two-reel episodes that ended each Saturday with the hero at risk and a teaser as to the improbable rescue that would begin next week's episode. Not that A movies did not pull in their share. Ranging from musicals such as *Golddiggers of 1933* (1933); to political tracts such as *The President Vanishes* (1934) and *Gabriel over the White House* (1933); to westerns such as *Billy the Kid* (1930) and *Stagecoach* (1939); to message movies such as *Black Fury* (1935) and *The Black Legion* (1936); and to ever more sophisticated comedies, such as *Dinner at Eight* (1933), and movie versions of the slick novels of the day, such as *Imitation of Life* (1934) and *Grand Hotel* (1932), A movies still played the flagships of the studios' chains and remained the heavy money earners they had been since the end of World War I.

If movie audiences changed at all in the Depression, it was only in their taste in heroes, according to Nick Roddick (*A New Deal in Entertainment: Warner Brothers in the 1930s* [1983]). In the first days of Roosevelt's New Deal, heroes ran to group leaders rather than to lone wolves, that is, to Tom Keene in *Our Daily Bread* (1934) rather than, as later, to James Cagney in *Angels with Dirty Faces* (1938). Early in the Depression, the bad guys seemed to prefer cabals and conspiracies as their modus operandi, a choice that obliged the heroes to form their own "secret sixes" in such movies as *The President Vanishes*. Later, when the economy stabilized, political conspiracies persisted, even into the halls of Congress, but the heroic defenders against them had become lone populists, the prime example being, of course, James Stewart in *Mr. Smith Goes to Washington* (1939), the defining scene of which is Stewart's croaking filibuster before an unheeding Congress.

The shift from collective to individual heroism was also seen in fictional movies set in foreign locales, such as *The House of Rothschild* (1934) and *The Life of Emile Zola* (1937), two movies that took up the theme of anti-Semitism. In the earlier film, anti-Semitism is confronted by the collective, with old Nathan Rothschild and his dutiful sons pitting their family banking empire against imperious Napoleon himself. In the later film, the novelist hero Zola, standing as though alone against the French Army, uses his celebrity as a writer to rally opinion on behalf of a Jewish artillerist unjustly charged with treason and sent to Devil's Island.

Did moviegoers attend movies because of the qualities of these genres, themes, and styles, or were they merely, to use *Variety's* word, "sure-seaters" who went to see anything on their nights off? Were the studios correct then in seeking to steady their marketplace by obliging exhibitors to "blockbook" or even "blindbook," that is, to rent movies in blocks that included duds and risks or, indeed, to rent movies that were not even in the can yet?

Perhaps the audience readily took to the individualist politics embedded in the movies of the Depression, or perhaps they gave them another spin, derived from the particular venue in which they viewed them. It is also possible, though the least likely, that they surrendered their class and group interests and gave themselves over to a false consciousness, prostrating themselves before the goddess of the status quo. In any case, few would have subjected their movies to political analysis. Of course, if Lacan was correct, many moviegoers entered the theater ready to embrace the politics of the movies in much the same way that children's openness to experience brings them shocks of recognition by which they make their way from a sense of puerile self to a sense of themselves as "other" yet with a place in a family circle. Then again, perhaps what the audiences "recognized" on the screen amounted to nothing more than how to hold a cigarette or kiss a lover's hand.

Clearly, however, moviegoers who were conscious of the movies' tenuous link with real life and refused to be taken in by them easily vented their cynicism against the pat endings and easy denouements. They giggled aloud, catcalled at the screen, and otherwise stood up to the movies' attempts to manipulate their emotions. Recent culture critics who have found in movies an efficient vehicle for conveying a politics of either self or society have missed the irreverent contempt, the hooting derision with which adversarial movie-goers greeted screen fare that violated their sensibilities, based as they were in the real world of nabe, class, race, or group. And of course, as always, a good movie might have been simply a good movie, nothing more, nothing less.

But what of the psychologists' cant about escapism? Was *Stand Up and Cheer* (1934) no more than a means of flight from despair by Americans too shattered by the Depression to do more than stare vapidly at a screen full of the white telephones and money that their own lives had disallowed them? In part yes, write Mast in *A Short History of the Movies* and Andrew Bergman in *We're in the Money: Depression America and Its Films* (1971). But the escape route was also a source of examples of "human grit and triumph over suffering" that gave people plausible hope that "eventually good people would make bad times better." So even if some movies diverted attention from the era's social despair by means of "subtle propaganda" or even "overt manipulation," still others stammered out alternative meanings. For example, in *Movie-Made America* Sklar argues that Mae West's flaunting of sexuality not only flew in the face of middle American convention, but also arrived "in time to catch the movie public in its disenchantment with traditional values." Contrarily, moviegoers might have also stiffened at Capra's sentimentally optimistic movies. Other resistance to facile hope may even have derived from seeing the despair set forth in other movies, like the federal government's documentaries *The River* (1937) or *The Plow That Broke the Plains* (1936) or John Ford's sentimental (it must be said) version of John Steinbeck's populist fable *The Grapes of Wrath* (1940).

If the politics of such centrist movies seemed too spineless, there was a more polemical alternative cinema to which a politically left moviegoer might turn. Its ranks included the grainy tracts of America's two most radical filmmakers, the Marxist, even Stalinist, Nykino and the Film and Photo League; the films of industrial unions such as Walter Reuther's United Auto Workers; and the movies of other agencies that provided narrowcasting for the faithful.

The onset of World War II did not change everything, but it did change a few things. James Feibleman, in *Theory of Culture* (1968) argues that the tightening of defensive circles against foreign enemies resulted in a socialization of political subcultures into a cohesive domestic alliance, as well. On its face such coalescing might seem the occasion for narrowing the range of dissent and diversity. But as Antonio Gramsci (cited by Stuart Hall in "Gramsci's Relevance for the Study of Race and Ethnicity" in the *Journal of Communication Inquiry* [1986]) argued in the case of Sardinians and Sicilians in Italy, moments of cultural crisis also result in confluences of goals, for example, the majority's aim for victory, as against a minority's wish for a renegotiated status. Indeed, as though tutored by Gramsci, the black *Pittsburgh Courier* mounted its "Double Victory" campaign during World War II, calling for simultaneous victories over foreign fascism and domestic racism, a formulation that blacks and their liberal allies would carry into peacetime as an anticipation of the goals of the civil rights movement.

After the war, a newly anomic, suburbanizing drift thinned the ranks of the movie audiences. Wishing to thank its citizen soldiers for giving it a victory over the Axis powers, the U.S. government provided several avenues of social mobility loosely grouped under the rubric "the GI Bill." As generous as the Marshall Plan to reconstruct ruined Europe, it provided for higher education and retraining for new positions in a changed economy; individual houses on vast tracts in new suburbs; loose cash for the purchase of new cars; and the expansion of roads on which to drive those cars. The result was that the cities began to empty. The resulting sprawl coincided with a judicial trend known most famously by the decision made in "the Paramount case," which decreed that studios must be separated from theater chains, thereby dissolving the vertically integrated script-to-screen system of making and selling movies. The audience and its suppliers never again resumed the old linkage.

Instead, the audience grew less ethnic, less Italian or Greek if you will, and followed in the footsteps of the prewar Germans, who already had leached into the general social fabric. Even African Americans, burdened as they were by law and custom that proscribed their behavior, found ways to migrate from former ethnic ghettos. The movies' clientele, then, scattered by wealth, mobility, and growing interest in an increasing diversity of forms of amusement, grew choosier and less cohesive. Rivaling the movies for people's attention were newly revived baseball, the maturing professional sports of football and basketball, and a rise in tourism induced by the widened awareness of the world that the war had brought. The taming and modulation of older feelings of class, group, and ethnicity coincided with the arrival of a new attraction—the blandly domesticated medium of television. Thus the audience who had as a matter of habit gone to the movies at least once a week, and their children twice as often, found ever more reasons for turning away from movies. The declining attendance; the closing of thousands of theaters; the studios' selling off of old movies to television; and, finally, the shift of Hollywood's main business from making cinematic features to making television fare revolutionized the use of leisure time.

With the passing of the great movie audience and of the movies as an oligopolic medium of entertainment, there passed a form of expression that had simultaneously provided a prismatic spectrum of the politics of entertainment and spoken as though on behalf of a mythic universal American. Classical Hollywood had come to its end, perhaps victim of its own part in the very myth—that of a white bread America—it helped to create, by means of its narrative form and gilded downtown palaces.

Here at the end of this narrative history of the audience in the classical era of Hollywood, the reader should know something of the theoretical terrain that is now being contested by a variety of theorists who have drawn from Marxist, Freudian, and feminist canons of commentary on popular culture. The result has been a small body of literature collected under the rubric "reception theory." In providing my account of the audience in this chapter, I have been informed by some of this writing but have not tethered myself to it.

The reader will recall that the concept of the audience has been only imprecisely defined and that the tools for its measurement remain relatively blunt. Students of the medium have put forth their own particular ways of examining the changeableness of the audience. Among these scholars, a loosely defined Wisconsin school of socioeconomic history emerged, marked by Douglas Gomery's inquiries into the impacts of air cooling and even popcorn, Janet Staiger's work on the judicial aspects of oligopoly, Kristin Thompson's study of Hollywood's foreign conduits, Russell Merritt's and Gomery's pursuit of movie history as local history, and Robert C. Allen's work on the change from vaudeville to movies.

Still open to debate is whether the audience can be defined simply as a receptor of an ideology. Following the lead of the early work—partly recanted—of Theodor Adorno of the Frankfurt school of Marxist sociologists, some critics, such as the popular journalist Vance Packard, have argued that media constitute a cadre of "hidden persuaders" possessed of uncanny manipulative skills that perform miracles of persuasion in both advertising and politics. Other critics, such as Elizabeth Cohen and Miriam Hansen, have borrowed from Habermas in arguing that movie theaters were a sort of *bürgerliche Öffentlichkeit*, a public space that gave worker audiences the privacy of anonymity to see and think what they wished. This notion of the liberty provided by public space colors, if not defines, the work of those historians who have struggled to analyze audience behavior by class and group. By means of this theory, they have revealed the limitations of the idea of movies as a tool of an omniscient ruling class.

Still other historians have studied movie history as the story of an economic system that, like an engine that drove a machine, fed viewers' expectations by means of word of mouth, advertisements, fan magazines, and the daily press; displayed their wares in theaters fed by exchanges (described in Chapter 2); and delivered the products through a vertically integrated factory atelier in Hollywood.

Thus in response to the question Sklar poses in "Oh! Althusser!: Historiography and the Rise of Cinema Studies" in the *Radical History Review* (1988), that is, whether the "audience constituted an autonomous working-class public sphere or was . . . the site of the absorption of hegemonic domination," we must answer, "both." The Hollywood apparatus may have been feeding audiences messages from a ruling class, but the audiences, in the privacy of the darkened houses, were giving the movies spins of the ideological wheel unintended by their makers. They were, to use Galbraith's term, "countervailing" against rather than falling for the movies on their minds.

As we have seen, historians have disputed the universality of the audience, with more recent historians preferring a polyform model, arising from the fact that exhibitors strove for a more affluent audience even as the poorer audiences dominated the nabes. Historians investigating this social complexity have examined Sanborn fire insurance maps; business directories; and advertisements to define the variegated dimensions of the audience and the growth of, as *Variety* put it, "fewer, bigger, cleaner" houses at the expense of the marginal grind houses in changing neighborhoods.

This often brilliant reference to sources and spheres outside the channels of moviemaking and distribution has become the hallmark of this generation of historians. Moreover, when their sources have run dry, they have resorted to forms of modeling, inference, and hypothesis that have carried the resulting literature beyond the limitations of empirical evidence. Yet, they are still far from the end of the road in their analysis.

Hansen, for example, has carried such inquiry to imaginative conclusions while only rarely missing insights to be culled from sources outside of movie history. The "classical spectator" was also increasingly drawn from a getting-and-spending middle class, whose taste-culture included Thorstein Veblen's "conspicuous consumption." Arriving at this conclusion, apart from its brushing incautiously close to Adorno's notion of a feckless spectator sitting helpless before the power of the moving image, Hansen's work is a tour de force in imaginative, inferential history. In *Babel & Babylon,* she presents Edwin Porter's 1907 adaptation of "Goldilocks and the Three Bears" as an echo of an event in Theodore Roosevelt's political career as well as an instance of introducing audiences to consumption as a social and personal value. Goldilocks and Baby Bear are "allied," she contends, "by the common cause of consumption." How does she know? Pure inference, without reference to Porter's own intentions. But that is the point. "This kind of reading may not correspond to Porter's intentions," she writes, "but it does proceed from conflicts and contradictions that shaped the historical horizon of perception." Pressing on, she sees quotations of Jacob Riis's photographs of "the other half" in D. W. Griffith's *The Musketeers of Pig Alley* (1912).

The result of the movies' openness to an omnibus of readings, she asserts, was an audience increasingly sophisticated, capable of seeing nuance even at an ironic distance and thereby contributing to the "illusionist voyeurism of the classical cinema." Here she enlists Thompson, coauthor with Staiger and Bordwell of *The Classical Hollywood Cinema* (1985), to show the result in later "classical narration," which "tailored every detail to the spectator's attention" in order to, as Eileen Bowser puts it in *The Transformation of Cinema* (1990), "control the vision of the audience." Taken together, they imply an eventually highly apt mass audience open to varied readings of movies.

For example, Hansen identifies certain political references to President Theodore Roosevelt that any au courant moviegoer might have read into *The Teddy Bears* (1907). At issue were America's persistent entanglement in matters of race and ethnicity and their exacerbation by the nation's entry into the imperialism that characterized the Gilded Age. In Hansen's preferred reading, there is an echo of Roosevelt as compassionate leader who was famous for, at the end of his disappointing hunt in Mississippi, his refusal to shoot a bear cub that had been tethered for the purpose of providing him with an easy target.

But any faithful black Republican might have taken an entirely different reading of the movie. Roosevelt had enjoyed a solid reputation among black voters and in fact owed his easy nomination in 1904 in part to their bloc vote in the party's convention. They remembered his service in Cuba with not only the fabled Rough Riders, but also two regiments of black regulars; they loved the flap caused by his entertaining Booker T. Washington at a White House dinner; and they appreciated his six-year fight to confirm his appointment of a black customs collector to the port of Charleston and his closing of a post office in Indianola, Mississippi, after nightriders harassed its black postmistress.

In refusing to violate the rules of sportsmanship on the bear hunt, Roosevelt clearly provided African Americans with an alternative reading of the movie. In 1907, the movie would have provided visual evidence that Roosevelt, in standing up for the bear cub, was standing up against all forms of oppression of the powerless, including that directed against African Americans, and might be returning to his former racial ideals. The point, of course, is not to find Hansen remiss but to suggest that any analysis of movie audiences, including the present chapter, remains open to new methods and fresh data.

PALACE THEATRE OF VARIETIES

Manager - - - - Mr. CHARLES MORTON.

30/8/97.

Programme - - - - **6d.**

1. OVERTURE ... ... "The Naiads"	*Bennett.*	8.0
2.	EDIE ROSS. Serio Comic.	8 8
3.	HARRY DREW. The Celebrated Welsh Basso.	8.17
4.	EMMELINE ETHARDO in her Mélange Artistique.	8.27
5.	WILL CRACKLES. Comedian.	8.37
6.	MAY HOWARD. Vocalist.	8.49
7.	GUS ELEN. Comedian.	8.57
8.	THE DE FORESTS. Whirlwind Dancers.	9.7
9.	LES GARDENIAS. Opera-Bouffe Quartette.	9.20
10.	SADIE JEROME. Comédienne.	9.36
11.	WILSON AND WARING. Grotesque Dancers and Comedians.	9 46
12.	DEYO. Dancer.	10.1
13.	WILLIAM E. RITCHIE. Tramp Bicyclist.	10 9
14. Orchestral Intermezzo		10.16

"Masque" (As you like it) ... ... *German*

No. 1—Woodland Dance.   No. 2—Children's Dance.   No. 3—Rustic Dance.

By permission of Messrs. Novello & Co.

15.
THE AMERICAN BIOGRAPH.   10.28

Invented by HERMAN CASLER, of New York.

LIST OF PICTURES TO BE SHEWN.

Sleigh Bells.	The Eclipse Stakes, Sandown Park, 1897.
New York Fire Department.	The Diamond Jubilee Procession.
A Hard Wash.	The Naval Review at Spithead.
A Cavalry Charge.	The Military Review at Aldershot.
A Pillow Fight.	Afternoon Tea in the Gardens of Clarence House.
Henley Regatta.	H.R.H. The Prince of Wales leaving Marlborough
A Motor Fire Engine.	House
Pussy's Bath.	The Pennsylvania Express, Ltd.
	The Empire State Express.

The Music Composed by ALFRED PLUMPTON.

16.	MAYS AND HUNTER in their unique Banjo Entertainment.	11 0
17.	SHAWLINE. Siffleur and Mimic.	11.10
18.	THE LORRISONS. Song and Dance Artistes.	11 20

Musical Director, Mr. ALFRED PLUMPTON.

The order and composition of this Programme may be varied as circumstances require.

DOORS OPEN 7.45.   **COMMENCE 8.0.**

The Pianofortes used at this Theatre are by Messrs. JOHN BRINSMEAD & SON.

POPULAR PRICES.—PRIVATE BOXES from 1 to 3½ Guineas.   FAUTEUILS (numbered and reserved). 6/-   ORCHESTRA STALLS (numbered and reserved), 5/-   ROYAL CIRCLE, 2/-   FIRST CIRCLE, 2/-   AMPHITHEATRE 1/-   GALLERY 6d.

This program for a summer's night at the Palace (London, 1897) suggests that, far from being chasers, the movies shown under the rubric of "The American Biograph" held a set place in the bill just before the live entertainment returned to stage. (Frank Holland)

William S. Porter's *Uncle Tom's Cabin* (1903) combined rudimentary editing for narrative with a product drawn from a popular stage production. (Library of Congress)

As Hollywood became HOLLYWOOD, picture palaces in cities across America moved uptown and left the nickelodeons behind in the declining neighborhoods, where they became "grind houses" such as this one in Baltimore's infamous Block. The house began as the Comedy Theatre in 1907 and became the Globe Burlesk in 1927. (Farm Security Administration Collection, Library of Congress)

A Pacific electric "red car" on Hollywood Boulevard, before the founding of the "movie colony." In only a decade or so this sparsely settled land would sprout with the studios, picture palaces, and stars' villas that marked the maturing of Hollywood. (Special Collections, University of California, Los Angeles)

D. W. Griffith's *The Birth of a Nation* (1915)—this frame portraying the mulatto brute at the core of the film's dramatic conflict—was a *cause celebre* as a synthesis of movie art, as the subject of a national advertising campaign, and as a racial polemic that drew moviemakers toward self-censorship, all eventual traits of "classical" Hollywood. (Author's collection)

"Average" moviegoers line up for a night at the movies in the New Garrick, neither grind house nor palace but merely a nice "ten, twen', thirt'" house, well kept, appropriate to its well-turned-out clientele. (Special Collections, University of California, Los Angeles)

An often-used image among historians of film, this photograph reflects much of the social reality of Hollywood: the shabby side-entrance, the "colored" balcony, the white B-movie fare, and the ten-cent prices that lumped black hoi polloi and riffraff into the same crowded, classless balcony. (Farm Security Administration Collection, Library of Congress)

Grauman's Chinese Theatre on Hollywood Boulevard served as an icon of Hollywood as "movie capital" in 1933, the year of Garbo in *Queen Christina*. (Special Collections, University of California, Los Angeles)

The famous center "Hollywood and Vine" epitomized Hollywood socioeconomic life in 1936: on the left is the landmark Taft Building and on the right a typical chain theater, the Hollywood Pantages. (Special Collections, University of California, Los Angeles)

Major movies such as *Captains Courageous* (1937), known as "prestige pictures," were drawn from many sources, in this case from a Kipling novel, and engaged achievers such as writer Marc Connelly (*The Green Pastures*) and director Victor Fleming (*Gone with the Wind* and *The Wizard of Oz*); stars such as Spencer Tracy, who won an Oscar for his role; winsome kids from the studio's stable of familiar players, such as Freddie Bartholomew; and black regulars such as Hattie McDaniel's brother, Sam. (MGM/UA)

In "race movies" such as *Spirit of Youth* (1937), low-budget films produced for African American audiences, black heroes were played by celebrities such as boxer Joe Louis. Black comedians, such as Mantan Moreland (next to Louis), had the opportunity to take meaty roles; bit players, such as Clarence Brooks (center, wearing hat), stepped into character roles; and actors such as Clarence Muse (not shown) had the chance to direct. (Author's collection)

Hollywood blew with the political winds: to the left during the World War II alliance with the Soviet Union, to the right during the ensuing cold war. Here on the steps of his own studio (ca. 1950), Louis B. Mayer exhorts his "family" to support the "Crusade for Freedom," a private lobby against Soviet cold war ambition.

One sign of the breakup of Old Hollywood was the challenge to it in the form of an East Coast documentary style marked by reducing the scale of moviemaking to a personal level, as shown here in the filming of Shirley Clarke's *The Cool World* (1964). (Author's collection)

CHAPTER FOUR

Red Flags, White
Thighs & Blue Movies

In times of rapid social change and crisis, there always seems to be an observer who describes the situation as a war between two cultures. Certainly the Civil War and, closer to our own time, the Berkeley free speech movement and the civil rights movement have been portrayed in this way. Often this cultural polarity is sharply etched into black versus white camps of cultural yang and yin, with no gray nuances to be found. In the case of the movies, which began coincident with urbanization, a culture war flared into a nationwide struggle. At issue was the moviemakers' right to play to a national, rather than parochial or sectored, audience versus the local clergy's right to define and legitimize regional or sectarian morals. The national scale of movie distribution, which emerged not long after the birth of movies, flew in the face of local preachers' sense of moral territoriality. They had little choice but to use local law to erect barriers against the movies' seeming threat to local moral standards.

For a while before World War I, the tide ran against the movie men, who fought each other over patents and territories with far more bitterness than they showed in taking on the preachers. The preachers were joined by not just mossbacked puritans but also liberal urban Progressives, and, testifying to the political unity of local forces, a flurry of state and local censorship laws was passed. The movie men at first bent to the will of local reformers, claiming that as purveyors of mere entertainment, they expected no protection of their free speech. After World War I, however, they formed the Motion Picture Producers and Directors of America (MPPDA), which formulated a list of "don'ts and be carefuls" with which it tried to reflect a national taste-culture as well as guide moviemakers in moral matters.

After World War I, movie men readily consented to, even sought, some form of censorship within their industry as a means of standardizing the wide range of local moral codes into a national code that all might tolerate, if not agree to. Accompanying this strategy for assuaging local fears of aliens (in particular Jews, in the opinion of Main Street Protestants) tampering with American values was a wish to narrow the political spectrum to exclude the color red. At the end of Hollywood's classical era, on the eve of the "Paramount case" (1948) that would require "divorcement" of the studios from their theaters, America was dealing with the major shifts in politics and morale World War II had brought, and the age of "the thinking picture" was coming, according to James J. Shotwell, the historian, internationalist, and president of the Carnegie Endowment for Peace. This energized period between the two world wars in which classical Hollywood matured was a field of moral combat in which the stakes appeared to be smelting down America's parochial and regional moral and political codes into a national creed to which movies might subscribe. According to Richard Maltby in "The Production Code and the Hays Office" in Tino Balio's *Grand Design: Hollywood as a Modern Business Enterprise, 1930-1939* (1993), if such a creed were established, the resulting moral and political order, apart from its impact on moviegoers, would ensure that the movie industry was safeguarded from organized criticism.

Implicit in this debate was local preachers' and Progressive reformers' (and later Catholic activists') sense of loss of their role as moral stewards, a loss, it must be reasserted, that they viewed as a defeat at the hands of Hollywood Jews. The stakes seemed nothing less than, as Maltby puts it, a transfer of "the possession of cultural power" from local to national forces.

As for Hollywood, it sought only freedom from writing, shooting, and cutting every movie to fit every whistle-blower's idea of rectitude and decorum.

At first, as we have seen, the coming of movies brought with it only a fear of the new—a transformation of a seemingly progressive social order by means of movie shows unmediated by church, school, or family. By 1907, for example, a quarter of a million moviegoers entered New York nickelodeons each day, a figure that nearly doubled on Sundays. By 1910 there were ten thousand theaters in the nation that were fattening on, as *Harper's Weekly* called it, the "nickel delirium." In other words, early on the problem for the moral stewards seemed only a matter of monitoring a passing fad, rather than a struggle for cultural power. After all, movies *could* be a few minutes of good clean fun for workers after their shift, kids on their way home from school, and families after church on Sundays.

Yet this was also the heyday of urban, bourgeois Progressivism, when social workers and reformers imagined an expanded leisure time being put to use in more civic ways. Part of their movement was a "City Beautiful" campaign inspired by the glorious "White City" built for the Chicago Columbian Exposition of 1893. They envisioned the cities of the future as classically beautiful, richly rewarding social organisms whose reformed environments precluded slums and other urban dysfunctions, relieved the strains of industrialism on the family, and restored the values of Victorianism.

Many Progressives saw movies as having a place in this utopian setting and thought of their work as simply reforming movies, not stifling them. Their instrument of choice for this purpose was the licensing power of local government, through which movies, like food and drugs, might be regulated for the common good. Yet at the conservative pole of reformist thought were those who saw movies as a "new and curious disease" (Gregory Black, *Hollywood Censored* [1994]) that afflicted American cities, or devil's work offered to idle hands, or a siren leading youth astray. For them, prohibition, not regulation, was the weapon of choice. The conservative reformists' campaign reached a climax at Christmas in 1908, when George McClellan, the mayor of New York, shut down all theaters in a draconian measure that obliged exhibitors to reapply for licenses under a more rigid set of hygienic and building codes. Obviously, this was the most difficult for the slummy marginal movie houses that served the poor and immigrant neighborhoods. Thus under the guise of toughened regulation the city had essentially embraced prohibition of movies for the lower classes.

In its way, McClellan's rule by fiat helped reformers see the difference between regulation and prohibition and to formulate a private form of regulation that state and municipal legislation might emulate. A coalition of ten New York social agencies formed the New York Board of Motion Picture Censorship (later renamed the National Board of Review), which strove to find a middle ground upon which movie men and reformers might meet. The Board, led by the reformers Frederic C. Howe and John Collier, imagined movies as "democracy's theater" and therefore saw their duty as restricted to shielding only "children, or delicate women" from the worst that moviemakers might offer.

Unlike the private New York Board, with its more urbane constituency, reformers elsewhere searched for tighter, more prescriptive, even proscriptive, control of movies. In Pennsylvania, Ohio, Kansas, and other states, as well as major cities (led by Chicago's police department–governed Board), these "political" censors linked movies to the well-being of society and banned portrayals of crime, seamy morals, crooked cops and politicians, and various forms of civil strife and injustice.

One would think that protecting political figures from criticism stifled freedom of expression, but by 1915 only a single case challenged the trend. It was filed in Ohio by Mutual Film Corp., a distribution firm owned by Harry Aitken, one of the angels for *The Birth of a Nation*. Arguing that movies were entitled to the same First Amendment protection accorded the printed word, Mutual insisted that movies were "publications" that broadcast knowledge, drew forth opinions, and took up important social issues, all in an environment analogous to libraries. Portentous of things to come, the Supreme Court of Ohio found against Mutual Film Corporation, arguing that movies were "a business pure and simple" and, because "they may be used for evil," were indeed open to censorship.

Thus the debate over the soul of America pitted the moguls, who wished to have their way under the banner of "mere entertainment," against the clergy, who were trying to cling to their local authority under the guidon of "national ideals." Beyond local taboos, Maltby argues, the debate "was about the cultural function of entertainment and the possession of cultural power." The politics of censorship revealed itself only at times, however. One of those times was the 1920s, when there was a growing licentiousness in the movies, particularly the epics of Cecil B. DeMille, which usually included a long unfolding of the decadent mores of Rome or some other ancient empire before, in the last reel, the empire converts to Victorian virtue.

Accompanying the rising incidence of such movies was a spate of scandalous incidents involving Hollywood stars, the most notorious being the comedian Fatty Arbuckle's wild party in the St. Francis Hotel in San Francisco, during which a budding actress died in bizarre circumstances. Coupled with a cycle of licentious movies and a string of other off-screen scandals involving drug addiction, casual divorces, and even murder, Arbuckle's case spurred the moguls to organize in 1922 into the MPPDA, which would be under the direction of the "czar" Will Hays.

Hays came to his work with almost godsent credentials: ordination as a Presbyterian elder, a reputation as the only "clean" member of Harding's disreputable cabinet, membership in the usual fraternal orders, and status as a midwestern Republican of consequence. With his slouch hats, serge suits, and plain, open face, he seemed the perfect champion of rectitude. Conservatives everywhere were pleased to honor his potential by imputing the powers of a czar to "the Hays office." They had already seen what influence such a czar could wield in the person of Judge Kenesaw Mountain Landis, newly named czar of organized baseball following a betting scandal in the 1919 World Series.

As the Republican decade unfolded, Hays found himself at the center of an unexpected institutional evolution. On the one hand, he was seen by many Gentile publicists as the tutor who would teach those alien Jews of Hollywood the values of Gentile America, while serving as mediator between middle American Protestant ethics and the more institutional and obligatory ethics of Roman Catholicism. Mainly, this antagonistic alliance was made necessary by the increasing pressure on Hollywood brought by Martin Quigley, a Catholic lay activist and publisher of a pioneering trade paper, and Father Daniel Lord, a St. Louis Jesuit and prolific writer on popular ethics. Together, the moguls, the Catholics, but mainly Hays's own office, hammered out the fragile "don'ts and be carefuls" that were meant to guide American movie morals through the Jazz Age, a decade that seemed to assail every last Victorian moral tenet. At stake was the formulation of some pragmatic moral code for movies that might reflect Hollywood's wish to play to both a shared national moral sensibility and the traditional morality of the local divines, who still feared the erosion of their authority. The inevitable compromises not only did little to soothe the clergy, but also raised fears of a Jewish plot. The contributor to one Episcopal magazine claimed that Hays was merely a "smoke screen" behind which "shrewd Jews" could operate.

As we have seen, the studio bosses wished only to trade in the same national marketplace in which other corporations, such as Ford, Sears Roebuck, Piggly Wiggly, A&P, Woolworth's, the National Broadcasting Company, and the Radio Corporation of America, offered their wares. They saw their theater chains as units in a sprawling system that was little different from a five-and-ten and therefore hardly threatening to the moral order of the hamlets of America.

Nonetheless, the resulting struggle between local forces and national motion picture distributors took on the aspect of a clash of ideologies. Indeed,

Marxist scholars, particularly during the era of Lenin and later after the Marxist revisionism of Louis Althusser, saw the outcome as a "state apparatus" that broadcast the ideology of a national ruling order. Never mind that the struggle was cast as a matter of morals; at bottom, the movies, privately owned as they were, spoke for a bourgeois order. The movies, so went the argument, framed their images as though "quoting" from, for example, Renaissance artists whose paintings made use of the optical illusion of perspective to give viewers a seemingly privileged vantage. Augmented by its use of seamless narratives that precluded debate, the movie industry's politics grew single-minded. This vision of movies as purveyors of conventional morals (and thereby politics), although not adopting the extreme position of the Frankfurt school that movies were coldly efficient "hidden persuaders," ironically also allowed conservatives to fear movies as an endangerment to traditional America.

To conservatives' way of thinking, a farm woman might trade in a national marketplace of *things*, ordering her yard goods or shotgun shells from the Sears catalogue or getting her Sanford B. Dole pineapple tins from her Piggly Wiggly, but she should not be allowed to derive her ideas from William Fox's *A Fool There Was* (1914). The result, heaven forbid, would have been her absorption of an ethic administered in strong doses by Jews residing in licentious Hollywood rather than by Main Street preachers. Meanwhile, the hapless, modern, other-directed moviegoer, having been cut free of local moorings, would have been rootless, detribalized, and vulnerable to movies' slick, modernist messages. Somehow, movies opened themselves to being the heavy in this plot—perhaps because of Arbuckle's party and other scandals; perhaps because of the Jews thought to be at the bottom of the plot; perhaps because, as Garth Jowett writes in "A Capacity for Evil: The 1915 Supreme Court Mutual Decision" (in *Historical Journal of Film, Radio, and Television* [1989]), "the movies dramatically symbolized the diminishing power of [communities'] *localized* control over their own lives"; or perhaps because the movies were openly hawked on Main Street at the Bijou. The moral relativism of the Greenwich Villagers who bobbed their hair, read Freud, smoked Fatimas, and saw Marcel Duchamp's "Nude Descending a Staircase" at the Armory Show in 1913 passed far less noticed.

In any event, in the 1920s Hays seemed to have brought a semblance of order to the scene, placating local moral forces and channeling moviemakers into the broad political center of American culture, where they probably wanted to be, anyway. By disarming early antimovie reformers like Canon William Sheafe Chase of Brooklyn, the most vocal reformer, the Progressives bent on civic uplift, the National Board of Review's pressure for "better" films, southerners defending their "way of life," Bostonians acting in the name of waning puritanism and emerging Irish Catholicism, and even the more than half dozen cities and states that had passed local "political censorship" laws, the Hays office helped neutralize prickly local taste-cultures into the national culture that movies needed in order to survive.

Not that Hays was ever the czar that Landis became after baseball's "Black Sox" scandal. It only seemed so in the press releases of the Studio Relations Committee of the MPPDA. For the most part during Hays's first decade, all sorts of amorality crept into movies. For example, the 1920s saw a remake of *A Fool There Was* (1922), stories of prostitution in *The Painted Lady* (1924) and *The Pace That Kills* (1928), and the rakish lives of *Our Dancing Daughters* (1928) and *Our Modern Maidens* (1929) come to the screen.

As early as 1914, William Fox startled the squares from Peoria to Azusa with the bohemianism and protofeminist sexuality of his *A Fool There Was*, starring Theda Bara as a predatory vamp. "Kiss me, my fool"—a line from the movie—became a tag line for the age and spurred a cycle of movies that painted the rich as sodden with excess yet sunken into despair and ennui. Cecil B. DeMille's *Manslaughter* (1922); Erich von Stroheim's *The Merry Widow* (1925), *Blind Husbands* (1919), and *The Wedding March* (1928); and dozens more like them filled the screens with predatory lasciviousness followed by last-reel atonements.

Clearly, the "don'ts and be carefuls" issued from the Hays office led to little measurable change. This was partly because although a new generation of sociologists had rediscovered movies as a cause of "juvenile delinquency," publishing their findings as the voluminous "Payne Fund studies," they blunted the impact of their report by their scholarly hedging. They found in movies only "suggestibility" rather than causation and, like Robert and Helen Lynd in *Middletown* (1929), recommended only that movies for children be "better." Indeed, in surveys of criminals, less than 1 percent cited movies as the cause of their taking a wrong turn. Thus there was no alarmist body of social literature to charge movies unequivocally as culprits.

Nonetheless, in forming the MPPDA in 1922 and appointing Hays to front it, the moguls had begun to define a broadly Americanist taste-culture somewhere between the zealous reformers and timid social scientists. Hays became a sort of Presbyterian pope, who demanded of his producers that they avoid "depreciation" of public officials and religion. The MPPDA got through the 1920s placating but not pleasing themselves, their fans, or their critics.

It is here in the thickets of ambiguity that we find the politics of entertainment. Would movies under Hays's shaky code eternally speak a stuffy Victorian cant that had long since given way to a modernist moral ambivalence? Critics certainly thought so, as they ribbed Hays for obliging every bedroom on the screen to be furnished with twin beds and insisting that every police officer be as stainless as molybdenum. And certainly, the rural folk who felt offended by Hollywood and diminished in their power to exclude it from their communities persisted in their struggle. Effectively the two camps—Hollywood and Main Street—constituted the countervailing forces that John Kenneth Galbraith found in American capitalism. And like most players in the game of movie politics, they could not dominate the game but only share in defining its terms. Like Napoleon at the height of his power in 1806, they still could not dictate history but only participate in it.

To miss this point is to miss the residual power that local censors held and the extent to which their local differences, if left untrammeled, would have made a national cinema impossible. A glance at the efforts of Lloyd Binford, the censor in Memphis, and therefore the arbiter of what much of the Mississippi Valley population saw on its screens, is illustrative. Binford spent much of Hollywood's classical era cutting scenes or even banning entire movies in the service of shielding southern whites' eyes from the changing racial mores outside their region. Sometimes he snipped sequences merely because of his personal aversion to a black performer. With the onset of sound his excesses worsened, not only because spoken language heightened movies' impact, but also because trimming sound sequences often ruined sequencing, continuity, and meaning. To the moviemakers' exasperation, Binford's powers derived only from Boss Ed Crump, an archetype of southern urban bossism.

In Atlanta, the librarian Christine Smith wielded similar power over movies that threatened the slightest departure from southern racial etiquette. However, her authority derived not from wardheeling but from her institutional connection with Atlanta's Carnegie Library.

Indeed, every local censorship board enjoyed some link to a local power source. In Memphis it was Crump's smoke-filled office; in Atlanta, a library;

in Chicago, the police department; in Pennsylvania, a commission whose members were drawn from the professions; in Maryland, a coalition of Jewish, Catholic, and Protestant politicians, joined occasionally by the publisher of the *Afro-American*. En masse, these survivors of a deeply felt localism provided a countervailing force that opposed Hollywood's quest for a national marketplace along the lines already drawn by nationwide retailers.

Even worse for Hollywood, the censors in many large communities, such as Memphis or Atlanta, were able to impose their mores and politics on vast hinterlands, simply because of the high cost of restoring censored films. Having to pay the censors a fee per foot of film to cover the cost of their scene-slashing labor as well as the costs to restore the cut scenes once a film was returned was too much for many hardpressed distributors, who economized by sending the film on to the next community without restoring the scenes cut by the censor in the previous community. Censors in small towns often received their films in the diminished, even incoherent, condition in which they had left the previous censor's cutting room.

Thus one of Hays's most nettlesome problems was to find a way to contain or standardize the powers of local censor boards. Throughout his tenure, he blanketed the nation with lobbyists who portrayed the MPPDA as guardian of "the highest possible moral and artistic standards," hoping to undercut many communities' dependence on the local boards, each with its own political and social agenda. Yet, as Gregory Black writes in *Hollywood Censored* (1994), even as the age of dialogue-on-film approached, which put untrained censors in the position of having to cut both sound and image while preserving continuity, the issue would still not die down. Canon Chase testified before Congress that movies were a "threat to world civilization," prompting the New York censor to take steps to remedy the situation, in 1928 slashing thousands of scenes from some six hundred submitted movies.

By the end of the Republican era, local moral arbiters and Hollywood remained as apart as ever, unable to define a broad center on which all could stand. The locals maintained their drumbeat against Hollywood excess. The moguls agreed with Carl Laemmle of Universal Pictures that movies, with their obligatory last-reel atonement scenes, had grown "too damned clean" for Jazz Age sophisticates. Worse yet, the newspaper publisher William Randolph Hearst, it was reported, favored federal censorship, a view shared by a few members of Congress, who considered assigning the regulation of Hollywood to the Federal Trade Commission.

In 1932, as soundfilm took hold and Republicans departed the White House, a third force joined the moguls in seeking some sort of national political aesthetic for movies: a group of Roman Catholics. Why were Catholics involving themselves with the Jews of Hollywood? Easy. Both were interested in defining a nationally shared ethics of the center, not only rooted in some accepted bedrock of American sociopolitical values, but also acceptable to the local preachers who stood against a rampant national secularism. Besides, Father Daniel Lord, who, like James Cardinal Gibbons and Bishop Fulton J. Sheen, enjoyed a following among Protestants and who had long harbored a fascination with Hollywood, had already helped shape the "don'ts and be carefuls." Moreover, a veteran trade paper publisher, Martin Quigley, enjoyed growing fame as a Catholic lay activist and publicist.

At issue for these Catholics was the search for a core of Catholic moral suasion in a debate that so far had seemed between Jewish cosmopolites and Protestant squares. Quigley's agenda, for example, seemed not so much to dominate or even to sway the debate but to serve as a third force to, according to Leonard Leff and Jerold Simmons in *The Dame in the Kimono* (1990), "harness the movies' power over American culture and morals" by simultaneously increasing the influence of his *Exhibitor's Herald World* in the industry while seeming to fans a "moral barometer of the nation."

The Catholic hierarchy was by no means giving its blessings to Quigley and Lord's efforts. Why should the church meddle in what seemed a spat between Protestant divines and a Presbyterian elder over the issue of reining in the power of the Hollywood Jews? To do so was surely to risk a surge in the anti–Roman Catholic sentiments that had always lurked in the corner of the Protestant psyche.

After seeing a film of Hays addressing a "Eucharistic Congress" in Chicago, Quigley believed that Hays had tied up the picture business with the churches for all time. By 1929, prelates in the church had steered Quigley toward Father Daniel Lord, whose own public role as friendly Catholic with no wish to possess the soul of America provided him with an iconic figure who might help cast the moguls into teddy bears with whom Southern Baptists might live in peace.

Hollywood, for its part, had just entered its period of recovery from the Great Crash. Shaken by its time of troubles, sell-offs, retrenchment, and reorganizing, Hollywood almost unavoidably lent an ear to these voices, in effect giving its attention to theologians whose sense of ethics was painted in the stark black and white drawn from the staid centers of American life. Inevitably, their vision of what was good for America leaned toward movies that were uplifting; foursquare; and, unfortunately for the sophisticated, hopelessly mired in redemptive pap. And yet, by agreeing, the moguls might save their movies from endless costly rewrites and retakes and from the local censors' scissor work.

In other words, if the moguls failed to reach an accommodation with a national moral *voice*, their quest for a national *market* would forever be lost to the powers of the local censor boards. The "don'ts and be carefuls" had achieved only a modicum of success in synthesizing the practice of the local boards, but even this would be lost with the arrival of sound. Dialogue film brought with it moral "problems"—divorce, adultery, poverty, indeed social dysfunction of all sorts—and with them the prospect of open political debate on the nation's screens. Accompanying these portrayals of social malaise was a rising chorus of objection to everything linked to Hollywood: its presumed Jewishness, its oligopolic structure, its remoteness from middle America, and its playing to "the tabloid mind" (as the *Churchman* declared).

In response to the transformation in the social content of movies that dialogue-on-film had brought, the MPPDA moved toward a new accommodation to localism that ended with Hays welding an alliance with nationally focused Catholics against the Chicago censor board. The occasion was an MPPDA conference in New York on "the community and the motion picture" in 1929. There they tinkered with Hays's toothless code of 1927, while their counsel pressed George W. Cardinal Mundelein of Chicago to lobby for repeal of the local police-driven board. Soon thereafter Quigley, in his *Exhibitor's Herald World*, urged a more detailed code and suggested that Father Lord draft it. Father Lord, perhaps unknown to the principals, had embraced a notion that provided the basis on which the moguls and priests agreed: that "theaters are built for the masses" and therefore the moguls, unlike artists who spoke only to a small art world of sophisticates, owed their broad-based flocks a "correct" entertainment that might "improve the race" (as Maltby quotes Lord in "The Production Code and the Hays Office").

Jason Joy of the Hays office certainly agreed that movies were a medium for the masses, but he added the caveat that movies might offer nuances that delighted cosmopolites but "would mean nothing to the unsophisticated" (as Maltby quotes him). For their part, Quigley and Father Lord stiffened Hays's limp taboos while masking their Catholic sources behind a more universal ethic. Thus they played to Hollywood's own wish for a codified consensus of the center, the bankers' wish for box office steadiness, their own desire for a role in shaping movie morals, and the wish of "patriotic gentile Americans" for a national ethic to replace the eroding local moral order.

"My eyes nearly popped out when I read it," recalls Hays in his *Memoirs* (1955). "This was the very thing I had been looking for." At last, writes Raymond Moley in *The Hays Office* (1945), movies would cease spreading "the clink of highball glasses, the squeal of bedsprings, [and] the crackle of fast conversation to a thousand Main Streets." And apart from a few flashes of journalistic cynicism and a few pangs of angst within the walls of the movie lots, everyone relaxed. In Leff and Simmons's *The Dame in the Kimono* Joy, for example, reports that various local censors "gave us the encouragement which made it possible for us to keep control of production under the Code." And after all, that had been the point: to centralize censorship in a Hollywood agency that thereafter was to serve as national priesthood/rabbinate. Or, better, as a sort of Sears Roebuck or Woolworth's that retailed a national ethic.

Then sound and dialogue came, and the ecumenical spirit crumbled. Sound intensified every shading of moral deviance. The local watchdogs, nettled by the apparent betrayal, resumed their slashing, even of movies that arrived with the Production Code Administration (PCA) seal. A cycle of urban crime movies—*Scarface* (1932), *Little Caesar* (1931), *I Was a Fugitive from a Chain Gang* (1932), and others—played Cecil B. DeMille's old game of wallowing in violence and crime and then piously atoning for it in the last reel. Accompanying the gangster movies was a round of sexually nuanced movies. Led by Adolph Zukor's fiscally shaky Paramount, which offered both literary fare such as Hemingway's *A Farewell to Arms* (1932), with its pregnancy out of wedlock and burlesque in the form of Mae West's purring, and campy parodies of sexual mores in *She Done Him Wrong* (1933) and *I'm No Angel* (1933), Hollywood played both sides of the moral street—high and low.

Desperate for a ramrod who might restore the moral and political order that had been thrown into disarray by the power of sound, Hays hired Joseph Breen. Breen was Catholic and then some. Following his graduation from St. Joseph's College in Philadelphia, he had devoted much of his life to secular Catholic causes as well as to a form of anti-Communism that embraced antiunionism, anti-Semitism, and antimodernism.

Breen's all-encompassing conservatism came to the PCA just as the nation itself, embarking on the New Deal reformism that Roosevelt offered as a life preserver to the struggling economy, turned toward a compensating social conservatism. The signs of its revival were unmistakable: Local censors resumed their adversarial rhetoric. *McCall's* ran a few pages from the multivolume Payne Fund studies on the effects of moviegoing on "juvenile delinquency." The Roosevelt government itself mulled over the possibility of regulating movies under the aegis of the "blue eagle" logotype of the celebrated (and eventually deemed unconstitutional) National Recovery Administration (NRA). Catholics, perhaps prodded by Breen, joined in the general antiliberal antipathy. The Episcopal Committee on Motion Pictures enlisted lay Catholics in a national "Legion of Decency" that chose the boycott as its weapon; parish priests joined in, sometimes so vigorously that even Breen thought them a "lunatic fringe"; powerful lay figures joined in, such as A. P. Giannini, whose Bank of America had become an angel for Hollywood.

Recognizing the trend, Hays tightened the existing guiding formulas, hoping to head off censorship-inclined critics of the "problem" pictures that seemed a "dangerous" spreading of "alien" (read Jewish) values to America's small towns. By the summer of 1931, the studios were obliged to submit to the MPAA both scripts and release prints, giving the Hays office two opportunities to cut offending material. On the first day of 1932, Joseph Breen began his job as censor for the Hays office, complete with a reputation as a "crusader" with a mission to save the industry from itself. His ideology, and that of other lay Catholics such as Quigley and Wilfred Parsons of the Jesuit weekly *America*, deployed Catholics in a skirmish zone between the demonized Jews of Hollywood and "America's enfeebled Protestant Main Street," as Maltby calls it in "The Production Code and the Hays Office." Year by year, the pace of Catholic "cultural assertiveness" picked up by means of open letters in the press and protests over specific movies such as *State Fair* (1933) and *Ann Vickers* (1933), both of which featured challenges to the "don'ts."

The year of crisis was 1934, the middle of Roosevelt's first term. The Church hoped to force his government to include moviemakers in the roster of industries with self-created "codes" by means of which the NRA was to monitor corporations' efforts to combat the effects of the Depression. Breen solicited the commitment of bishops in his crusade; Father Lord and others proposed their Legion of Decency and its capacity to invoke boycotts, an idea Breen tested by calling for local boycotts in selected cities. For their part, the studios muted Mae West's sly innuendos and set in motion a cycle of so-called prestige pictures such as *Little Women* (1933) as well as adaptations from Shakespeare, for which they began to supply schools with study guides.

Thus by the middle of the Great Depression the Catholic Church had, improbably, become a third force in the struggle to define a national form of moral and political rectitude. The Protestants had become ciphers in the cause. Indeed, a prescient joke of the day went, "How come they never make movies about the Protestant clergy, only Catholics?" "Sure they do. What about *Rain*?" (referring to the movie based on Somerset Maugham's novel about a fallen preacher who commits suicide).

To appreciate the impact of the Catholics, simply compare Mae West's stock role in *I'm No Angel* (1933) with her later flops, such as *Klondike Annie* (1936). Gone, too, were the African American lowlifes who had peopled the first generation of soundfilm musical shorts such as *St. Louis Blues* (1929), in which Bessie Smith and Jimmie Mordecai danced in a shamelessly, fluidly erotic style and Mordecai said about his digs, "This ain't Bessie's room; she just pays for it." And never again would Marlene Dietrich smokily intone lines like "It took more than one man to make me into the Shanghai Lily."

As if the censors did not have their hands full trying to standardize morals, they also did battle with the varieties of political expression on the screen. At first, they focused their attention on the spate of gangster movies (two dozen per year, on average) made during the early 1930s, contesting their contemptuous treatment of police and other authorities and decrying their impact on social behavior (in light of the Payne Fund studies that found links, albeit tenuous ones, between moviegoing and criminal behavior). "Chi Censors Rank Gun Play Ahead of Sex in Their Taboos," blared a *Variety* headline. Yet in 1932 during his last days, Hays stood up to the local censors, hoping to persuade them to let pass Howard Hughes's *Scarface*, with its echoes of the life of Al Capone.

As long as the debate focused on whether movies affected children's behavior, as the Payne Fund studies suggested they did, politics consisted only in whether or not the government enjoyed a constitutional right to censor. But with Warner Bros.'s release of *I Was a Fugitive from a Chain Gang* (1932), a first-person account of the callousness and corruption of penal systems in

Georgia and other southern states, journalists' attention was drawn to the trend of which this movie was a part, the calling to the bar all sorts of government malfeasance. Movies about prison in particular had pulled up especially dirty corners of the nation's rugs. Here the MPPDA revealed its wish to link the box office with the political right by pressing the studios to soften their indictments of southern justice as a shield against not only the scissors of the Binfords of the South, but also the wrath of touchy southern newspaper editors and ticket buyers. In fact, while Mervyn LeRoy was shooting *I Was a Fugitive* on the lot at Warner Bros., the production boss, Darryl Zanuck, was pressing the writer, Howard J. Green, to soften the blow by writing in "sincere arguments in favor of chain-gang systems" (as Gregory Black quotes Green in *Hollywood Censored*). When the movie was released, everyone from Hays to the Warners hid behind their collective achievement of having made a movie "free of propaganda," a course of action challenged by Pare Lorentz in his review in *Vanity Fair* in which he argued for using movies as a forum for social justice.

Meanwhile, the right-wing newspaper publisher William Randolph Hearst offered his own form of social justice. His Cosmopolitan Studios reflected the aimless, almost feckless, American politics of the early Depression years, when the humanitarian Herbert Hoover seemed an empty husk in the White House while his Democratic rival, Franklin Roosevelt, was taken to be a nascent dictator. Hearst himself was torn between a populist impulse and an authoritarian urge to act against it (an ambivalence that Orson Welles later caught in *Citizen Kane* [1941], widely regarded as a roman à clef of Hearst's career). As though playing to American confusion and playing out his own political fantasies, only weeks after Roosevelt's inauguration Hearst brought out *Gabriel over the White House* (1933), a movie centered on a composite political character who possessed qualities of the cronyish Harding, the feckless Hoover, the activist Roosevelt, and even a Hitler in mufti, as though calculated to offend the faithful of any party. Its extravagant solution to issues of war, peace, economic depression—almost any political dysfunction—called for the sort of saber rattling that marked the then beginning careers of Hitler and Mussolini. Political opinion of every stripe seemed slandered, forcing MGM, which had allowed Hearst's movie to slip through minus the attention of the Republican Mayer, to rewrite its substance. But at bottom, the politics of Hollywood were revealed as conservatively rooted in earnings. As Fred Herron of the foreign trade desk of the MPPDA "exploded" (to use Gregory Black's word), "We have a hell of a nerve to put any-thing like this in one of our pictures, and at the same time beg our various Embassies to constantly help us out with foreign governments."

Hollywood seemed to have tripped over its own ideological innocence in retailing a movie whose melodramatic devices were meant to seem above the squabbling of party politics but that ended by advocating fascism. The domestic stake in economic recovery, coupled with a national despair, pro-vide a fertile ground for a widening of the range of political perspectives. Well-meaning citizens—in minority numbers, to be sure—admired the ap-parent successes of totalitarian governments ranging from Stalin's Soviet Union to Mussolini's Italy in pulling their countries out of the economic slough, thereby alerting censors to nervously seek paths toward some safe consensus of the center. Moreover, this politics of the center emerged from Hollywood itself, forcing the ranks of the liberal left (and the anti-Nazi right) to form opposing groups. For example, the Hollywood Anti-Nazi League took an anti-Hitler stance that drew both the leftist intellectuals among the writers as well as anti-Nazi Jews such as Jack Warner.

When *Potemkin* (1925), Sergei Eisenstein's famous reenactment of the re-bellion of the Russian czar's Black Sea fleet, came to America before the Great Crash, it faced the scissors of only the Pennsylvania censor board, en-joyed a friendly press, profited from Hays's decision not to seek the sort of bans that the British and Germans had enacted, and earned a place on the Ten Best Movies list of the *New York Times*.

After the Great Crash the mood changed, the rising of a militant left hav-ing stirred a thermidorean, anti-Marxist right. Eisenstein came to the States in the early 1930s at the invitation of Paramount to make *Sutter's Gold* (1936), in which the California Gold Rush was to be a metaphor for unrestrained capitalist greed. However, he found himself a pariah, branded by various politicians and movie men as the "Red Jew." In fact, the reception of a do-mestic variety of utopian socialist fable, King Vidor's *Our Daily Bread* (1934), anticipated the coolness with which the Russian director would be greeted. Vidor, then at the height of his powers at MGM, had regarded his pet theory of a communal, not to say collective, response to the Depression as a timely topic for a movie. But the conservative Mayer squelched the project until Vidor agreed to commit his own funds and even then found ways to play it off with only a pallid campaign. In keeping with the centrist mood, when Upton Sinclair, a homegrown socialist, ran for governor of California, the movie moguls, led by Mayer, raised funds for his opposition and helped make an alarmist movie that predicted the decline of California if Sinclair won. He lost.

This is not to say that this homogenizing and centralizing of the national movie market sequestered the nation's screens from all but MPPDA products. After all, even at the zenith of their oligopoly the Hollywood chains owned but a small percentage of the nation's screens. This meant that in every major city with an immigrant population, small houses showed foreign-language movies, among them works of political advocacy that no Hollywood studio would have touched. The pious *La Passion de Jeanne d'Arc* (1928), whose French chauvinism was lost on most Americans; the politically radical German-language films *Kuhle Wampe* (1932) and *Niemansland* (1932); and the race movies of Oscar Micheaux, with their implicit calls for black aspiration, all played without PCA seals to little ghettos of like-minded moviegoers.

As regards what Hollywood was sending overseas, the studios strove for a politics of the center that skimped on any cultural detail at which moviegoers (and censors) in foreign markets might take offense. Indeed, until the onset of the more brutal forms of Nazi anti-Semitism, the studios often accommodated the demands of the German consul in Los Angeles, George Gyssling. Not that they played unctuous victim of Nazi brownshirts; rather, they simply responded to German pressure much as they had responded to America's more genteel anti-Semitism: by enameling over Jewishness. The cashbox and Hitler shared their attention. Two movies specifically about anti-Semitism, *The Life of Emile Zola* (1937) and *The Mortal Storm* (1940), managed to take up their themes without ever uttering the word "Jew" (although in the former, viewers are allowed to read it over a policeman's shoulder). Only oddments such as *Lancer Spy* (1937), *Confessions of a Nazi Spy* (1939), and Chaplin's independently produced satire *The Great Dictator* (1940) withstood foreign pressure.

Of all the movies on which Hollywood caved in to foreign pressure, one stands out: Walter Wanger's *Blockade* (1938), an adventure yarn set in the Spanish Civil War. Although the movie had originally been intended to be a warning that this civil war was a rehearsal for an impending world conflict, the moviemakers caved in to both PCA and diplomatic pressures and managed to avoid mentioning Spain, the rival Loyalists and Falangists, and any of the foreign belligerents. It was hazed by the critics.

Pressure from the British came from within Hollywood's own ranks. The politically articulate "English colony" of Hollywood acted as a go-between, speaking to the moguls for British diplomatic interests, who also happened to own heavy investments in the United Kingdom. Indeed, Cedric Hardwicke earned his knighthood far more for his work on behalf of the Crown than for his crisply professional but seldom electrifying movie acting. Led by its dean, C. Aubrey Smith, the colony cultivated a circle of Anglophiles, such as the scriptwriter John L. Balderston, who lobbied Mayer and others to release such pro-British movies as *The White Cliffs of Dover* (1944) and *Mrs. Miniver* (1942).

The Anglophiles led to a strand of imperialist movies that sycophantically advocated imperialism. These included *Clive of India* (1935); Warner Bros.'s *The Charge of the Light Brigade* (1936); and MGM's string of celebrations of Queen Elizabeth's reign over the English Renaissance (and the world's sea lanes): *The Sea Hawk* (1940), *Captain Blood* (1935), and *The Private Lives of Elizabeth and Essex* (1939). Typically, the Englishness of the hero (often the Australian Errol Flynn) surfaced in his victories over Pakistani chieftains or oily Spaniards, while his subliminal Americanness took the form of a streak of independent-mindedness that served to teach proper British martinets the value of enterprising liberty.

Few of these movies sullied the Crown's image as benevolent bearer of the white man's burden. MGM dutifully removed the more mutinous scenes from its *Mutiny on the Bounty* (1935)—a movie *about* mutiny. Even the professional Irishman, John Ford, exalted the British in his movies: in his *Drums along the Mohawk* (1939), the heavies of the American Revolution are not Redcoats but rather darkly ominous loyalists (complete with piratical eyepatches). Similarly, in George Stevens's *Gunga Din* (1939), a saga of the Anglo-Indian War, the climax comes when three British soldiers, abetted by an unctuous Indian waterboy, thwart a massive revolt led by an Indian whose sentiments are made to seem driven only by a steel-eyed cruelty, not by a sense of nationalism.

As may be seen, as movies passed through the hands of the PCA and the moguls, they risked becoming no more than voices of an official apparatus. Still, within this circumscribed politics a degree of play remained in which to debate the alternatives.

The Depression-born dysfunctions of American society similarly could be examined only within strictures imposed by Hays and Breen. Moviemakers, both liberal and conservative, were allowed to portray only a vaguely Americanist social politics, in which heroes won because of their individual acts of heroism, rather than their specific social stances, and what they won was usually something personal (such as "the girl") rather than political.

As discussed in chapter 3, Nick Roddick in *A New Deal in Entertainment* (1983) identifies a shift in the type of heroes seen on the screen during the Great Depression. He observes that early in the Depression movies featured collectivist heroes and situations and that as confidence in the country returned, the more familiar lone heroes began to reappear. For example, in Warner Bros.'s early-Depression *Cabin in the Cotton* (1932), a callow hero comes to see the injustice of sharecropping and peonage, and the movie ends with a vague promise of a sharecroppers' union that might stand against callous landlords (who, nonetheless, get to tell "their side"). The rootless heroes of *Wild Boys of the Road* (1933), set adrift by joblessness and at the mercy of brutal rail yard cops, are rescued in the last reel by the aroused conscience of the American polity. However, when the nation's confidence was somewhat restored in Roosevelt's second term, the heroes in Warner Bros. movies returned to their former mode as loners. Problems were once again resolved by the lone crusading newspaper reporter, the empathetic judge, or the good cop, rather than by a cohesive citizenry.

A star such as Humphrey Bogart played both sides of the law, but in either case he was the driven loner. In *Crime School* (1940), he was the crusading DA who exposes the corruption that oppresses the inmates of a boys' reformatory. In *The Petrified Forest* (1936), he was Duke Mantee, a deadly killer on the run who, in a wry ending to Robert E. Sherwood's play, kills an effete poet whose life insurance policy sends a young poet (Bette Davis) to Paris for her season in bohemia. In another spin of the wheel, in *Angels with Dirty Faces* (1938) James Cagney plays a murderer whom a priest persuades to go to the chair looking like a craven coward, rather than the arrogant cock o' the walk his youthful fans imagine him to be, thereby smelting redemption into social issues. Obviously, Breen had a penchant for last-reel denouements; it was a penchant audiences shared.

Eleventh-hour atonement, penitence, and mortification might have arisen from the conservativism of Hays or Breen (or the Republican moguls), or it might simply have derived from the formulations of classical Hollywood style. For example, in *The Dame in the Kimono,* Leff and Simmons report that David O. Selznick left Russia's economic problems out of the movie version of *Anna Karenina* (1935) because he knew a large part of the audience would go to the movie just to see its stars, Garbo and Fredric March. Chaplin's hazing of industrial capitalism in *Modern Times* (1936) seemed the mildest of indictments but, nonetheless, earned a gibe from Martin Quigley in a letter to Breen: "Amongst our Semitic brethren, there seems to be . . . an acceptance of the idea of radical propaganda on the screen."

Regardless of whether they were about mere style or presumed Jewish radicalism, the debates among moviemakers or occasionally between the monitors within the PCA drew movies toward a nettle-free cinema. In a particularly enigmatic movie, Walter Wanger's *The President Vanishes* (1934), the producer seemed as one with both the pacifist left and the isolationist right. At the time, both the left and Republican Gerald Nye's Senate investigating committee believed that conscienceless munitions makers had been the central cause of World War I. A reworking of one of the angles in *Gabriel over the White House,* Wanger's movie likewise mounted a "bitter attack on . . . ruthless munitions makers," as *Newsweek* reported. Breen's dismay at the movie lay not in its treatment of munitions makers, but in its portrayal of a "drunkard" president who acted as dupe for "a gluttonous group of capitalists," a dismay that he overcame to give the movie a PCA seal. Hays, however, stiffened at the sight of Wanger's "communist propaganda" that so opposed the American social order as to be "perhaps treasonable" in its failure to "reflect correctly our own institutions." Fearing its impact abroad, Hays removed the seal.

Such solicitude for the images of public figures managed to cloud even the politics of movies that were explicitly about politically controversial issues. A case in point is Warner Bros.'s *Black Fury* (1935). Not only was the movie inspired by the true story of the murder of a coalminer by a hired company goon, but its source was a memoir written by a judge in the case. Nevertheless, Breen, not wanting to heighten "industrial unrest," urged the scriptwriters to dampen the struggle between the bosses and workers by shifting the onus of violence away from both factions and onto some fictional "crooked agitators." Furthermore, he persuaded Jack Warner, who was then in the midst of his own labor strife, to authorize the rewrites. The result was, as the *New York Times* observed, "a handsome defense of the status quo."

Subsequent movies that suffered at the hands of the PCA or like-minded moguls, with the results ranging from having their politics reduced to personal little stories to being withdrawn outright from production, were *Fury* (1936) and *They Won't Forget* (1937), movies that assailed American-style lynching; *Black Legion* (1937), which focused on a hate-group; *It Can't Happen Here*, Sinclair Lewis's eventually thwarted dystopian tale of fascism's arrival in America; Sidney Kingsley's drama *Dead End* (1937), with its stark set that contrasted the lives of the rich and poor; the Federal Theater's production of *One Third of a Nation* (1939), a ringing call for government action on behalf of public housing; and Robert E. Sherwood's Pulitzer Prize–winning pacifist play *Idiot's Delight* (1939). As was typical of his handiwork, writes Gregory Black in *Hollywood Censored*, Breen's treatment of Steinbeck's angry populist novel *The Grapes of Wrath* rescaled it from a story of the plight of sharecroppers whose lives were ruined by the Dust Bowl the Midwest became in the 1930s to "a story of mother love" that closed with an "uplifting ending."

Oddly, the system chugged along not so much because of its totalitarian nature as because of the ambiguities seeping through its cracks. On the one hand, it seemed in control—"By the end of the decade Breen had effectively muted political and social commentary from the movies," writes Black. On the other hand, Breen himself wambled, sometimes moved by his own populism, other times influenced by his membership in the Catholic Church, which, being based in the cities, was sympathetic to the malaise of city life. For example, he let the movie based on Sidney Kingsley's *Dead End* slip through with only a few shavings of language, prostitution, and venereal disease missing and, moreover, touted it to Hays as bearing an important social message. Much of the play's class conflict, urban despair, and baldly asserted squalor survived in Samuel Goldwyn's movie, which the liberal-left press praised for both its politics and its artistic level. Sometimes, ambiguity crept into movies merely as a result of a sly greasing of the wheels with innuendo that, as Jason Joy anticipated, cosmopolites would catch but would be lost on the masses. Slipping in such material often earned a winking reproach from a PCA man.

With the onset of World War II, censorship took another turn of the screw in the form of the development of the Office of War Information (OWI), whose motion picture branch seemed to ensnare Hollywood between an urge to serve the nation as its propaganda arm and its fear of the resulting cozy link between state and movies. In general, Hollywood cooperated with the government, albeit often losing the point of the war in implementing its

own conventions: the loner hero; the cartoonish portrayal of foreign enemies, particularly a race-based assault on the Japanese; and a failure to per-
sonalize larger war aims. Some individuals in the OWI thought the result
would be a collective inability to define the terms of victory or to treat with
the enemy after the war.

As though echoing the adversarial rhetoric it had spouted to the PCA before the war, Hollywood at first took a similar stance against the OWI. But
national polls confirmed a collective wish for some form of social control of
entertainment. Thus little seemed lost in obliging the OWI, except for, perhaps, some sleep among those on the left who feared that Hollywood would
become even more the state apparatus that the Marxists saw it as.

As for American citizens' mood during the war, it was optimistic, based
on the belief, partly induced by their own government's propaganda, that
the postwar era would provide a materially better life. As a Ford commercial
sang on the radio, "For the Ford in your future you will have to wait."
African Americans expected to be in on the spoils of war, as though adapt-
ing to their own uses Gramsci's notion of bargaining for gain during a crisis.
As mentioned earlier, William G. Nunn, publisher of the black *Pittsburgh
Courier*, called for a "Double Victory," that is, simultaneous victories over
foreign fascism and domestic racism. Hollywood joined in this futurism, offering such fare as the B movie *Gangway for Tomorrow*.

Hollywood's new role as tubthumper for a nation unified by a vision of a
postwar future was not without its glitches. The reality of warfare jangled
against Hollywood's formulas in ways that polarized those who wished to report the texture of combat and those who wished to censor its worst images.
The army's censors, for example, clashed with John Huston's infantryman's
view of the war in *The Battle of San Pietro* (1945), much as Marine officials
objected to civilians' viewing their dead on the beach at Tarawa. They argued
that missing from the story told by the localized shots of soldiers pinned
down, taking casualties, and stalled in awful terrain, their dead and wounded
exposed to view, was the sense of impending victory.

Yet the military censors' demands and the OWI's pressures confirmed the
movie men in their customary relationship to the PCA. So Walter Wanger,
Chaplin, and the rest deferred their dueling with Breen until after the war.
Howard Hughes was the one exception, making a stand regarding his sopho-
morically censorable *The Outlaw* (1947), the ad copy for which offered its
well-proportioned star by asking, "Would you like to tussle with [Jane] Rus-

sell?" As for the rest, they anticipated that the war might change mores and politics and so stored up movies against a more liberal future. Only occasionally was the calm ruffled, as when Preston Sturges's *The Miracle of Morgan's Creek* (1944) toyed with the PCA's "don't" regarding premarital sex, inducing a waggish comment from James Agee: "The Hays office has been either hypnotized into a liberality for which it should be thanked, or it has been raped in its sleep" (quoted by Leff and Simmons in *The Dame in the Kimono*).

At war's end, the entire industry was confronted with an all but revolutionary wave of change. The fragile sensibilities that military censors and the PCA imagined they were protecting when they blocked the showing of, say, Huston's *Let There Be Light* (1945), a documentary on the psychic damage caused by combat, or the prominent display of Jane Russell's breasts in *The Outlaw* had all but evaporated under the heat and pressure of warfare. If for no other reason, this was so because the veterans began to return from worlds of experience they could not have imagined in their small towns before the war. Hollywoodians muttered over their lunches at Lucy's or Musso and Frank's about "the new audience" that had "grown up out of the war," as the director Robert Rossen described the new mood, and "the thinking picture" that soon would result. Leff and Simmons report that even Eric Johnston, the conservative former president of the U.S. Chamber of Commerce and recently appointed successor to Hays, expected "more adult" movies.

But with postwar change came renewed conflict between the mossbacks and the avant-garde, the city mouse and the country mouse, the pious and the rakish. All stereotypes, of course. But all containing, like any good stereotypes, their simplistic point. Deeply embedded in the essence of the opposing sides was an agreed upon sense that the intense idea of individualism in America needed some restraints. After all, the most radical reformers in American history, the Progressives who gave their name to an era and the New Dealers who gave theirs to yet another, favored not overthrowing the order but rather reforming it to save it from itself. That is, men and women like Frederic Howe, Florence Kelley, and the Roosevelts carried *two* sociopolitical genes, political reformism *and* social rectitude.

Unavoidably, then, the postwar sensibility brought with it a drive for more freedom of expression but within constraints worn more loosely. Seemingly at every turn, the moguls challenged the PCA during the crucial last days of the war and the first giddy days of peace. Kathleen Winsor's lurid novel of the English Restoration, *Forever Amber* (1947); Niven Busch's western *Duel in the Sun* (1947); and James M. Cain's erotically driven murder yarn *The Postman Always Rings Twice* (1946) ("as amoral as zoo exhibits," one critic labeled it); not to mention the rereleased *The Outlaw*, all challenged the PCA's surviving authority.

Yet in a sense, this rising challenge to the PCA was no more than a replay of prewar ways. It was the political movie that really shook the system, mainly because the distributors of political movies took the fight to the courts, where defeats began to erode the PCA's legitimacy. At issue was the plaintiffs' insistence on relief from censorship on the grounds that political movies were entitled to the protection of the First Amendment. The challenges came from two sources: the American distributors of foreign movies, with their gritty "neorealism" and Marxist overtones, and the NAACP, with the support of the makers of Hollywood message movies, who insisted that racially reformist movies such as *Intruder in the Dust* (1949), *Lost Boundaries* (1949), *Pinky* (1949), and *No Way Out* (1950) have access to southern audiences. The distributors of foreign movies, none signatories to the renamed Motion Picture Association of America, filed suits, and the NAACP filed *amicus curiae* briefs against several southern censors.

Italian movies, with their earthily blunt view of social breakdown, their faces cast for type rather than star quality, and their avoidance of pat endings, conveyed a distinctly "realistic" Euro-Marxism that shook the PCA. Vittorio De Sica's *The Bicycle Thief* (1949), for example, arrived in America complete with a child protagonist who casually pisses on a wall. Its distributor, Joseph Burstyn, had been trying for years to find an audience for European movies and had at last found a mix of art house venues and lurid advertising that pulled in a viewership characterized by suburban drift. Their habitual moviegoing phase over, Americans had begun turning to the television and to new outdoor leisure diversions. In other words, they needed to be drawn into movies on their merits and on the bold appeal of the new. Burstyn not only reached them, but scored an ideological coup that laid bare the stark differences between the old and the new. The coup was not so much that critics raved and sophisticates stood in line to see it. It was that on the one hand the Catholic Legion of Decency condemned the movie, while on the other the Academy of Motion Picture Arts and Sciences gave it an Oscar!

Breen was powerless. Not only did Burstyn proudly advertise *The Bicycle Thief* as running uncut and without a PCA seal, but no fewer than three theater chains that had recently been divorced from their parent studios by a Supreme Court order picked up De Sica's movie.

In a couple of years, the Supreme Court would affirm Burstyn's right to play *The Bicycle Thief* in the equally famous "*Miracle* case." *The Miracle*, an Italian movie that arrived in the United States in December 1950, concerns a peasant woman who is impregnated by a man whom she believes to be St. Joseph. To escape religious fanatics, she flees to a country church, where she gives birth to her ironic Jesus. Roberto Rossellini's film, yet another Burstyn import, opened at the Paris in Manhattan and immediately drew a blast from the Legion of Decency as "a blasphemous and sacrilegious mockery," a threat by Francis Cardinal Spellman of a boycott, a crowded picketline led by Catholic war veterans and priests, a flurry of harassment by city agencies in search of fire code violations, and threats of bomb plantings. Moreover, the Church's forces used the skirmish as a means of negotiating cuts in other pending domestic movies, such as Elia Kazan's *A Streetcar Named Desire* (1951). Breen and his office stood their ground in view of the added strength provided by these allies within the Church, but by 1954 Burstyn's case had worked its way to the Supreme Court, which, in a narrowly cast opinion, found in favor of *The Miracle*.

For their part, black Americans, or at least Walter White and the NAACP, reversed a 25-year history of advocating censorship and began filing *amicus curiae* briefs on behalf of southern theater owners who were trying to break their local censors' grip on controversial racial material. Reversing the approach they had taken in 1915, when they had assailed *The Birth of a Nation* by using censorship as a weapon, in 1949 they made use of an alliance they had formed during World War II with the OWI and the leftists in the movie studios to influence the racial content of wartime movies. White reopened his contacts, even seeking money to support a Hollywood bureau of the NAACP, and began to influence movies at their source. He praised or damned current movies in his newspaper columns and letters, lunched with the moguls, and addressed Hollywood agencies. In the case of Darryl F. Zanuck and Elia Kazan's *Pinky*, White, through his daughter, Jane, actually wrote NAACP goals and ideology into the script. The NAACP's success in this cycle of message movies, as they were called, seemed to derive not so much from shifts in Hollywood's corporate behavior as from the position of strength it had attained in World War II. Not only had the ideology of the war and its aims invited attacks on racism but the NAACP had increased its membership tenfold during the war. Although the resulting opinions were far from precedent setting and often heard on the narrowest of grounds, together with the *Miracle* case they constituted a platform on which more defining cases would be built in the future.

Thereafter, movie after movie in one way or another revealed fissures in the formerly unbreachable walls of censorship. The cause célèbre was Otto Preminger's *The Moon Is Blue* (1953), an innocuous comedy by a director with a lengthy Hollywood pedigree. Breen opposed the movie on the basis of its "low moral tone," symbolized by a single word—*virgin*—and thereby risked the prestige of his office on a chimera. Preminger not only played it off without a PCA seal, but, once he knew that the sky would not fall, turned to Nelson Algren's novel of drug-ridden Chicago, *The Man with the Golden Arm* (1955), casting Frank Sinatra, who was at the height of his acting career, in the title role. As such challenges proliferated, the PCA and the Church sometimes flubbed their lines. For example, the PCA gave a seal to Kazan's *Baby Doll* (1956), a southern gothic that featured a coyly erotic juvenile, while the Legion condemned it. When the movie played to good grosses, the take all but gave Hollywood permission to laugh off the Church's last-ditch weapon, a boycott by the faithful. At the same time, it spoke as an omen of the end of Breen's, then Jack Vizzard's, and eventually Geoffrey Shurlock's office that Hays had wrought in the 1920s.

In effect, the postwar taste-culture rode on the comet's tail of an increasingly liberal federal judiciary. It had also grown more affluent and more educated, had moved away from the downtown rialtos, was now fickle in what it chose for leisure activity and intrigued by foreign alternatives to Hollywood, and was being drawn to the electronic domesticity of television. Hollywood, in the face of declining revenues, suffered a self-inflicted wound when the major studios sold their libraries of old movies both to the television networks and to hundreds of local stations. Thereafter, Breen's successor could do little more than resist only the grossest breaches of the PCA code.

Even the Legion of Decency felt the change in the air when the polltaker Leo Handel found that in the decade after *The Miracle* there was a general stiffening of Catholics against the Legion of Decency. The agency was compelled to alter its stance by setting up two codes, one for adults and one for children, anticipating a similar change within the PCA.

As for the movies themselves, they had become like music: a medium with a sectored audience with discrete and sometimes countervailing tastes, no single one of which enjoyed hegemony enough to dominate the market-place. Gone was the presumption of a broad, consensual center of American politics. Under the hand of Jack Valenti, a politician who had been Lyndon Johnson's chief White House aide, the PCA inched toward a system of letter ratings that signaled to parents and moviegoers that the content of movies was "suitable" for adults or children or adolescents (with parental counsel). The concept of moviegoing mediated by censorship had given way to the concept of moviegoing by informed consent. And with the decline of the PCA's brand of prior censorship, the concept of a classical Hollywood cinema also began to give way.

CHAPTER FIVE

The Sound of
the System

What was the first talkie? Every movie fan knows the answer: *The Jazz Singer*, which came out in 1928. What many movie fans do not know, however, is that movies came with sound long before Al Jolson uttered his famous line, "You ain't heard nothin' yet."

It is inaccurate to divide silent film and soundfilm into separate epochs. All through the first decade of classical Hollywood, and even earlier, movie-goers were often enveloped in sound, although not from the screen. As the nickelodeons grew into picture palaces and ticket prices along the rialto increased to pay for the capital improvements, picture palace audiences expected not only more sophisticated movies, but also amenities—cool auditoriums, plush seats, and some form of sound. All the downtown palaces housed a "mighty Wurlitzer" or its equivalent pipe organ, and for grand occasions (such as the first run of *The Birth of a Nation* in 1915) they might have even included a pit orchestra; the better nabes offered a house pianist or maybe an organist. Sometimes, exhibitors provided narrators, or even actors, who read lines in synch with the action on the screen, particularly to accompany "reality" footage such as *Hale's Tours*.

While the house pianist was playing, electrical wizards and entrepreneurs such as Lee DeForest and E. H. Armstrong were off in their labs, working on transmitting sound electronically. Their goal was mainly to improve on Morse's telegraph, first by broadcasting sounds wirelessly and then by transforming the human voice into electrical impulses transmitted in the form of sound waves of various frequencies. Along the way, DeForest took a detour and used his "audion tube," among other innovations, to record sound in a way that could be amplified in synch with projected moving images. Among these images were the often excerpted sequences of the black musicians Eubie Blake and Noble Sissle and the black actor Abbie Mitchell, performing for both camera and sound recorder. Although these images were never seen as part of the daily theatrical bookings of the day, they must have held open a hope for an eventually normative, commercially viable soundfilm.

Certainly, the scientists at Bell Laboratories, Western Electric, and various German labs harbored this hope. Moreover, all Americans had already come to regard Alexander Graham Bell's telephone as a part of every comfortable home and every corner store. Many knew that it had taken less than half a century for Bell's instrument to become ubiquitous, having just been demonstrated at the Philadelphia Centennial Exposition of 1876. Less well known but central to the culture of technology that helped define the 1920s was the fact that Bell's progeny—American Telephone and Telegraph (AT&T); its manufactory arm, Western Electric; and its eventual broadcasting arms, the Radio Corporation of America and the National Broadcasting Company—were increasingly dedicating their resources to discovering the technology of soundfilm with the goal of selling it to Hollywood. For movie fans, the result was the celebrated commercial debut of soundfilm in the summer of 1926, when Vitaphone showed a seven-act demo of the prospects for a future sound cinema.

The point is that the prospects for a cinema enriched by sound were enhanced by public expectation (though, to be sure, the topic was primarily taken up in engineering trade journals and *Popular Science*). Thus the moviegoers of the 1920s formed an anticipatory audience that was as one with the audience of the 1930s, for whom soundfilm would become conventional. Furthermore, the corporate culture that made possible such an investment in scientific research also possessed resources that enabled it to withstand the worst of the Great Depression by investing millions in installing sound systems in thousands of theaters. Thus the technology, enterprise, social readiness, and systemic superstructure of soundfilm not only permitted movies to shift their aesthetic basis to entirely new ground, but also allowed for a generational continuity of audiences. The quarter of a century from the end of World War I to the end of World War II was in many ways all of a piece, and so too was its audience.

The corporate presence in Hollywood in this epoch had a history; it did not merely enter as a deus ex machina holding out a juju to Warner Bros., the producer of *The Jazz Singer*. From this angle, the great man was not, say,

Lee DeForest, but rather Waddill Catchings, the banker whom Douglas Gomery ("Warner Bros. Innovates Sound: A Business History" in Gerald Mast's *The Movies in Our Midst* [1982]) puts at the center of the deal that brought together a research lab, a studio, and the corporate will to prevail against competing sound systems. It was Catchings who stood at the confluence of profit, consumer acceptance, technics, and deep corporate pockets.

In this story, the coming of sound was not so much the result of flashes of scientific imagination as an episode in techno-corporate history. Indeed, it was an almost predictable outcome of the propelling of underwritten research from lab to engineering to prototyping. In a way, movie sound served Hollywood both as a machine tool that could be used to make products and as a consumer product.

As an institution, Hollywood joined in this cycle of corporate-sponsored invention, asserts Gomery and his colleagues. Apart from the studios themselves, each new guild of engineers and technicians subscribed to its own trade papers that informed its members of new advances in, for example, sound technology. Furthermore, each guild issued manuals on shop practice that standardized operations, served as study guides for licensing examinations, and handed on precautionary advice and rules of thumb. In concert with the management practices of the movie lots, such routinization by practitioners encouraged normative Hollywood behaviors. Thus, in the world of soundfilm, research, engineering, banking, and shop practice all served as agents of technological and eventually aesthetic change on the movie lots.

As mentioned, into this picture of institutional Hollywood we must also sketch an audience with a readiness for the profound change in movie culture that sound would bring—just as important as the sources of venture capital and factors of production. Just as a bank might have refused a loan to an exhibitor who wished to wire his theater for sound, so the prospective clientele might have rejected the aesthetics of sound, preferring, as did the literary critic Edward Wagenknecht, the romance of the silent film over the sound film's similarity to the realism that had begun to dominate the Broadway stage.

Not that these risks were unique to the marketing of movies. Even the yo-yo could not have succeeded in America had investors not been positive about its prospects, had tool-and-die men not been able to create machine tool settings for milling mass-produced parts, or had the traveling Filipino drummers who sold yo-yos not been able to persuade American boys away from marbles and mumblety-peg.

Movie men faced similar crises of faith, technology, and marketing. Each new refinement of the system, and the rationalization of work routines, standardization of product, and management of product flow it required, constituted what Thomas Schatz calls "the genius of the system." Into this changing yet stable system the arrival of sound was less like an unexpected thunderclap than like hearing the telephone operator's voice after inserting your nickel.

In much the same way, printmakers had introduced their art world to the grey shadings and values that once had been open only to sketchers and painters. Much as painting and drawing had created an anticipatory market for such modeled figures, so centuries later the "stereotypers" of newspaper composition rooms accomplished a similar union of art and commerce in the form of the fin de siècle "rotogravure" section of Sunday newspapers, which introduced the photograph to the mass-printed newsprint page.

At issue in this halting path toward soundfilm were the capitalists' predictable anxieties: the costs of research and design; the factoring of cost into price; the constraints on equipping every theater for sound; the bold advertising needed to assure moviegoers that the new augmented, rather than spoiled, the old; and, finally, the agonies of standardization of the competing systems. The costs of wrong decisions were eminently ponderable, because history was already littered with the wreckage of wrong choices: projectors whose deviant speeds never became standard, half-baked coloring processes (such as maddeningly slow handwork or the bathing of whole strips of film in mood colors, red for rage, blue for sadness, and so on), and wide screens and three-dimensional stunts that appeared before audiences were ready for them.

The chronicle of soundfilm was no more risk free than the stories of other technologies. But the manner of its success differed from almost all other cinematic achievements. Neither the adventurers in the banks nor the visionaries in the lab could have predicted soundfilm's tremendous success after a vaudevillelike snippet of it premiered in the summer of 1926.

True, during the ensuing couple of years moviegoers would demonstrate their readiness to accept sound. But more central to the Hollywood system was the corporate nature of the arrival of sound. According to Tino Balio in *Grand Design: Hollywood as a Modern Business Enterprise* (1993), the studios, being institutions, behaved according to norms of institutional conduct that "as a whole constitute a group style." It follows that, as David Bordwell, Janet Staiger, and Kristin Thompson write in *The Classical Hollywood Cinema* (1985), "social processes . . . translate filmmakers' goals and standards into new materials, equipment, and procedures." Thus, "just as the Hollywood style is a group phenomenon, so is technological change." Bordwell and his coauthors are describing a social process within the institution of Hollywood, but their conceptualization also applies to the interaction between moviegoer and moviemaker. In this instance, as Bordwell and Thompson report, "sound had to be integrated into an existing set of stylistic priorities," mainly in the form of a restoration of the fluidity of silent film style that had been momentarily frozen by the rigidities imposed by early recording technique.

By now, the fey tinkerer writing up his lab notes by the light of an oil lamp had gone the way of the Stutz Bearcat. Now heaps of capital, not the romantic visions of the lone eccentric, drove research and development. From the outset, sound and film had seemed a natural union to some. As early as 1889, W.K.L. Dickson worked to synchronize sound with Edison's Kinetograph. And in 1912 Edison synched a Mother Goose rhyme to a thread of sound and hoped to wire up four Keith–Orpheum houses in New York. Kinetophone, he called it. Abroad, another system played the Paris Exposition of 1900. In 1923, Lee DeForest formed Phonofilm in Pittsburgh to apply his self-promoted audion tube to movies. Although Phonofilm was eventually a technical succès d'estime, it was never a commercial success. DeForest lacked faithful backers; an audience open to Phonofilm's possibilities; a cheap means of replicating the system in chains of theaters; and, finally, a solution to a tinny timbre, a metallic "wow" in the circuitry, and amplification that was not up to filling cavernous theaters.

During the boom years after World War I, an invincible optimism drove the stock market to uncommon heights, a shift to the political right brought in a Republican era, and corporations embarked on a rush toward expansion and merger (and overproduction, it would later be discovered). The time was ripe for new things.

Clearly, in the view of recent economic historians of movies, the era of soundfilm awaited only the catalytic agent that would set in motion a symbiosis of research, capital, audience, and window of opportunity. Such a marvel of social organization had already happened and, furthermore, would contribute to the debut of soundfilm. Alexander Graham Bell's telephone, which had been introduced at the Philadelphia Centennial Exposition in 1876, might well have remained simply a classroom audio aid for Bell's deaf pupils were it not for the entry of various Wall Street banking houses into the field as angels. The resulting AT&T Company and its Western Electric manufacturing arm would eventually stimulate the creation of still other communications giants, such as Radio Corporation of America and its National Broadcasting Company network. As early as 1923 the infant AT&T moved from the lab to making demos for the purpose of selling its sound technology to Hollywood.

Thus the eventual result, movies that talked, arose not from a simplistic fable, such as the legend of a Warner Bros. studio made desperate by imminent collapse, or, as the Marxists would have it, the yoking of science to capitalism's needs. Moreover, the movers and shakers in the plot were not the moguls as much as the gnomes in their banks acting in concert with Warner Bros.'s search for an aggressive weapon. In keeping with this strategy, the studio negotiated a line of credit from Goldman, Sachs with which they expanded their plant, bought enough theater chains to join the ranks of the giants, increased the budgets of their A movies, and bought a radio station (through which they learned of AT&T). So mundanely corporate were their interests, Robert C. Allen and Douglas Gomery report in *Film History* (1985), that part of their plan was a wish to shoot vaudeville acts to introduce Warner Bros. movies to vaudeville theater owners as a way to cut the labor costs inherent in maintaining pit orchestras.

It was at this point that Waddill Catchings became involved in the project in his capacity at Goldman, Sachs. It was he who brought together Warner Bros.'s corporate plans, AT&T's history of both research and attention to Hollywood, and the resources of Goldman, Sachs. Without the fiscal arrangement, the union of studio technicians and AT&T's engineers and scientists could not have happened, and neither would we have the entertaining but inaccurate fable of Warner Bros.'s being saved from destitution by soundfilm that came into being after word got around that the studio's annual report of March 1926 revealed a short-term debt of $1 million. Far from the threat of bankruptcy, Warner Bros. had aggressively formed Vitaphone to exploit the research of Western Electric in an arrangement that gave exclusive license to each party to make commercial use of sound. This classic agreement founded in prescient decisions permitted exploitation of the new technology and eventually its presentation to an urbane audience who had already been prepared for it by advertising.

Ironically, it was the *other* studios that had misjudged the situation, by overextending themselves in theatrical real estate, betting their futures on the survival of silent film, or adopting sound in some limited form, such as Fox's *Movietone News* newsreels. In contrast, Warner Bros. entered the Great Depression in command of the Vitaphone studios in Brooklyn, its own lot in Hollywood, fifty exchanges at home and abroad, and its arrangement that Catchings had assembled, all of it underwritten by both its own resources and $3 million in revolving credit from Goldman, Sachs. Coupled with other leases and purchases, Warner Bros. at the height of the Depression grew from a small outfit to the size of the fabled but shaky Famous Players–Lasky–Paramount–Publix group.

The show that resulted from all this endeavor became a legend. In its premiere of soundfilm on August 6, 1926, Warner Bros. treated movie fans to a seven-act vaudevillian *Vitaphone Prelude*, which included Will Hays's twangy introduction to the medium, Giovanni Martinelli in an aria from *I Pagliacci*, the overture to *Tannhäuser*, and a one-man "duet" for harmonica and banjo, all of it serving as an overture to *Don Juan*, a silent movie to which a Vitaphone music track had been appended. The program played theaters in Atlantic City, Chicago, and a half dozen other cities in which theaters had been wired for the occasion. The success was marred only by a quarrel among the principals: Western Electric hoped to buy Vitaphone, rather than be a member in an exclusive partnership, as the Warners wanted. The former course would have reduced the studio to no more than a supplier of product. In fact, Western Electric had already created a subsidiary, Electrical Research Products, Inc., through which it intended to offer its wares to an open marketplace.

But the impact of the event on movies far outlived this clash of corporate wills. Warner Bros. built four new soundstages in Hollywood, complete with motor-driven cameras mounted in soundproof blimps and incandescent bulbs to replace the hissing carbon arcs that had vexed early sound men. A year later, *The Jazz Singer*, blessedly near the last in a century-long cycle of assimilationist movies, became yet another achievement of the guild of sound men. At a nut of a half million dollars, it was Warner Bros.'s costliest movie ever, but the studio put every dollar on the screen: Al Jolson's cocky charisma, Samson Raphaelson's schmaltzy script about a Jewish family rent by the conflict between an assimilationist son and his traditionalist cantor father, energetic yet sentimental blackface routines that some African Americans tolerated because of the empathetic charm that Jewish performers brought to them, some snappy echoes of the music of the Jazz Age, and a paean to motherhood. Granted, a few flaws revealed *The Jazz Singer*'s ideological debt to its forebears, Israel Zangwill's *The Melting Pot* (1908) and Anne Nichols's *Abie's Irish Rose* (1922), two old-time stage plays that had defined the sentimental assimilationist genre. Despite its faults and its well-deserved mediocre reviews, however, *The Jazz Singer*'s four Vitaphoned segments earned enough revenue that the Warners signed Jolson on for more of the same.

The resulting rush to soundfilm caught everyone short—even Warner Bros., which needed cash to grind out a cycle of soundfilm shorts and part-talkie features and still more cash to meet its mortgage notes on its newly acquired Stanley theater chain, which it had bought to catch up with the number of downtown picture palaces that the other major studios owned. Moreover, they then picked up another movie lot, First National, as well as the Skouras chain of theaters in the Midwest.

In fact, some studios were never to collect on the bet they made on soundfilm. RKO, for example, had stirred to life like Frankenstein, cobbled together from the detritus of fiscal Hollywood and New York: a fragment of Joseph P. Kennedy's small lot, called FBO; capital drawn from John Hertz's rental car firm; John Hay "Jock" Whitney's personal fortune; and the Keith–Orpheum vaudeville circuit, which had been hastily joined to RCA and its broadcasting technologies. RKO struggled through the Depression on the coattails of a brief run of urbane Fred Astaire musicals, including *Flying Down to Rio* (1933), *Top Hat* (1935), and others; an occasional classy oddment, such as George Stevens's *Gunga Din* (1939), Merian C. Cooper's *King Kong* (1933), and Orson Welles's *Citizen Kane* (1941); during World War II, Val Lewton's neat package of film noir, *Cat People* (1942), *The Curse of the Cat People* (1944), *The Body Snatchers* (1945), *Isle of the Dead* (1945), and *I Walked with a Zombie* (1943); and a few fine postwar genre films, such as *Murder My Sweet* (1945) and *The Set-Up* (1949). Easily identified by its distinctive logo of an airplane circling a sparking radio tower and its mottled, angularly lit black-and-white photography, RKO nonetheless never attained the ranks of the majors.

For the others, soundfilm proved a marvelous engine of prosperity that saw them through the Depression. Among the majors, only Paramount suffered, and that was mainly from overextension during the most enervated years of the slump. Aggressively, Adolph Zukor and Jesse Lasky used Paramount's status as "a Ford or Woolworth's" (to quote Gomery) to convert all their movies to talkies. They backed up their decision by setting up a music division, buying a piece of CBS, and attempting a grand merger that would have netted them yet another thousand theaters, a half dozen studios, and a covey of ancillary enterprises. Only a threatened federal antitrust suit headed off the merger.

Then the Great Crash made itself felt with a vengeance, and Paramount almost went under. Hertz, retired pioneer of the automobile rental business, member of the board at Lehman Brothers brokerage, an early player in RKO, and eventually a member of Paramount's finance committee, stepped in, rescheduled the mortgage burden, cut salaries and unit budgets, and sold off the weak links in the theatrical chain and the firm's CBS holdings. Even so, after a brief upturn, the studio still registered a 1933 loss of $20 million. Part of the problem, advised Kennedy, a principal in the founding of RKO, was Hertz's seemingly sound decision to stock the upper echelons with businessmen, rather than movie men (save for Zukor, the founder). "Get rid of their quality businessmen," Kennedy wrote, "or prepare for another receivership." At last in 1936, the board hired Barney Balaban of the Chicago chain of Balaban and Katz theaters, the first time an exhibitor had been appointed to the position of Hollywood studio chief. With Zukor in charge of production, Balaban embarked on a spare regimen that by the latter days of the Depression had restored the firm to solvency.

Everyone in Hollywood faced similar, though less dire, threats. MGM, for example, entered the sound era late, hurried to catch up, and stumbled into an antitrust suit when the founder, Marcus Loew, died and his widow set out to sell her stock just as Nicholas Schenck saw an opportunity to merge MGM with Fox. Snared in his own problems, Fox had done little toward entering the soundfilm era, save for its *Movietone News* and the showcase olio *Fox Movietone Follies*.

In the final analysis, however, all of the majors not only survived the Great Crash, but won back many fans in search of cheap entertainment amid the rubble of the nation's economy.

My point in providing this information is not to give a lesson in fiscal survival, but to show the effect on the Hollywood system of not only sound but also the interaction of optical/aural/electronic scientists, inventive financiers, and audiences open to the new. Together, these forces brought into being an institutional network that defined what came to be called the sound era. Suppose, for example, the symbiosis among financial backers, moviemakers, and consumers froze in 1928, the year Warner Bros. made *Lights of New York*. The camera would still be locked in its blimp today; editorial cuts would still be linked to the ends of spoken sentences; choice of settings would still be curtailed by the requirements of the engineers' microphones; the writing would still be long and expository, referring to off-camera events; and actors would still be a tableau of talking heads, their speech taken by mikes hidden in vases. These strictures would dictate matters of pacing, movement within the frame, cutting, and even the range of theme and subject. Suppose further that, like fans of opera or cat shows, moviegoers had come to prefer sameness rather than change. The moguls, their backers, and their scientists would have left off pressing against the limits of the medium.

But the symbiosis did not freeze, and adaptation to the new became the norm—new within the limits of convention, of course. By this I mean that each new movie was bound by conventions but was free to move within them and even to press against them in ways mutually agreeable to budgeteers in search of the risk-free product and moviegoers who knew what they liked. In other words, as mentioned in earlier chapters, each new movie was to be the same, only different. King Vidor's *Hallelujah!* (1929), for example, so violated the emerging canon of rules that Mayer refused to make the project unless Vidor put up his own "earnest money." Vidor stretched the new medium by recording exterior and wild sounds and laying them over studio-made recordings of dialogue. His hope that the primitive mixing of ambient sound, music tracks, and the spoken word would be accepted by the audience was more than fulfilled in the ways in which he married image with sound and caught the folk idiom of black southern music, all the while making an uncommonly fluid movie.

Another genre that came to life as a direct result of soundfilm was the short performance film, sometimes bonded by a thin plot and other times offered as a visual record of a bandstand gig. The genre, which lasted for the rest of the classical era of Hollywood, was at its best in Dudley Murphy's *St. Louis Blues* (1929). In her only appearance on film, Bessie Smith sang

W. C. Handy's title song accompanied by a bourgeois-looking chorus who had been gathered for the purpose at New York's Gramercy Studio. Not only are the rhythm and pace of the cutting set to her performance, but also other cuts tighten the focus on Jimmie Mordecai's flashing feet, waiters spinning trays as they work, and a pan shot of the chorus (in the role of drinkers in a saloon). In one particularly nuanced sequence, we see Bessie in her room, where, having been cuffed by her caddish man (Mordecai), she pours herself a slug of gin and begins "The St. Louis Blues" just as the screen fades to black; the next cut fades up on Bessie standing at the bar, still singing without having missed a beat.

Such shorts became standard fare as a cheap way of introducing the new. Indeed, at the Milwaukee debut of *The Jazz Singer*, a local exhibitor scooped Jolson by playing Vitaphone shorts and a feature augmented by a music track. "Milwaukee Liked the Vitaphone," crowed the local *Journal*. The shorts units provided a broad range of performance styles: Jolson's arch rival, Georgie Jessel; the wry comic Fred Allen; the bandleader Fred Waring and his Pennsylvanians; the operatic tenor John Charles Thomas—the bits seemed limitless.

As to feature films, the most important change that followed from sound-film was the creation of a new genre, the backstage musical, which provided an imaginative merger of dialogue and performance art. Leading the pack were *Rio Rita* (1929); *Sunnyside Up* (1929); a restrike of *Showboat* (1929), Jerome Kern and Oscar Hammerstein's groundbreaking Broadway vehicle; and what eventually became the paragon of the genre, Warner Bros.'s *Gold Diggers* series (1933–37). Of course, once the knob-twiddlers mastered post-synching, rerecording, looping, and such, any genre, be it western, jungle yarn, or gangster movie, became possible.

This apparent ease of adaptation and the splashy journalism and advertising that accompanied it quickly fused into the legend of the smash hit—*The Jazz Singer*—that supposedly single-handedly transformed the medium overnight, pulled Warner Bros. from the brink of extinction, and blighted the careers of actors and directors who failed to measure up to the rigors imposed by the new. Every movie buff knows the legend of John Gilbert's fall from being Vilma Banky's romantic partner in silents to the ignominy of flopping opposite Greta Garbo in soundfilms. The story has been exaggerated, as many legends are; Gilbert's failure probably was more a matter of having a voice that did not match his image, rather than having the shrill voice legend gives him, and MGM's impatience with his reluctant change-over. However, it does confirm that changes in convention, performance, pacing, studio style, and setting were made unavoidable. More accurate was the story of Dolores Costello's defeat at the hands of talkies. "The most beautiful woman in the world" ran the ads. Alas, from the first line this clear-eyed beauty spoke in *Tenderloin* (1928), it was clear that her day had ended. "Merthy, merthy, have you no thisther of your own," Alexander Walker reports her as saying in his *The Shattered Silents* (1979).

As perhaps befits the profession, the legend of the arrival of sound is long on drama and short on substance. It begins in 1926 with reports of a box-office in bad shape made worse by price-cutting gimmicks, movies unable to compete with the emerging radio stations, and Warner Bros. acting desperately to forestall its doom and ends with audiences cheering wildly when Jolson utters the line, "You ain't heard nothin' yet," and moviemakers' subsequent stampede to wire up theaters, build soundstages, and hire voice coaches and East Coast writers.

In fact, the confluence of invention, underwriting, exploitation, and reception by the targeted audience that was required to produce sound on film proved to require more perspiration than inspiration, report Allen and Gomery in *Film History* (1985). Theater owners in Milwaukee, for example, took slowly to sound and, as we have seen, challenged *The Jazz Singer*'s claim to be the first talkie by showing Vitaphone shorts. In fact, even after one theater had run *The Jazz Singer* for a month, the other Milwaukee theater men only grudgingly moved toward wiring their houses. Except for *Movietone News* newsreels, no new talkie arrived until the spring of 1928, when a second run of *The Jazz Singer* satisfied demand. At this point, Fox hesitantly announced the wiring of five of its larger nabes as a trial before it wired its downtown palaces. By the end of summer, all of the downtown Milwaukee palaces had been wired.

Allen and Gomery further illustrate that the story of soundfilm is not the stuff of legend by arguing that, indeed, *The Jazz Singer* only lamely qualified as the first talkie, because it was only in a few segments that an actual word was uttered. Jolson's next gig, *The Singing Fool* (1928), had better credentials in that it was truly an all-sound film and one that audiences embraced as such; in one New York run of six weeks, fans bought 400,000 tickets. Again, what defined this project was the alliance between bankers, moviemakers, and moviegoers. The Morgans and the Rockefellers who controlled Western

Electric and RCA readily lent their capital to the development of sound technology, having accepted the reception of the Warner Bros. movies as an indication of future patronage for soundfilm. As though closing the circle, by 1930 ticket sales had reached 90 million per week, a rise since 1927 of some 30 million.

Clearly, no single engine drove the movement toward soundfilm. Rather, in "a climate of acceptance," to use Nicholas Vardac's description of the mood at the time of the changeover from vaudeville to nickelodeon, prudent investors had anticipated the receptivity of a new technology and acted on their intuition. Jolson's brief fling as star of the new medium provided the occasion for investors to recover their stake, engineers to polish their craft, and audiences to display their readiness for the new. In fact, engineers quickly forged ahead by modulating their touchy mikes; muffling motors so well that blimps soon disappeared; and introducing the Movieola, which allowed both sound and image to be cut. And moviemakers wasted no time in pressing against the uncertain codes of shop practice. In 1932, only a couple of years after *Hallelujah!* and *The St. Louis Blues*, W. Duncan Mansfield, the editor of Somerset Maugham and Lewis Milestone's *Rain*, introduced a cut in which he lapped a preacher's voice reading The Lord's Prayer over the tartish image of Sadie Thompson, a previously unthinkable stroke of dramatic cutting. Only Charles Chaplin remained resolutely committed to silent film; as late as 1936 his *Modern Times*, although graced by a music track, calculatedly avoided dialogue.

On the sets, actors who had trained in the theater, vaudeville, and burlesque quickly filled the void left by the departing Gilberts and the Costellos, many of them entering the movies while remaining in New York and using the old studios in Astoria and Long Island, New York, and Fort Lee, New Jersey, and even the stages of big theaters like the Metropolitan Opera House. The Marx brothers brought the zany, pun-filled aural humor of *Animal Crackers* (1930), *Duck Soup* (1933), and *Coconuts* (1929) to the screen, while the Hollywood regulars survived only if they followed the examples of their fellow actors Stan Laurel and Oliver Hardy and were able to combine their silent visual humor with personas they created out of their readings of lines. Musical performers such as Sophie Tucker, whose theme song was "Some of These Days," and Texas Guinan, with her brassy "Hello, suckers," enjoyed brief vogues purely by playing wisecracking soubrettes. Some of them, like Helen Morgan or Jeanne Eagels, were one-trick ponies capable only of wistful renditions of torch songs. Men brought to the screen region- or class-specific accents: Lee Tracy's staccato New York style; the urbanity of Warren William, whose stock in trade was his Barrymore-like profile; and Joel Mc-Crea's and Stu Erwin's hayseeds. If they could manage it, they adapted to a long cycle of drawing room melodramas by learning to wear black ties and dinner jackets as though born in them. And they groused about the absurdities of moviemaking in comparison with The Theater. Helen Hayes hated the delays required by the light men. W. C. Fields and John Barrymore wore out their welcomes because of their alcoholism, which lent itself to the late rising and ritual performance of theater but not to the early hours that moviemaking required. Adolph Menjou was vexed by the engineers' muttering "Mississippi" over and over as they took mike checks.

Of course, all the stars from the silent era who had alien accents were obliged to find a niche in which they could get regular work, and this was rarely as the stars they had been in the silents. Pola Negri, Vilma Banky, and Renee Adoree seemed too alien, too heavy, and they either retired or went home to Europe, as did Emil Jannings, who was burdened by both a German accent and an un-American girth. Greta Garbo's Swedish purr gave her a fey quality that enabled her to last ten years in talkies, a fate also enjoyed by the Englishman George Arliss, whose accent and foxy grandpa manner found him a home in biopics of Voltaire, Alexander Hamilton, Nathan Rothschild, and other historical figures. Maurice Chevalier's French accent seemed perfect for the task of endlessly playing himself, a charming, winsome, rakish "continental." Later, the accents of Bela Lugosi, Maria Ouspenskaya, Victor Francen, and eventually an entire stable at Warner Bros. gave credibility to multiethnic or exotic locales. None of this, of course, would have been at issue before the development of soundfilm.

The case for soundfilm as the mold for recasting the role of directors is more difficult to make, and yet the evidence is there. It must be added that ancillary factors not specifically related to sound technology but nonetheless given weight by the coming of sound also altered the hierarchy of moviemaking. Directors had entered the post–World War I era as intuitive bosses who had learned at the feet of the pioneers, many of whom, like Griffith, still clung to their hopes of recapturing the achievements of halcyon days. But as Bordwell and his coauthors argue in *The Classical Hollywood Cinema*, much of the routine stuff of classical Hollywood film practice derived from technology and its conventions that were set forth in technical trade papers that some of the old-timers could make little sense of. If the result was standardization of everything right down to the lightbulbs, then not only would directors learn to systematize their work, but producers would supervise the process. Even as the technicians organized into the American Society of Cinematographers; the Society of Motion Picture Engineers; and the company union, the Academy of Motion Picture Arts and Sciences, the studios themselves combined to make impending changes normative. At the same time, the studios encouraged the large independent labs—Kodak, Bell, and Du Pont—to take up specific problems of moviemaking that would, as horseplayers say, "improve the breed." As a result, directors had less control over, for example, lighting, which was now in the hands of lighting specialists.

The results were startling in both their immediacy and the transformation they brought to soundstage practices, which once had been directed by directors theatrically gotten up in puttees or boots or other motley that echoed the romance of command, as though Culver City sat on the banks of the Somme. Faster panchromatic film; coolly efficient incandescent lights; mike booms; Movieolas that permitted sound and image editing; and standardized, edge-numbered film stock all made for precise editing, matching, and conforming of image and sound. Bordwell and his coauthors observe that in the trades, artifice followed technical change, as, for example, when engineers told each other of new ideas such as the illusion of distance achieved by the lowering of volume as an image fades. Bordwell and his colleagues call this sharing of ideas the "entrenchment of techniques."

In this new setting, directors gradually relinquished authority to others, not only producers but voice coaches and even writers. And the spoken word itself, of course. Many directors turned out silent movies rich in the imagery of life on the bottom: *The Cohens and the Kellys* (1926), *Kosher Kitty Kelly* (1926), and *Sailor Izzy Murphy* (1927) and other such movies were thick with ethnic comedy and melodrama, featuring the musketeers of Pig Alley, the Salomes of the tenements, and squabbling biethnic families. Why did their cycle come to an end? Perhaps hearing the accents of immigrant culture abraded the senses of the broad center of the audience and therefore obliged studios to soften otherness into mere difference, ethnicity into sentiment, and hardship into nostalgia. In any case, ethnicity became too much for classical Hollywood to handle and was easily rendered into a "structured absence," a prime example of which is the absence of any utterance of the word *Jew* in *The Life of Emile Zola* (1937), a movie about anti-Semitism.

Sometimes things just happen; styles become old hat. Marshall Neilan enjoyed a flashy, irreverent career in silents, climaxed by directing his wife, Blanche Sweet, at a high moment in her career as Hardy's *Tess* in 1925. But too easily could the cocky celebrity become the merely "difficult" has-been. Neilan possessed both an attitude and a dated style, and both proved lethal in the new technocratic age.

The directors who were able to make the transition from silence to sound were different; they shifted from one cinematic code to another or they adapted their shtick to fit new tastes. Edward Sutherland, for example, played the local colorist in both his silent film *A Regular Fellow* (1925) and his soundfilms *Mississippi* (1935) and *Dixie* (1944). Frank Capra, in a way, learned to change by watching his silent star, Harry Langdon, resist changing his eerie wistfulness that had once charmed audiences. What's more, Capra seemed to be under a lucky star in that his best work was in movies written by smart, witty writers such as Robert Riskin, with whom he won an Oscar in 1934 for *It Happened One Night*. Still other directors, like King Vidor and Rouben Mamoulian, not only survived the talkies but, in the spirit of innovation, actually pressed against the limits of the new medium. During the long sessions it took Vidor to manually mix wild sound, ambient sound, music, and dialogue for *Hallelujah!*, he went into rages at the pathbreaking task. Mamoulian had a flair for introducing theatrical effects, such as his tour de force opening of *Applause* (1929), in which street noise was used as a percussive symphony of urban life.

The most prolific of the directors who crossed into sound were those who worked uncomplainingly as smithies, doing what they were told, bringing their movies in under budget, spinning them out like jute: W. S. "One Take Woody" Van Dyke; B. Reeves "Breezy" Eason; William Witney; and Sidney Franklin, who made more than 50 movies, ranging from *The Forbidden City* in 1918 to *The Barretts of Wimpole Street* in 1934, and won an Oscar for *The Good Earth* (1937). In four decades, Allan Dwan made perhaps 100 films, among them *David Harum* (1915); *Robin Hood* (1922); *Rebecca of Sunnybrook Farm* (1938); and *Sands of Iwo Jima* (1949), in which he directed John Wayne. It was these directors who defined the conventions of moviemaking, which later artists became great for having broken. Collectively, they helped remake classical Hollywood by refusing to greet the arrival of sound merely by mourning the loss of silence.

Thereafter, these directors' experiences were used in every genre of movies, save for westerns, which did not reemerge until John Ford's *Stagecoach* (1939); Henry King's *Jesse James* (1939); Cecil B. DeMille's bio pic of Calamity Jane and Wild Bill Hickok, *The Plainsman* (1937); and William Wyler's *The Westerner* (1940), the last two of which raised Gary Cooper to the height of his iconic western style.

As to other genres, gangster movies came into vogue on the urban jangle that sound gave them: the stutter of tommy guns, the bursts of wisecracking dialogue, and the wail of sirens. *Scarface* (1932), *Public Enemy* (1931), and the rest would not have been the stunning successes they were without sound.

Musicals were divided between Busby Berkeley's intricately contrived *Gold Diggers (1933, 1935, 1937)*, *Dames* (1934), and *Strike Up the Band* (1940) (not that he did not make his own forays into the city streets, in movies such as *They Made Me a Criminal* [1939]) and the sound-induced revival of the old-fashioned operetta, which seemed made for the team of Nelson Eddy and Jeannette MacDonald in, for example, *Rose Marie* (1936), *Naughty Marietta* (1935), *Maytime* (1937), and *The Girl of the Golden West* (1938). Just as sound created a musical form for this duet to work in, better miking and looping provided an expansive stage upon which Fred Astaire and his partners brought insouciance and grace to song and dance forms that would have been unthinkable before sound.

Another new genre that silent film could only hint at was the witty social drama: *Dinner at Eight* (1933), *Dodsworth* (1936), *Our Betters* (1933), *Grand Hotel* (1932), *Design for Living* (1933), and *The Women* (1939). These sleek, repartee-filled movies gave a generation of directors reputations as Hollywood's sophisticates: George Cukor, Edmund Goulding, and Ernst Lubitsch, to name a few.

Not so much genres as older forms enhanced by sound were those movies in which noisy engines enhanced peril much as music might have, but with the extra touch of reality that ambient sound gave. These included *Hell's Angels* (1930), *Ace of Aces* (1933), *Submarine D-1* (1937), *King Kong* (1933), and a hundred sagas about mail pilots, race car drivers, and cadets at military academies.

Finally, among the animators, Walt Disney quickly embraced sound, spurring a train of followers. He even won a couple of Oscars by combining the visions of Mack Sennett, Louis Melies, and his own sketch artists. In little more than a decade, he put out *Steamboat Willie* (1928), Ub Iwerk's prototype of Mickey Mouse; *Skeleton Dance* (1929); *Who Killed Cock Robin?*

(1934), an Oscar winner; his *Silly Symphonies* series; *Snow White and the Seven Dwarfs* (1938), his first feature; and his tour de force of sound and music, *Fantasia* (1940).

Apart from technological developments, the Great Depression brought a renewed attention to dysfunctions in the social fabric, which found its expression in the cinema in the form of the "social problem movie." Obviously, this genre had its roots in the earliest days of Progressive-era reformism and a lineage that extended through the Republican era after World War I.

Yet, because its rhetoric embraced the word as well as the image, sound-film gave the movies an increased ability to advocate reform. To the extent that the resulting movie rhetoric led to easy last-reel resolutions of problems, it also invited the depressed nation to adopt a sentimental (rather than political) collectivist solution to the dysfunctions faced by the nation. Marxist critics, of course, could not help but find in this movie-made optimism the hand of the ruling class exercising its powers through manipulating mass culture. *They Gave Him a Gun* (1937), for example, limned the problem of veterans of World War I returning home to idleness and poverty, armed only with the lethal skills they learned in combat. One of these unfortunates, the protagonist, turns to a life of crime. However, this late in the New Deal era, such movies focused not on groups and their problems, but on the individual hero or bad guy and his woman. Thus the denouement gives meaning to the protagonist's wasted life and death by linking it to the happiness of his friends, rather than by solving the problem—the man with a gun—with which the movie began.

Granted, the reformist politics that social problem movies offered was not one that the leftist magazine *New Masses* might have put much stock in, but, as Andrew Bergman reckons in *We're in the Money* (1972), these movies at least drew Americans into what James Agee called a "collective dream" in what Arthur Schlesinger termed "the operative center of the nation's consciousness." In *A New Deal in Entertainment* (1983), Nick Roddick sees a more manipulative, not to say malign, "Hollywood style [that] rested upon the individualizing of social issues [and] exercising the maximum control over . . . the story, while disguising such control." Not that this notion of voicing discontent while also controlling it began with soundfilm. Kay Sloan argues in *The Loud Silents* (1988) that simply by legitimizing city dwellers' frustrations, silent films often stilled their dissatisfaction.

Regardless of what contemporary historians think, the audiences and critics of the 1930s saw these newly talking movies more as fables of optimism than as the covert voice of a ruling class. Indeed one could say of the 1930s what Kevin Brownlow writes of the 1920s in *Behind the Mask of Innocence* (1990): "One of the contributions of the twenties' movies is that, like baseball, jazz, and national magazines, they brought Americans together again after years of severe—and by 1919, hysterical— divisiveness."

Whether one sides with the leftists, who argue that movies were the apparatus that taught the "false consciousness" Lenin warned of, or with the centrists, who insist that movies taught a progressive national consciousness, it is clear that, as a rule, movies in Hollywood's classical era proffered an open-ended catholicity. Together, the scientists, capitalists, technicians, actors, directors, and writers created a synthesis of the center that also allowed for alternative readings based on class, group, gender, and political bent. Moreover, the heightened realism that sound brought to the screen made possible a conscious political rhetoric expressed in the social problem or message movie.

This debate is more than an academic pillow fight. After all, either the ticket buyers who saw fifty movies annually are seen as possessing a countervailing veto power against the men in the countinghouses, or they are viewed, as by the Frankfurt scholars, as simple sponges who accepted ideological handouts. Keeping these opposing views in mind, we can clearly see how soundfilm enhanced the social realism of movies, perhaps even drawing toward the harsh naturalism of Zola's or Stephen Crane's novels, in which implacable nature takes command of plots as though giving a hero a thorough shaking and then asking, "Little man, what now?"

Crane and Theodore Dreiser had already brought such a mood to American fiction, and later Ernest Hemingway and Dashiell Hammett would add to it. But critics early on believed that soundfilm, seamless editing, and the movie's easy resolution of the social problems that the Depression had brought into vogue would seduce moviegoers into seeing movies as ideologically uncontested ground. "Something immovably banal," the critic Edmund Wilson said of talkies, and Margaret Thorp suggested that they were made for "the average citizen's wife." Gerald Mast accounts for it in *A Short History of the Movies* (1971) by asserting that Hollywood had become "totally dependent upon Wall Street brokerage houses to underwrite the costs of production [which] necessarily pushed movies . . . toward more conservative themes." Yet, as though granting that the players in the game were indeed countervailing powers, Robert Sklar (*Movie-Made America*, 1975) praises this techno-capitalist-cinematic "revolution" as "smooth, progressive and generally beneficial."

Whatever their politics or circumstances, moviegoers, after a hesitant start, took to talkies not so much as a revolution but as an almost predictable enriching of the movies they had already embraced as their own. For critics like Edmund Wilson, for whom movies had become little more than the studios' "favorite formulas," alternative readings and alternative cinemas provided relief from the bland. Hollywood did share the grind houses, if not the picture palaces, with "red movies" from the USSR, race movies from Oscar Micheaux and his circle, Yiddish films from Joseph Seiden and his school, and various exploitation movies. Outside the system, in union halls, film societies, and political cells, an aesthetic and political avant-garde scene persisted in the form of sponsored films of advocacy; New Deal films such as Pare Lorentz's famous *The Plow That Broke the Plains* (1936) and *The River* (1937); and leftist films from Frontier Films, Nykino, and other cells of socialist activism.

Thus as Hollywood grew more dependent on corporate sources of capital; more businesslike in its folkways; more capable of resisting incipient trade unionism in its ranks; more monoethnic (Zanuck's was the lone Gentile studio) and yet sometimes more Catholic than, if not the Pope, then Joe Breen; more imperialist in its dominance over other nations' cinemas; and more sure of its voice, it remained open to and yet sealed off from contending, alternative, countervailing voices. Mainstream in its outlook and the idiom of its product, it also was so unable to predict what particular movie would succeed that despite its rationalized methods, Hollywood remained open to each new cycle of movies, whatever it brought.

CHAPTER SIX

Others' Movies

Throughout the classical era of Hollywood, what moviemakers put on the silver screen was determined by the box office; by the mores formulated into the Production Code Administration's censoring system and its forerunners; and by a slyness on the part of some moviemakers in slipping in references to racial, sexual, and political material that the first two forces precluded explicit mention of in the movies. This meant that African Americans, Jews, and other ethnic groups; political ideologues on the extreme left or right; and people whose sexual preferences thrust them into a corner of American life found only undertones of lives on Hollywood's main screens. Indeed, Hollywood often denied the presence of even the undertones, as Vito Russo claims in *The Celluloid Closet: Homosexuality in Movies* (1981). Howard Hawks did in an interview about his classic western *Red River* (1948), in which he denied the gay undertones that homosexuals imputed to the male bondings portrayed in the film. "A goddamn silly statement," Hawks said.

Only blacks, socialists, homosexuals, feminists, members of other subjected minorities, or activists acting on behalf of one of these groups decoded the moviegoing experience, focusing careful attention on small bits so as to tease out tonal meanings that mainstream viewers might have missed. Indeed, meanings other than the ostensible ones had a way of slipping into the frame, through moviemakers' inattention or naivete or sly willfulness—or viewers' imagining. For example, in 1943 a Richmond newspaper critic complained that the camera doggedly, incongruously sought out black Ethel Waters in *Cairo* (1943), as though for some unstated racially driven reason. Glenn Ford recalled that in making the sexually charged noir film *Gilda* (1946), he and George MacCready knew that "we were supposed to be play-

ing homosexuals," but the director, Charles Vidor, could only ask in disbe-
lief, "Really?" A few fleeting shots of the white guitarist Barney Kessel in sil-
houette were an in-joke for the knowledgeable jazz fans among the viewers
of *Jammin' the Blues* (1946), a movie ostensibly about the mores of an all-
black jazz ensemble. For homosexual moviegoers on the lookout for a witty
parody of gay life, there were always the mincing scenes of Franklin Pangborn and Fritz Feld; there was also the game of rushing to see the latest film
by the reputedly homosexual George Cukor or Mitchell Leisen in order to
ransack it for fey asides directed at the homoerotically inclined. Lesbians on
the lookout for a nod in their direction could find Eve Arden playing the
wisecracking buddy who has been through a lot with the female star. The
slim canon of Dorothy Arzner was also fruitful, not only for the movies but
for her "bourgeois butch" mode of dress, a boldly mannish jacket and tie.
Feminists searching the frame for signs and omens were rewarded with Rosalind Russell on an adventure in Bombay, alleviating the effects of polio, or
even slugging some bad guy with an uppercut. Other offerings for feminists
were Zona Gale's Lulu Bett throwing off the harness of domesticity with far
more rage on the screen than in the book; the biopic of Marie Curie; and the
many movies in which the star walks alone when she chooses (Lauren Bacall
in *To Have and Have Not* [1944], Marlene Dietrich in *Blonde Venus* [1932] or
Shanghai Express [1932], Barbara Stanwyck in *The Bitter Tea of General Yen*
[1933], and Jean Arthur as Calamity Jane in *The Plainsman* [1937]). Along
these same lines, John Schuchman, the historian of Hollywood's treatment
of deaf persons, closes *Hollywood Speaks: Deafness and the Film Entertainment Industry* (1988) with not only a ringing appeal for movies worthy of "a
society committed to a policy of equal access," but also a forty-nine-page filmography of bits and sequences that politically centered deaf persons may
wish to seek out.

Hollywood's exclusionary posture toward these individuals for whom life
"ain't been no crystal stair" and who have responded to this fact with a
heightened political consciousness resulted in alternative cinemas only for
blacks, Jews, and political extremists (feature films by blacks and Jews and
documentaries by political groups). Almost no alternative cinemas for feminists, homosexuals, or persons with physical impairments. It is these alternative cinemas that are the focus of this chapter, rather than Hollywood's sly
hints and inadvertent leaks, whereby it, for example, through Katharine
Hepburn's androgynous character in *Sylvia Scarlett* (1936) merely "intro-

duced the possibility of homosexual activity into the film for a covert gay audience while providing laughs for the majority," as Russo writes.

In addition to these political subcultures was another taste-culture, one that was driven by an appetite for the erotic and was hellbent on violating convention. Indeed, its tastes serve as a loose definition of pornography, the medium that titillates by violating prevailing norms of taste, behavior, and expression. Catering to its fans' insistence on pressing against the limits of convention, this genre drove them through an endless cycle of first arousal by violation of norms, and then jadedness as violation became norm, and then revival of arousal by the next round of deviance from norms already stretched. These films suggest not so much a common taste that impelled a politics as a politics of alienation symbolized by the lone, joyless men who patronized pornographic movies. The movies warrant our attention not as an alternative sociopolitical cinema on the model of African American race movies or Nykino's politically radical movies, but as an example of a cystlike subculture within the main culture.

An outlaw form of cinema, pornography films have stood outside the protection of the First Amendment, and to their devotees that is part of their allure. Before the existence of the present system of rating movies by letter grade, with X indicating the intent to trade in the porn houses, most porn movies played in private venues, such as a war veterans' post, a political clubhouse, or a stag party. In its marginal forms—striptease movies, nudist camp frolics, patently fraudulent "educational" films, and anthropological films unerringly focused on brown-skinned breasts—such fare played the side streets of urban rialtos. The west 40s in Manhattan, "the Block" in Baltimore, south State Street in Chicago, and Turk and Eddy in San Francisco were a few of the notorious scenes. Even when censorship began to crumble in the late 1960s, purveyors of pornography preferred their side-street grind houses, perhaps for the anonymity they provided. Since its earliest days it was here that pornography in all its genres—skin flicks, nudies, exploitation movies, and burlesque reels—offered its nips of arcana, curiosa, erotica, and fetishism in perpetual sideshow seediness. Neither the puritans who assailed these movies nor the fans who knelt before them cared whether the movies were beautiful; roués and puritans alike shared an interest only in their excesses.

In *Sinema* (1974), Stephen Zito and Kenneth Turan report that such movies were offered in the penny arcades as early as 1908 and were not driven underground until the age of the Hays office began in the early 1920s.

Thereafter, in the grind houses they always promised more than they delivered, a fact that helped stimulate their audiences' obsessive behavior. Apart from the censors who constantly sought to restrain them, the movies generally drew only a passive aggregate of loners, typically men who took the streetcar downtown to, for example, Baltimore's cavernous yet all but disused Rivoli. In the audience were also various geezers and down-and-outers seeking a haven from foul weather, kids who had chained their bikes to the lamppost on Baltimore Street, rummies from the flophouses and missions, and dedicated onanists in their raincoats settled into their squeaky pews. The regulars brought their lunches, perhaps a couple of Coney Island hot-dogs from the lunch counter at the end of the Block. Topping the bill might have been *Jungle Siren* (ca. 1935) starring Ann Corio, a sometime stripper who might have been playing in the flesh across the street at the Gayety, followed by a well-worn print of Armand Denis's *Goona Goona* (1932). Closing the show might have been a burlesque reel with Hinda Wassau removing far less of her clothing than she would have in one of her shows at the Gayety.

Such fare reached all the way to the 1960s and the implementation of the Motion Picture Association of America (MPAA) ratings system. Thereafter, pornographers displayed a movie's X rating as prominently in its ads as if the movie had won an Oscar, and there was actually a movement among pornographers to attain styles, forms, and conventions of the old classical Hollywood style. No longer restricted to back rooms and grind houses, the "blue movies" were shot in color; were plot- and even character-driven; and were structured in classical linear fashion with beginnings, middles, and ends.

The person responsible for bridging the old and the new was Russ Meyer, a former combat photographer who combined a voyeuristic sensibility with a knack for recruiting and casting women with outrageously, almost pneumatically, endowed bodies. He arrived at his formula as early as 1959, with *The Immoral Mr. Teas.* In this movie he linked his voyeur's eye to the threat of censorship by offering a sort of erotica interruptus in which the plot began with a sexually frustrated man, desperate to satisfy his lust, and ended with the urge thwarted. Replicating Meyer's typecasting of the audience, the protagonist was a wool-gathering nebbish who, while on his rounds as a delivery man, mistakenly receives an anesthetic that provides him with the voyeur's nirvana—the power to see through clothing! The result for Meyer: a $1 million return on a $24,000 nut, earned partly because the film broke into the disused downtown palaces (which soon would fill with black kids in search of "blaxploitation" movies) and the flagging art houses that the end of World War II had brought about and partly because it broke into the columns of the daily press. "More female nudity than ever before," said *Variety*. Such movies scratched their clientele's itch (simple to do, really, when one considers that it was entirely innocent of any ethnic, political, or gender loyalty and driven only by anomic obsessions) and became the most persistently successful of alternative movie products.

The other alternative cinemas, those based in political and ethnic taste-cultures, had a more difficult time of it in serving their audiences, who were sectored and poor and made fickle by Hollywood slickness. The inexperienced alternative moviemakers and their scant budgets made the creation of an alternative aesthetic elusive. Moreover, these moviemakers were often driven by cross-purposed ambitions to be both objective and advocative, authentic and propagandistic, magisterial and engaging.

Turning first to the documentary, until World War II there was no political tradition in this cinema. A couple leftist groups attempted to change the apolitical stance of the documentary in the 1930s, and the right wing occasionally attempted an ideological movie, but it would take World War II to create a strong political vein of documentary.

At the mercy of corporate sponsors, most documentarists adopted a pose of disinterested objectivity that disqualified them from asserting a politics. By default, they spoke for the status quo. (Even Joris Ivens, a lifelong Dutch leftist, made commercial reels for Philips Radio.) In addition, their urge to document cultures in the rimlands could not help but confirm in their viewers a sense of cultural chauvinism. Whether it was Edison making his early vignettes of black Caribbean life, featuring women bathing babies and men coaling ships; Robert Flaherty making his long-lived classic, *Nanook of the North* (1922); or even the more raffish makers of "adventure yarns," most documentarists edited their subjects into Procrustean beds in order to contrast their savagery with Christendom.

In making *Nanook,* Flaherty trekked north of the Arctic Circle in search of the Inuit he had known as a boy; his sponsor was the furrier Revillon Freres, who expected an image-enhancing film. The mixed motives could not help but lead to bread buttered on both sides, an outcome Flaherty achieved much as the photographers for the Farm Security Administration would do later in recording the responses of American folk to the Great Depression: by dressing, posing, cropping, and otherwise shaping his subjects into images fit for America's gaze. Sometimes Flaherty went so far as to put his Eskimo subjects at risk, rolling film beyond the moment when a prudent walrus hunter would have called "cut" and sectioning igloos in order to shoot their interiors. However, "authenticity of result" was these moviemakers' goal, even though, as Erik Barnouw explains in *Documentary: A History of the Nonfiction Film* (1974), their tools included the "machinery of the fiction film."

Although upon its completion in 1922 *Nanook* was not picked up by Hollywood, its opening at the Capitol in New York reaped a "substantial profit" as well as the praise of critics, who found it "in a class by itself." Only then did Hollywood chase Flaherty, if only to do another *Nanook*. The moguls' enthusiasm soured, however, after Paramount sent Flaherty to the South Pacific, where he shot *Moana* (1926), an idyll that lacked the dramatic danger of life inside the Arctic Circle. After having a go at other cultures of the rimlands, in F. W. Murnau's *Tabu* (1931) and Merian C. Cooper and Ernest B. Schoedsack's *Grass* (1925) and *Chang* (1927), Hollywood resumed business as usual, symbolized most patently by Cooper and Schoedsack's reward—the opportunity to make *King Kong* (1933) for RKO.

The only exception to Hollywood's retreat from the genre was the occasional film of an actual anthropological expedition, which, for the sake of heightening interest (at the expense of verisimilitude), would be shamelessly recut until it bore little resemblance to its makers' intentions. It was as if the studios' credo became, as one mogul said, "Let's fill the screen with tits." In the late 1920s, Martin and Osa Johnson roamed Africa, often at great risk, recording its peoples, only to arrive back home and lay in voiceovers dripping with racial humor. Among their imitators, Frank Buck won a following for his "animal pictures," the most famous among them *Darkest Africa*, which played the Century of Progress Exposition in Chicago in 1933. Buck's pseudoscholarly detachment from the "childlike," even "weird," subjects in his staged fragments of African culture encouraged his audiences' sense of cultural superiority. At the bottom of this chauvinist heap were the exploitation films that played urban grind houses, teasing their lounging male audiences with the promise of bare-breasted women pursued by horny gorillas. Together these movies doomed Flaherty's vision of a semblance of cultural relativity (the anthropological notion of equality among cultures) only slightly dramatized to appeal to thoughtful viewers. Even worse than the documentary was the "educational film," which was so beholden to corporate and civic donors that avoidance of controversy became its defining trait and benign topics such as hygiene, heroic inventors, and exotic tribes its stock in trade.

While in Europe a documentary avant-garde was breaking new ground, with the Germans Walther Ruttmann making *Berlin: Symphony of a Great City* (1927) and Leni Riefenstahl shooting hypnotic Nazi party films, such as *Triumph of the Will* (1936); Dziga Vertov making *The Man with the Movie Camera* (1929) in the Soviet Union; and John Grierson and his peers in the film units of the British government post office and the Empire Marketing Board turning out socially conscious films such as *Coal Face* (1936), the best America could muster was Flaherty's *Nanook* and the Yale Chronicles of America series, which included *Dixie* (1924), a film that portrayed slavery as a benign socioeconomic system. If a filmmaker dared to take a political stand in a documentary, a teachers' trade paper reviewer was sure to urge, as the nationally known William Hartley did, that "the teacher should also see that the [other] side of the story is told."

In the 1930s some documentary filmmakers to the left of this mainstream tried to take the documentary beyond fluff. William Alexander begins *Film on the Left* (1981) by conveying the hopes Lenin and Seymour Stern had for the cinema. "The cinema can and must have the greatest significance," said Lenin. "It is a powerful weapon." Stern called for "a working-class cinema" free of capitalists, censors, the merely pink left, and Hollywood. "What a possibility!" he wrote in 1931. "What a vision!"

Though leftist documentarists struggled to gain access to the theaters, they often had to settle for preaching to the converted in union halls and church basements. Typical of those on the left was the Marxist Film and Photo League, which, as part of its cultural activities, one evening might have shown Sergei Eisenstein's *Battleship Potemkin* (1925) or one of its own films, such as *Fighting Workers of New York* (ca. 1932), or a *Worker Newsreel* that covered strikes, "Hoovervilles," and, in 1932, a national hunger march. In *Filmfront*, *The Left*, and other hand-cranked magazines, the left debated the place of film in dispensing "organically" grown ideology. And throughout the 1930s leftists working under the colophon of Frontier Films shot footage that ultimately became *Native Land* (1942), an alarm sounded about the shadowy interests conspiring against workers. As World War II approached, they directed their attention to the rise of fascism in Spain, rational city planning, and social justice.

Through it all, however, leftist cinema suffered not only from lack of access to theaters, but also from the divisiveness of the left. When Pare Lorentz's New Deal film *The Plow That Broke the Plains* was able to break into the theaters in 1936, for example, having been made with the help of a federal agency, it still suffered from the factionalism of the left. Although Lorentz had guarded his script against rewrites by cautious federal agencies, the Film and Photo circles still attacked the bland politics of *The Plow* as a sign of government control. Nonethless, Lorentz had the support of a few members of the Film and Photo League, King Vidor in Hollywood (whose populist *Our Daily Bread* had just appeared in 1934), and various federal agencies, and the movie's lyricism earned it a Broadway opening and bookings in three thousand theaters (bookings that often superseded those of its Hollywood rivals). Lorentz's second offer, *The River* (1937), enjoyed a tenfold increase in nut; was praised by Roosevelt himself; and won Lorentz not only the award for best documentary at the Venice Film Festival, but also the satisfaction of probably having influenced the tone of Ford's *The Grapes of Wrath* (1940).

Whereas the leftists tried to reach a left audience, the right wing aimed more toward the center. It had even less to say and, when it spoke, only muttered under its breath. So only in Hollywood Depression movies were any solutions offered, many of which were simply appeals to a führer. Sometimes they called for a populist rising against cabals who ran everything and championed the rise of authoritarian, even secret, leaders who knew what was good for the nation. In the first half of the 1930s, the repetition of the theme of a populist movement led by a "man on horseback" so closely paralleled the rise of Hitler and Nazism in Germany as to seem prescient. In *The Secret Six; Gabriel over the White House; The President Vanishes;* and even a musical comedy, *Stand Up and Cheer*, America's social dysfunctions are portrayed as the result of cabalistic villains (standing in for Hitler's Jews), rather than social forces. The apparently invincible heavies drive men to reckon that "there is no time for rules of evidence," the volatile mood leads to a publicly approved vigilantism, and finally a powerful lone figure rises to the presidency. In *Stand Up and Cheer*, a vast chorus rises to sing a rousing double-entendre song, "We're Out of the Red," as a voiceover to a shrewdly handled montage. Like the New Deal, the movie dismayed leftists by using radical means merely to save capitalism from itself.

More overtly ideological films that would have appealed to more rightist audiences rarely emerged from the right wing of Hollywood, if for no other reason than it would have sectored the audience and broken with the duty to earn profits. Here and there an exception emerged. Warner Bros.'s World War I hit, *My Four Years in Germany* (1916), a diplomat's autobiographical warning against Teutonic militarism, reached an alarmed audience. Al Woods's handmade *The Toll of Justice* (1924), a Ku Klux Klan tract, managed to offend almost everyone, including Thomas Dixon, the literary source for *The Birth of a Nation* (1915). No chance of even "a nickel," said *Variety* of this extremist flop. Hollywood's one successful attempt at overt rightist politics was one of Felix Feist's *Metrotone News* films, which Mayer and Thalberg (and others) commissioned to defeat the candidacy of the socialist Upton Sinclair for governor of California. Surprisingly, Sinclair had carried the Democratic primary, and Feist's film, a string of talking heads of Californians, successfully challenged him in the general election by stacking the opinions of clean-cut citizens for the Republican candidate against those of the pro-Sinclair forces, who seemed uniformly to speak for the vagrants and hoboes of the state.

Not until World War II approached did the right wing attempt another movie of political advocacy, and this offering conveyed not so much an explicit rightist ideology as a preparation for war. Throughout the late 1930s, Henry Luce's *The March of Time* series had provided an unrivaled movie magazine that met theaters' need for "shorts." In a strident voice that seemed to speak for a broad American center, the series twitted or viewed with wry irony almost any cultural expression that departed from the sentiments of middle America. The producer of Luce's series, Louis DeRochemont, gradually assumed a degree of control and used it to prod the nation to prepare for war. Indeed, as Raymond Fielding reports in his book *The March of Time*, DeRochemont mounted a feature-length *March of Time* film entitled *The Ramparts We Watch* (1940) in which he warned of impending war. Senator Burton K. Wheeler charged DeRochemont with warmongering, to which the filmmaker replied by branding Wheeler and his clique "intemperate and reckless" in their ignoring of the "tragic fate of millions who have come under the tyranny of the Nazis."

A similar film greeted the throngs at the 1939 world's fair in New York. *Land of Liberty*, a patriotic pageant drawn from historical scenes from a dozen Hollywood features and presented by the Motion Picture Producers and Directors of America, offered only a butler as a black historical presence and described Americans' westward migration as seeking "a new home for the white man." Even a black biography, that of the agronomist George Washington Carver, suggested that the only proper political behavior was individual effort, either as a form of racial self-help or as a form of white "philanthropic efforts on behalf of the Negro." By inspiring individuals to aim toward personal goals, such films tended to endorse things as they were while at the same time paying homage to the oppressed, such as Carver, whose vision of personal achievement consisted solely of self-help. Of the antituberculosis tract (disease made a fitting enemy in a country that eschewed extremist politics) *Let My People Live* (1938), one reviewer said that in telling of public health measures against tuberculosis, the movie was also "useful in promoting tolerance"—tolerance being an individual, and thus preferred, goal of conservative race relations.

With the onset of World War II, both the left and right experienced a boom in documentary filmmaking, perhaps because, as both James Feibleman in *Theory of Culture* (1946) and Antonio Gramsci presciently argued, war against foreign enemies drew the citizenry together while at the same time the prospects of the oppressed were enhanced by the nation's need for their services. And of course, white America, caught up as it was in a war against Hitler's racism, suddenly found its goals conjoined with those of blacks.

Thus the propaganda celebrated the triumph of "teamwork" over robotic foreign enemies. William Wellman's *Memphis Belle* (1943) and John Ford's *The Battle of Midway* (1943), along with others that drew African Americans into the war, such as Stuart Heisler's *The Negro Soldier* (1945) and Edmund North's *Teamwork* (1945) are a few examples. Certainly the balance tipped toward the patriotic right. Nonetheless, the war brought forth a new agency, the Office of War Information (OWI), that differed from many peacetime agencies in that its lifers, career civil servants, were joined by "social engineers" (as they liked to be called) and liberals of various stripes for whom the war seemed a moment of opportunity. Almost predictably, the OWI and other agencies colored their official work of promoting the national war effort with a drop or so of the liberal change they promised would be an outcome of the war. Typifying the spirit, the New School professor Saul Padover, a wartime recruit in agriculture, proposed a film in which the African American appeared as "an average human being."

In the case of the Pentagon film *The Negro Soldier*, apart from its merely inclusionist goals, the National Association for the Advancement of Colored People (NAACP) viewed it as a prospective postwar voice of liberal advocacy and successfully demanded of the Pentagon that it prepare a version for civilians as well as soldiers. Echoing the NAACP's assertion that wartime propaganda could be used after the war to promote social change was Philleo Nash, an anthropologist in the OWI and a liberal whose work had resulted in an invitation from Lockheed Aircraft to use "wartime experience in the utilization of . . . physically handicapped, minor and overage, part-time workers, Negro, and Mexican workers." Optimistically hoping for a sort of peacetime version of the OWI that would carry American attitudes "away from the tolerance and good will aspects of minority group relations toward [solving] . . . an industry and community problem," Nash turned down the offer in anticipation of a more active postwar government.

The war was startling in its impact on documentary movies. Not only did it make racism a national issue for the first time since the *Plessy v. Ferguson* (1896) "separate but equal" decision, but it rendered it part of American propaganda. After all, ran the logic, Hitler had given racism a bad name.

The result was the training and political maturing of a generation of film-makers who advanced documentary from its noncontroversial roots into a postwar alternative cinema of liberal advocacy. *The Negro Soldier* stood out as an instance of the liberal drift toward using movies as propaganda. Orig-inally written by the black radio writer Carlton Moss as *Men of Color to Arms*, the War Department diluted its black nationalism, asked that it be re-worked into a call for national unity across racial lines, previewed it before a panel of black journalists, ordered its showing to all training companies, re-leased it rent free to civilian audiences, and at the end of the war gave it away as surplus to any liberal group who asked. Considered "painfully, pitifully mild" by James Agee, the film nonetheless became the NAACP's call for "liv-ing together . . . now and for the future." In a press release, the Congress of Industrial Organizations (better known as the CIO, the union that later linked with the American Federation of Labor to form the AFL-CIO) stated that because "commercial movies [promote] intolerance through stereo-typed characterization . . . perhaps the industry can profit" from a look at these government films.

Immediately after the war, advocates of social change through film, such as the American Council on Education, the Educational Film Library Asso-ciation, the American Film Center, and others, together formed an "audiovisual movement." "The whole AV field was starting up fresh," recalled Emily S. Jones, one of its leaders, "and new people were appearing . . . out of service in the armed forces." The studios themselves finished their war contracts with government agencies and released *It Happened in Springfield* (1946), *Don't Be a Sucker* (1946), and other films that turned racist incidents into little liberal victories. No longer dependent on corporate angels, filmmakers raised funds by turning to the NAACP, the United Auto Workers, the American Jewish Council, and other activists on the left. One survey indicated that one exemplary library acquired some two hundred movies that played to a quarter of a million viewers.

Joining this trend, various religious faiths put out their own advocacy films. Jews made a particular impact, because their films were more ecumenical than most and because some of them echoed the race movie movement. Indeed, Jews and blacks alike had first entered the documentary field by making lantern slide shows of Palestine. Two pioneers, Jewish Joseph Seiden and black Reverend Kieffer Jackson, shot their plates on location and then provided voiceovers to scenes of Old Testament parables, much as Catholic producers made continuities from the Stations of the Cross. By 1940, the black actor Spencer Williams and his white angel, Alfred Sack, had built on these frail beginnings to produce two feature-length race movies that caught the spirit of African American religion: *The Blood of Jesus* (1940) and *Go Down Death* (1946).

During their halcyon days, both groups released newsfilm to their clienteles. Seiden's sequences of Jewish life on the Lower East Side played to nostalgic dinner meetings of Jewish businessmen—"the Grand Street Boys," as one such group called itself. Leigh Whipper's Renaissance firm was a contemporary of Seiden's, to be followed by Bert and Jack Goldberg's studio, The Negro Marches On (named for a documentary of black soldiers in World War I); Claude Barnett's extension of his Associated Negro Press, which he called All America News; and, after the war, Liberty Films and an offshoot of Barnett's firm that made television magazine shows for Chesterfield cigarettes. Of this group, only Whipper and Barnett's colleague, William D. Alexander, was black.

This pattern was followed in the production of feature films: Jewish feature films reached some fifty in number, while the black total reached a few hundred. Other ethnic groups made do with a thin stream of imports from Europe. Jewish exhibitors played it both ways, importing a few and making a few more. The most famous of the European imports was Paul Wegener's *The Golem* (1913 and 1920), a sort of positive-thinking Frankenstein tale based on a medieval legend in which Rabbi Loew of the Prague ghetto heads off a pogrom by raising up a golem.

In its way, the golem story spoke for all the alternative cinemas, in that the heroes affirmed or defended the group, the heavies embodied negative traits meant to be scorned, and the plots consisted of each group's following a roadmap to its collectively defined Holy Grail. In addition to the main story, such movies often provided an anatomy of a ghetto social order and celebrated folkishness over assimilationism. For example, in *Bridge of Light* (1995) J. Hoberman praised Alexander Granovsky's *Jewish Luck* (1925), which although done in Soviet avant-garde style, caught the spirit of Sholem Aleichem's fables of shtetl life. Meanwhile in Jewish America, Seiden and Edgar G. Ulmer made a few Yiddish movies in disused studios on both banks of the Hudson. Ulmer, who spoke no Yiddish, shared direction with the theatrical actor Jacob Ben Ami in *Green Fields* (1937) and *Yankel dem Schmidt* (1938), for which they roamed New Jersey in search of shtetl-like settings.

What was the difference between Yiddish alternative movies and Hollywood fare? Easy, reports Patricia Erens in *The Jew in American Cinema* (1984): Movies like *The Cantor's Son* (1937) placed high value on the continuation of the Jewish ethos, whereas Hollywood's *The Jazz Singer*, of course, played an angle of assimilationism that echoed *Abie's Irish Rose* and *The Cohens and the Kellys*. "Most specifically, [Yiddish cinema] rejects intermarriage," concludes Erens.

Curiously, the year of epiphany for Yiddish films, and perhaps for all other ethnic cinemas as well, was 1939, which in the eyes of many critics was also Hollywood's pinnacle. For Roger Dooley, 1939 was Hollywood's "fabulous zenith," for Larry Swindell it was "the apogee," and Ted Sennett devoted an entire book to the year. Clearly, these critics spotted a transcendant moment in movie history, but perhaps their sense of Hollywood's having reached a crest also derived from a memory without pain, a nostalgia for the last year before the world plunged into war for the second time in twenty years.

African American race movies were shaped by the same forces that defined Yiddish cinema or, for that matter, any ethnic cinema: a sense of a common past, a setting forth of issues, a lightly sweetened nostalgia, and an anatomy of the group's interior life, all of it meant to cultivate a warm cultural chauvinism. They differed from European movies only in the details of their group's otherness. Along the way, the movies helped mediate between the pull-and-haul of opposing forces of assimilation and ethnic nationalism. On one hand, there were the "other directed" (to use David Riesman's term) African Americans who were bent on "making it" and lived in the cold wind of urban anomie, adrift from the warmth of the group. On the other hand, there were those who clung to language and culture, embraced religion as a conduit of culture, and ached with a nostalgia for community. The former ingested mass culture because it seemed more polished and grasped at mobility and its attractions, whereas the latter clung to folkish culture, rejected mobility, and stayed in the old neighborhood.

Only the black inventory of details seemed different. Their first culture came less from Africa or Europe than from "down South" or merely "down home." Segregation, by limiting interracial cultural contact, diminished the threat of assimilation, but upward mobility seemed an equal threat to cultural cohesiveness, in that the higher the black aspiration, the more likely that black bourgeois culture would intersect with the white, thereby setting apart the black riffraff from the black talented tenth. Moreover, just as the mafia or the tong provided Italians and Chinese with alternative, often criminal, paths to success, black outlaws often intersected with black bourgeois circles, sometimes even serving as their bankers and capital sources. The resulting claustrophobic social structure often thrust black respectables and riffraff into the same ghetto circles, and race movies necessarily struggled with how to handle the heroism of characters who also happened to be outlaws.

Black filmmakers considered how to take this into account while formulating a cinematic alternative to Hollywood. Should they admire indigenous black institutions at the expense of the increasingly sharply defined goal of integration? As a grudgingly liberalizing white America faced the social changes brought about by the Great Depression and war, would race movies behave like the black church or black baseball? Would they remain staunchly black, or would they, as black baseball did, fold up in anticipation of a surge of black athletes into formerly lily-white arenas?

At stake, for example, was black dignity. As discussed in Chapter 3, Mary Carbine and Gregory Waller have reported that blacks often went to theaters in Chicago and Lexington, Kentucky, respectively, not so much to see a movie as to be in clean and dignified surroundings remote from white rejection and black riffraff. Thus they carried with them to their movies an ideology rooted in both race and class. Paradoxically, class pride induced them to seek dignity within the situation of their rank, while race pride induced them to find movies that stressed black optimism and uplift.

Race movie firms outdid themselves in appealing to one or both of these urges while at the same time playing to differing tastes that had evolved in the black North and the black South. Northern and urban movies often seemed irreverent, jiving, even outlaw in their heroes' style, while southern and rural movies reached out to a folkish, pastoral, pious taste-culture. Each mode also acted as a sort of anatomical drawing of the social system of the other group. Thus a southern rural moviegoer might learn a bit about urban life from the Harvard-trained hero of the Lincoln Company's *The Realization of a Negro's Ambition* (1916), while an urban audience might relive the fervor of old-time religion in Spencer Williams's *The Blood of Jesus* (1940). Either way, race movies challenged Hollywood movies in that they took black aspiration seriously and formulated it into generic melodramas of scaling a black ladder of success, struggling against demons of cupidity within the race (never any off-screen white demons), and reworkings of white genres such as musicals, westerns, and film noir.

The first race movie that caught national black attention, *The Birth of a Race* (1918), grew out of a wish shared by Emmett J. Scott (Washington's secretary at Tuskegee), a committee within the NAACP, and a few whites in Laemmle's Universal studio to offer a rebuttal to Griffith's *Birth of a Nation*. At first financed in part by Julius Rosenwald of Sears Roebuck, a philanthropist of black education, the movie eventually fell victim to a "mammoth swindle" by shady brokers of its stock who scared off Rosenwald and his allies; a string of white directors, each of whom stirred in his own themes; and, finally, the onset of World War I, which resulted in a tacked-on justification of America's entry into it. Drifting every which way from Scott's original idea of the "strivings of the race" told from "the colored man's viewpoint," *The Birth of a Race* pleased no one. *Variety* called it "grotesque" and said it was remote from its original "preachment."

The most famous black pioneers, who are famous mainly for the simple reason that their archives survive (although their films do not), are George and Noble Johnson, whose Lincoln Company defined its ambition as "to picture the Negro as he is in everyday life" and to stand against the stereotype that "the brother is not up to the times in handling such fast business [as moviemaking]." If they failed in any respect, it was in garbling the success myth by failing to take into account off-camera white obstacles to its attainment, an ideological glitch that few black moviemakers were able to overcome. This is not to minimize their ideological rigor, but only to point out the political impediments embedded in an all-black genre in which whites were absolved by their absence of complicity in black plight and in which the race's goals seemed too linked to the sort of lone, laissez-faire hero that Hollywood movies offered.

Partly, they struggled with the black audience itself, which was divided into southern rural and northern urban taste-cultures as well as respectables and riffraff (the "talented tenth" versus "submerged tenth" as Du Bois put it). Moreover, it was tempted by the gloss of Hollywood movies, while wishing for better race movies, and was resistant to "colored theaters" that were too financially strapped to offer amenities. And yet, what else might have the race moviemakers expected? Except for the small group of employed, churched, socially affiliated black bourgeoisie, African Americans simply lacked the discretionary income and leisure for the movies. Moreover, politically, black audiences were of two minds. On the one hand, the Baltimore *Afro-American* praised "sensible producers like [Oscar] Micheaux," a black producer, and called for organized protest against Hollywood fare. On the other, the *California Eagle* praised a black western for its avoidance of politics: "No tragic race issue is involved; no tiresome sermon preached."

Oscar Micheaux most exemplified both the achievement and the plight of race moviemakers. Like the Johnsons, he insisted on a black identity apart from the white world, an identity often defined in his movies by a dramatic conundrum over whether to marry across racial lines. But like the *Eagle*, the Johnsons guessed that "our people do not care for propaganda." Between these two poles stood Micheaux, acutely black but seldom an overt advocate of a specific black cause, instinctively cinematic but too poor to be an artist, and avidly sensational and thus alien to the respectables, who thought him "not elevating" and short on the "high moral aim" of upbuilding the race.

Ambiguity colored Micheaux's entire life and thus his movies, so that the black respectables seemed at once appalled at his raffishness and lifted by his sense of bourgeois aspiration. Micheaux was both the primly correct Pullman porter and the lone wolf homesteader on the Dakota frontier, the suitor of a white fiancée and the husband of a solidly loyal black woman, the vendor of his own books to white midwesterners and a lifelong sojourner in black Harlem and the south side of Chicago. But it was his capacity for survival in the face of a countrywide influenza epidemic; the rise of white rivals; the black imitators who diverted attention from actual black achievers; and eventually the Great Depression, which forced him into bankruptcy, retrenchment, and indebtedness to white angels that marked him as a success. The dichotomies of his life leached into his movies in almost predictable ways. *The Homesteader* (1919) was an autobiography of life on the prairie (and on the border between black life and white life). *Body and Soul* (1924) challenged the hegemony that black preachers often held over their flocks. *Within Our Gates* (1921) assailed lynching by placing a white miscreant at the center of a plot. *Ten Minutes To Live* (1931), *The Girl from Chicago* (1932), and *The Exile* (1931) reworked in soundfilm the nagging theme of urban versus rural life.

These ambiguities that often exercised Micheaux's black moviegoers have, in recent years, caused critics to debate not only the merits of his work, but also the place of race movies in the canon of movies. At issue are such questions as whether race movies were an emergent African American art form or merely a blackface extension of Hollywood style. If they were a black art form, were they marked by specifically "black" shots, cuts, and other devices? If not, what made these movies black? Mere advocacy of uplift? If so, why did Micheaux often eschew uplift in favor of the lowlife? Were his movies "black" merely because they were peopled by Hollywood's "others"? If they were demonstrably black, how come the black press harped on the unfriendly audiences who laughed in the wrong places, catcalled, and, worse, often preferred the sleek Hollywood product? If the denouements were dictated by the group's collective wish for uplift or positive images, were their darkened versions of Hollywood happy endings politically sufficient? Or was the black essentialism of race movies embedded in the very fact of their poverty, their making necessity a virtue, their shameless pride in the benchmarks of one-take flaws? These issues have been raised in tandem with redoubled academic attention to race movies previously regarded as lost, unremarkable, or merely eccentric.

The issue matters to students of race movies partly because with each new rediscovery, these movies have been held up to aesthetic scrutiny against conventional critical canons that have found many in the genre wanting. For example, the Colored Players firm in Philadelphia, which had a white pro-

ducer-director team, turned out *The Scar of Shame* (1927), a startlingly polished social drama in the mode of the Hollywood problem movie. Some recent critics have debated whether its mise-en-scène and its tragic plot were
class or caste based, and others have debated its subtle congruence with
American stereotyping of African Americans according to light-skinned
virtue and dark-skinned vice. Finally, in the eyes of some critics the movie's
obvious cinematic polish has artificially called attention to its flawed race
movie rivals. In their view, to claim as an *Amsterdam News* critic did at the
time, that the movie attained "a new standard of excellence" or to find, as
one recent critic wrote, that it approached Hollywood quality was to miss
the point.

The quality of race movies varied more with the coming of sound, as may
be seen in, for example, the gulf between Micheaux's naturalistic silents and
his stagey soundfilms. Because soundfilms cost more to make, race moviemakers leavened their products with musical vaudeville turns that allowed
them to cut down on the expense of dialogue. Nonetheless, these jazzy scenes
provided a culturally blacker idiom. Paradoxically, soundfilm technology and
its costs also brought greater numbers of more experienced white entrepreneurs into the field, thereby blurring the definition of the race movie.

At the same time, as though anticipating the decline of the race movie,
many Hollywood studios spent the Depression years and World War II
adding increasingly sophisticated black roles to their product (while slowly
giving up their reliance on older forms of stereotyping). It began to play to
black audiences in 1929, with *Hallelujah!* and *Hearts in Dixie*; later came *The
Green Pastures* (1936), which strove for a black folk idiom played with quiet
dignity. Universal's film of Fannie Hurst's *Imitation of Life* (1934) treated the
taboo theme of "passing." *So Red the Rose* (1935) and *Slave Ship* (1936) toyed
with the theme of slave revolt. And Hattie McDaniel won an Oscar in 1939
for her "Mammy" in *Gone with the Wind*, the movie that David O. Selznick
changed from southern lost cause to a national *Iliad*. During World War II,
each of the major studios made a combat film in which a black character had
been integrated—*Sahara* (1943), *Crashdive* (1943), *Bataan* (1943), and
Lifeboat (1944). This trend persisted into civilian life in 1949 as a cycle of
movies with major black protagonists, including *Pinky*, *No Way Out* (1950
release), *Intruder in the Dust*, *Lost Boundaries*, and *Home of the Brave*, each
successive movie revealing audiences' increasing desire to see social drama.
Parallel to this trend and even anticipating it, the increasingly politicized

Paul Robeson appeared in his own cycle of British movies that featured a black hero, among them *Sanders of the River* (1935), *Jericho* (1937), and the overtly socialist *Proud Valley* (1940). Taken together, these movies of the Depression and war eras held out hope to African Americans that a national cinema might make ideological room for a black political aesthetic.

Clearly, the crises provided a moment of racial conscience that opened to the "other" a place in formerly white movies, thereby leaving open the question of the raison d'être of race movies. Increasingly, their former supporters in the black press reflected the anomalous place the movies had assumed. Critics either reckoned them, as the *Amsterdam News* viewed Bill Robinson's *Harlem Is Heaven* (1932), as "positively objectionable" or, as James Asendio did, praised them for conforming to Hollywood standards of "modern story, setting, and costumes." Those who made race movies increasingly touted them, as the Popkins did their *Bargain with Bullets* (1937), as "up to the Loew standard" and so devoid of "race propaganda" as to preclude "trouble" in the South. Indeed, at the height of the 1939–40 boom in race movies, the *Amsterdam News* praised *Mystery in Swing* (1938) and *Double Deal* (1939) as "the best to come out of black Hollywood" and dubbed their director Arthur Dreifuss "the Frank Capra . . . of the Colored motion picture industry." So ethnically ecumenical had they become that directors Joseph Seiden and Edgar Ulmer easily crossed over from Yiddish movies to race movies.

Unfortunately, its makers miscalculated in trying to become more like their Hollywood rivals; all this tactic accomplished was to unfairly thrust these movies into direct competition with the glossier Hollywood product. "Why have [race movies] failed to make the instantaneous hit with the public and what must be done," asked critic Dan Burley, to erode the black preference for Hollywood? Why, asked others, did black viewers laugh at scenes intended to be tense? Why support Micheaux's *God's Step Children* (1937) asked the Young Communists of Harlem, when it "creates a false splitting of Negroes into light and dark groups?" And as to standing up to Hollywood's production values, Hubert Julian, the black aviator and occasional movie angel, pleaded with *Amsterdam News* readers, "Don't expect the perfection of a Hollywood picture, but know that we have done our very best."

Thus after a brief boom, race movies went into a decline from which they never recovered. The impresarios who had led the boom wavered in these winds of change. David Starkman of the Colored Players drifted into other interests. Ted Toddy lived off retitling his older inventory and limiting current product to broadly comic two-reelers such as *Mantan Messes Up* (ca. 1940) and *Pigmeat's Laugh Hepcats* (ca. 1940). Emmanuel Glucksman and Claude Barnett (both of All America News) joined Chesterfield cigarettes in producing magazine shows for television. Spencer Williams flopped with *Go Down Death* (1946), a reprise of the religiosity of *The Blood of Jesus* (1940), and his angel, Alfred Sack, turned to skin flicks. Frank Schiffman of the Apollo and Robert Levy of Reol Pictures dropped out. The Popkin brothers formed a Hollywood B unit. Bert and Jack Goldberg turned to importing foreign films. Only William D. Alexander (of All America News) remained active, making film noir. In a final boomlet, race movies adopted Hollywood genres such as westerns and musicals to a black idiom.

The watershed year during which African Americans signaled an end to their support of race movies and the NAACP mounted an organized effort to affect movies at their Hollywood sources was 1944, in the midst of world war. As early as 1942, Walter White of the NAACP had held his group's convention in Los Angeles in the hope of pledging the moguls to succumb to the rhetoric of the war and amend their portrayals of blacks in movies. Some of them complied and produced parallel cycles of combat films and musicals in which black actors held roles to which they had never before had access. Abetting the NAACP campaign was the OWI. As mentioned earlier, the OWI pressed the Army to make a propaganda film, *The Negro Soldier*, and then prepared a civilian version of it. Horrified at surveys that revealed deep black disaffection, the OWI and the NAACP combined to block the efforts of the makers of race movies to retail their own propaganda films. The coalition denied race movies an allocation of raw film stock, used the courts to stymie efforts to promote race movies, and promoted Hollywood movies as harbingers of the improved racial arrangements that awaited blacks at the end of the war.

The impact on African America's alternative cinema was devastating. The combination of the demands for change asserted by William Nunn's "Double Victory" campaign, the implicit messages in the government's propaganda movies, and the strictures imposed by shortages of film guaranteed that race movies would engage in a struggle they could not win. Unavoidably, they faced the same fate the Negro National Baseball League faced after Jackie Robinson signed on with the white Brooklyn Dodgers: both Hollywood and major league baseball, by holding out a promise of black integration into a classier product than blacks could provide for themselves, ensured that the black audience would desert in favor of an integrated future. Not all black institutions faced such ruin; primary groups into which blacks were born rather than bought tickets to—such as the African American church—became instruments of future change, rather than its victims.

In this sense, the NAACP and OWI's collaborative wartime achievement anticipated the postwar era of Hollywood's message movie cycle, in which the studios made movies directly influenced by propagandists who believed, along with many social engineers, that prejudice could be irradiated by the light of reason and knowledge. Thus this peacetime outcome of the war's propaganda of liberalism helped create a taste-culture that drew its sense of advocacy from formerly stodgy Hollywood. This is not to argue that Hollywood was innocent of the charge leveled by the Frankfurt school of social critics that it acted as a form of state apparatus that spoke as the voice of the ruling class. Rather, in classic Gramscian fashion, World War II had provided the critical occasion when the social goals of the left and right, particularly with respect to race relations, briefly intersected, giving class and race antagonists an opportunity to bargain for change. The resulting postwar "thinking picture" was far more self-congratulatory than substantive, but nonetheless it provided a basis for hope that drew African America away from race movies.

Moreover, the war had matured documentary film from its infancy stage as sterile educational film into yet another voice of activism that eventually spoke to the television age. Indeed, the documentary became the voice and "the chosen instrument of the civil rights movement," according to the broadcaster William Monroe (quoted by William Small in *To Kill a Messenger* [1970]). Thereafter, despite a narrowing of the range of racial alternative cinema, documentary film found its voice as an advocate of, if not racial radicalism, at least a "liberalism of the heart."

Immediately after the war, educational institutions and other users of documentaries laid claim to the government's surplus documentaries that had taught Americans, as Frank Capra's War Department series put it, "Why We Fight." In the ensuing months, other signs of the birth of a documentary of persuasion appeared. In 1947, a British "docudrama" (to use a later coinage) entitled *Day Break at Udi*, an account of health agencies' assault on the tsetse fly in Nigeria, won an Oscar, while in the same year *To Secure These Rights*, the report of Harry Truman's Civil Rights Commission, was made into an animated film that provided a lexicon for teaching racial liberalism.

In a typical press release, the CIO urged its members to see *The Negro Soldier* as a weapon in "the battle against bias" and a call for "a better world for all the people."

Soon the American Jewish Committee, the International Ladies Garment Workers Union, the NAACP, and other advocates of leftist causes joined up as angels for documentaries. The American Film Center, the National Film Cooperative, the Educational Film Library Association, and commercial distributors such as Thomas Brandon ensured easy access to these films, which were not likely to reach mainstream theatrical screens.

Parallel to this movement, yet another alternative cinema emerged. This cinema consisted of foreign films made in a "neorealist" or documentary "style," and it immediately found an audience in so-called art houses, the small theaters, often independent from the major chains, that were locally owned by exhibitors intent on creating an ambience of understated amenities. These movies brought a new social dimension to American commercial movies. When Roberto Rossellini's *Open City* came to America in 1946, it took off at the box office, leading to a cycle of domestically produced, grainy, realistic movies such as Jules Dassin's *The Naked City* (1948).

Some of the imports, notably *Paisan* (1946), *Senza Pieta* (1948), and *Vivere In Pace* (1946), wove in black characters of such uncommon humanity that *Ebony* and other glossy black magazines allocated them equally uncommon coverage. As was typical of Marxist movies, in *Paisan* the black hero, a soldier made cynical by the thieving children of the streets of Livorno, comes to see in the poverty of the Italian proletariat a parallel with his own. The success of such gently political movies soon created a similar American genre in such movies as Helen Levitt and Janice Loeb's *The Quiet One* (1947), with their blend of fiction and location-shot documentary. Each new decade brought with it another *Nanook*, not of the North but of Harlem: Shirley Clark's *The Cool World* (1964), Gene Persson and Anthony Harvey's version of Amiri Baraka's *Dutchman* (1967), and Michael Roemer's *Nothing But a Man* (1964), each one a gem that diverted black moviegoers from any notion of a need for an essentially black cinema. Their sheer quality as well as box office take seemed to announce that black material had arrived and therefore the issue of an alternative cinema was moot.

CHAPTER SEVEN

The High Middle Ages
of the Movies:
The Great Depression

The rubric "classical Hollywood cinema" has acquired cachet in part because it graces the cover of an influential book by David Bordwell, Janet Staiger, and Kristin Thompson, *The Classical Hollywood Cinema: Film Style & Mode of Production to 1960* (1985). These authors view classical Hollywood as more than just the sum of almost a half century of movies seen through the prism of the idiosyncratic connoisseurships of the scores of critics in the popular press. It is also the sum of the sociopolitical effects of technology and artifice, consciously marketed, politically laden, and arrived at in a corporate version of the atelier.

Freed from the demands of wartime for the two decades after World War I and beneficiary of the New Deal, the interventionist/liberal strategy whose purpose had been to save capitalism from self-destruction, Hollywood movies served as bearer of a shared faith so pervasive as to warrant calling it Americanist. For good or evil, movies played to and helped define an American collectivity by means of an aesthetic that moviegoers *liked*. "The wonder is how many really fine pictures were produced within, or in spite of, the system," writes Roger Dooley in *From Scarface to Scarlett* (1981). "Even the most routine 'B' films still show a verve, pace, and vitality, a crisp professionalism all too seldom seen today." Politics could follow only from this duality of popularity and "fine pictures."

I know, I know, this confession of falling for Hollywood's self-proclaimed superlative works comes close to embracing the mere connoisseurship retailed by the journalists of, say, Arthur Knight's (*The Liveliest Art* [1957]) generation. Yet, as Dooley points out, "the relationship between art and commerce, after all, need not be a hostile one." I would add that the linkage of art, commerce, and politics need not make for overt conflict, as Louis Althusser and other theorists who have extended Marxism have pointed out. As regards moviemaking in Hollywood's classical age, such a linkage was not a deterministic superstructure or apparatus that blindly served the state, the status quo, or the ruling class. Perhaps the politics of movies in the 1920s, 1930s, and especially 1940s was a generalized politics, sentimental rather than programmatic. Referring to the shifting of racial opinions during World War II, I call this politics "conscience liberalism." A "liberalism of the heart" the screenwriter Philip Dunne called it.

On the face of it, to frame the issue in this way seems simply an avoidance of politics. However, I mean it as a way of focusing on a relatively circumscribed arena of politics, one defined as a cluster of feelings about the rightness of things rather than, say, a specific party platform. Obviously, movies would be more loved as a nationally marketed entertainment if they spoke in unifying generalities, rather than in platforms.

In any case, by the onset of the Great Depression the "genius of the system," to use Thomas Schatz's phrase, was in place, trimmed of fat and ready to adapt to the new technics of soundfilm and, though strapped for cash, even Technicolor. Throughout the Depression the system cranked out movies that spoke for an openly sentimental "Americanist" liberalism of the heart in which class conflict had no place. Unavoidably so, for they could hardly expect to offend the customers' partisan politics, else they might as well sell the factory and their chain stores, that is, the studios and theaters.

This seemingly innocent relationship between movies and their consumers remains controversial. In Tino Balio's *Grand Design: Hollywood as a Modern Business Enterprise, 1930-1939* (1993), for example, Balio views it as benign, whereas Richard Maltby views it as ominous. Quoting Margaret Thorp in her pioneering *America at the Movies* (1946), Balio states that movies were merely entertainments made for "the average citizen's wife." Maltby sees the same movies as part of Hollywood's grasping for "the possession of cultural power." In either case, moviemakers addressed a constituency they defined as a broad cross section of America, fickle toward particular movies but consistent over time in their moviegoing habit, so hungry for movies that the studios aimed to release one movie a week. The studios had already rationalized production into a producer-driven flowchart that diminished the authority of creators such as writers and directors (and actors) and emphasized decision by committee. This process did much to define the individual studio styles that together constituted a Hollywood style. However, other elements also made their way in, as a result of the fact that the system also took in refugees, most famously those driven from Nazism, such as Fritz Lang, Max Reinhardt, and Billy Wilder, many of whom were suspicious of heavy-handed systems. In addition, some Hollywoodians driven exclusively by aesthetics contributed their own particular apolitical gloss to Hollywood movies. Such an aesthete was MGM's art director, Cedric Gibbons, who, by virtue of his attendance at the Exposition Internationale des Arts Decoratifs et Industries Modernes in Paris (1925), helped define Hollywood style as starkly art deco in its architectonic, whitened set designs.

The confluence of all of these forces—the moviemakers' own gospel of success, the Production Code Administration's (PCA's) nationalized morals, the fans' mentalities, and the gesellschaft of the studios—set movies on their way down the middle of the road. The movie world also drew on the themes and formulas of older popular American literature: the lone heroes of Ned Buntline's dime-novel westerns; the stalwarts of the football grid, such as Frank Merriwell, whose name became eponymous for last-quarter heroics that snatched games from the jaws of defeat; the put-upon victims, whether Uncle Tom or self-sacrificing Stella Dallases; the rebels who sneered at the notion of living life by the book and whose heroic rashness in the last reel taught prim martinets that American life offered space for all sorts of people; the corrupt officials whose venality was susceptible to reform at the hands of, as Justice Frankfurter would say, "an aroused conscience"; and the "greenhorns," immigrants who learned their way out of their ghettos. Surely the PCA code helped define the forms that these historic images took, but at the same time the PCA watchdogs had themselves inherited a cultural baggage that included versions of the American virtues they had absorbed from the pious pens of the Catholic activists, such as Father Lord, Martin Quigley, and others.

How good were movie men at what they did? Was there enough slack in the product to allow for John Kenneth Galbraith's "countervailing" cultures of resistance to the status quo? After all, with its assemblage of social programs, its visible regulation, and the safety net it placed under the worst rigors of the Depression, Roosevelt's New Deal had seemed simultaneously to restore confidence and to tame capitalism in ways that lent themselves to movie images.

In this way, movies reflected more than one sensibility, often in unintended conflict with each other. The movie moguls' class affiliations loomed large, but they were compromised by their upward mobility from their own lower origins. Thus politics emerged mainly from the need to aim for the center: the ideals shared equally by the old middle class of entrepreneurial elites; the new middle class of newly licensed lawyers, doctors, and other professionals; and the workingman (never working *class*, in his view), whose hopes for his children were formed of the gospel of individual success. This faith in success, rather than some narrowly conceived class consciousness, was the mentality that moviegoers took into the theaters. Even Roosevelt's New Deal, with its tinkering, regulation, and experimenting that marshaled a temporary socialism in the name of saving capitalism, tried to raise individual hopes, rather than call for a permanent gemeinschaft collectivity. In such an ideological setting, movie men could hardly risk aiming for the far left or right of political life. They would have missed the middle, where most of the tickets were sold.

To make the case that the system defined a centrist Americanist politics that followed from its desire for a broad ticket-buying base, I prefer not to cite the investment, technology, industrial organization, and rationalization of production that Bordwell and his coauthors, along with Schatz and Douglas Gomery, have stressed, but to refer to the various supportive instruments that conveyed to moviegoers the assimilated, vaguely reformist ideology on which most movies rested.

One such instrument was the moguls' portrayal of their studios as "families," a stance that allowed them to minimize the labor strife that occasionally flared up on their lots. Moreover, movie star biographies were parables of the virtues of work and energy and pluck as well as the secular, hedonistic, anti-Victorian rewards of success. Reinforcing them were the gossip columnists, who served as watchdogs over deviant behavior. All urban dailies ran stories by these syndicated columnists. Among the first publishers to plunge into this virgin field was William Randolph Hearst, that bundle of populist impulses dressed up in jingoism. Perhaps he wished to cover Hollywood only as means of plugging the career of his mistress, Marion Davies. In any event, Davies's friend, Louella O. Parsons, who had been a show business reporter for the New York *Dramatic Clipper* and the *Morning Telegraph*, came to Hearst's *New York American* in 1923. After staying in California as Davies's houseguest, Parsons fell in love with the state and moved there to make Hollywood her beat. Parsons was not the only journalist to rake the gossip in search of scoops, but she more than any of her peers converted her stories into fables of soaring success or abject failure, all but inventing the formula of who was in and who was out. Although her work seemed apolitical on the surface, in fact it was a vehicle for the individual success myth and the notion that there existed an open playing field, on which average persons who got a break might win the game. Indeed, her own flagrantly limited journalism skills coupled with her soaring success allowed her to account for her own career by humbly claiming "I've just been lucky."

In no time, Parsons's syndicated column became Hollywood's town crier and, moreover, a sort of trade paper for movie fans—their equivalent of *American Cinematographer*, in whose pages camera workers learned the arcana of their craft. Like Hearst, Parsons was awed by power no matter who wielded it, but she was particularly caught up in how it was bestowed on those who were in and denied to those who were out. Thus she admired both Roosevelt and Mussolini, disdained "Eastern scribblers" because they did not learn the craft of screenwriting, praised Davies because Hearst insisted on it, but sneered at Garbo because her nativism required it. Her powers grew quickly: she could damn a movie because she disliked its makers or because it deviated from Hearst's politics. Her rewards were a house on Maple Drive, a Rolls Royce, and a chauffeur.

In 1937, Louis B. Mayer, acting on behalf of moguls who resented Parsons's erratic powers, found a rival in Hedda Hopper, an underemployed contract player on Mayer's lot. The lively column she turned out was picked up by the *Los Angeles Times*, a less shrill paper than Hearst's *Examiner* and one that the moguls read. Like Parsons a creature of the right, Hopper was a prewar isolationist; was slow to condemn Hitler's anti-Semitism; was an early cheerleader for Martin Dies's House Un-American Activities Committee; advocated the FBI's snooping into movie lot politics; and greatly admired Walt Disney's *The Song of the South* (1945), campaigning for a special Oscar to be awarded posthumously to James Baskette, who played Uncle Remus. In typical fashion, during the 1960s she boosted the career of Nick Adams, a journeyman actor, in exchange for which he went to Vietnam and sent back the reports of high morale and military success that her circle wanted to hear. In effect, Parsons and Hopper served as thought police in attempting to formulate a company town orthodoxy, broadcasting it to their readers, and replicating in print their barbed version of moviemakers' centrist ideology.

Less politically charged versions of Hopper's and Parson's work came in the form of the fan magazines, such as *Photoplay, Motion Picture Story, Silver Screen, Motion Picture,* and *Modern Screen.* In these colorful monthlies the ideology of puritan striving gave meaning to the capsule biographies and photographs of happy movie stars showing to the camera their winsome Americanism, their fortitude in the face of adversity, and their prayerful gratitude for the "lucky breaks" that had brought them stardom. Their stories confirmed in the readers a generalized certainty that life could be mastered, a sense of the rightness of things. In *Hollywood and the Great Fan Magazines* (1971), Martin Levin credits fan magazines with portraying the "movie dream crystallized" in a way that linked stars and readers in a symbiosis in which the stars' luxuries "inspired not envy but admiration and ambition [in] a permanent dream" that lifted the despair induced by the Great Depression. In addition, the stars kept the common touch by means of admitting their vulnerability, suffering, and victimization. After all, lucky breaks were often followed by unlucky ones, for star and fan alike.

Dozens of ghostwritten autobiographies testified to the universality of struggle, reward, and loss. For example, in her autobiography (as told to Mildred Barrington), Marie Dressler writes of her quick rise in a Hollywood that was "sophisticated, gay, [and] beautiful" and then of her equally quick descent to the point where "I would gladly undertake the smallest, feeblest role [because] my funds sank very low." Luckily, she concludes, "fate dealt a hand [and] talking pictures sprang into being"— MGM bought Eugene O'Neill's *Anna Christie* and cast Dressler as a "water-front hag." Such happy endings drew the stars into writing advice books, Douglas Fairbanks's *Making Life Worthwhile* being but one example. General circulation magazines soon joined in, publishing interviews with the stars at home and other inside dope, such as "What Joan Crawford Says for Herself" and "Why Garbo Is Making Her Last Picture."

Of course, to hold this high ground the stars were obliged to narrow the parameters of their personae to an instantly recognizable image, preferably one with a dash of American elan. Indeed, a division of labor akin to that in the guilds emerged: Adolphe Menjou or Charles Boyer could never wear a Stetson, while Gary Cooper could do Frederick Henry in *A Farewell to Arms* (1932) only by taxing his thin resources to their limits. Actresses fell into a similarly arranged typology, either as good girls or bad, the former impish and pert, the latter all feral glances through lowered lashes.

So compelling was this ancillary printed imagery that in *Screening out the Past* (1980) Lary May refers to the arrival of Douglas Fairbanks on the screen as "a cultural reorientation" for men based on a freshened 1920s optimism. Women too learned new mores and often taught them to men. "I am in effect a feministe," said Theda Bara in an interview after her splash in 1914. Later, this new order turned up a long cycle of screwball comedies in which wisecracking, pushy women played by Jean Arthur, Carole Lombard, and Rosalind Russell bent the old gender etiquette. At the turn of the century, William J. Gaynor, mayor of New York, had suggested that movies might even teach country girls how to "take care of themselves" in the city. A quarter of a century later, Douglas Fairbanks showed readers of his advice book how to extend these mere survival skills to embrace success and "the glory of play" that followed from it.

The moral power of this star quality that mingled real with reel revealed itself time and time again. A teacher admired Chaplin's and Mary Pickford's ability to sell liberty bonds during World War I and wished she held similar powers of persuasion over her pupils. Maria LaPlace saw this power in *Now Voyager* (1942), in which Bette Davis, though playing a conventional mother, brought an unexpected feminist subtext to the role as a result of her off-screen aura as a rebel. And after World War II, *Newsweek* used James Stewart's return from duty to herald the end of the war, featuring on its cover a cropped still from *It's a Wonderful Life* (1946).

How did the stars acquire such stature in a medium that had begun by masking them in anonymity? In *Stars* (1979), Richard Dyer finds the key in the nature of American society: hierarchically structured, bureaucratic, ordered, densely populated but open to feats of rapid social mobility, and driven by "commodification." Such a society, devoid of a folk culture and marked by a weak sense of the past, opened itself to acquisitive faddishness and an obsession with the presentation of the self. The young seemed particularly open to the excesses of loyalty and adulation that fan culture required. Yet adoration of icons carried with it no politics. Fans learned from Humphrey Bogart how to hold a cigarette but not how to embrace his liberalism; they aped John Wayne's reeling gait but not his jingoism. They accepted only that which they were already prone to do, and thus, for example, Kate Smith's "sincerity" was a reason for fans to buy war bonds that they were willing to buy anyway. Yet the easy, Americanish manner with which stars settled into their regal places added to their mythic, iconic quality that rose above the realistic mode of the movies that made their reigns possible.

If we ended the discussion here with the stars in their constellations, without taking up those stars who moved uneasily, even rebelliously, in Hollywood's galaxy, we would miss the point that movies included in their ideology a streak of rage at the anomic life that Dyer argues made stardom possible. For example, long after their youthful images of rebellion against convention had been tamed, Mae West and W. C. Fields spoke to their fans as rebels against Victorianism. John Barrymore drank his way into the hearts of movie fans long after his distinguished stage career had faded. Ted Healy's Three Stooges, the Marx bothers, indeed almost any physical and punning comedy rested in part at least on puncturing the pompous. And Bette Davis, aloof and catty in her roles, was similarly hard as flint in her clashes with Warner Bros. Did Fields actually drink more than a quart of gin per workday, smuggling it onto the set in a thermos bottle? To his fans the fact of the matter was irrelevant; his image as tippling rebel was truer than mere fact. Equally irreverent roles played by actors known for their own irreverence conveyed the same sense of delightful flying in the face of the restraints of convention. Bogart wisecracked, drank, and fought in saloons, and so did his Duke Mantee, Sam Spade, and the others. Errol Flynn and John Garfield often played the victims of worlds they never made, Garfield as the lone boxer or violinist who had risen from the tenements and Flynn as the rebel officer who breaks the chain of command that binds him in *They Died with Their Boots On* (1942) and *The Charge of the Light Brigade* (1936). Others played the same role as recalcitrant cadets in naval and military academies and flight schools, but the point was the same: the American social order may owe its efficiency to followers of the rule books, but the heart of the system lies in the mavericks who challenge it, revealing its remediable faults. They tutored the audience in the delights of thumbing its nose at the system.

In addition to the journalists and stars who represented Hollywood to its consumers, there were, of course, the moguls, the bosses of fiefs, the Jews into whose hands Americans had entrusted their mores. Indeed, its Jewishness defined Hollywood for both its friends and enemies: either Hollywood made engaging, winsome amusements, or it was a Jewish conspiracy to dominate Americans' minds. When they were not portrayed as crass, greedy, or bullying, they were ridiculed as unlettered. Cohn was the bully, growling to his internist, "I don't get ulcers. I give 'em!" Goldwyn was the verbal naif, telling dealmakers, "Include me *out*" and on another occasion making the pronouncement, "In two words, *im* possible." He was rumored to have introduced a famous British warrior as "Marshall Field Montgomery." Did he actually commit these verbal blunders? Doesn't matter. The image was truth enough.

Damned as either pushy Jews or ignorant Jews, some of the movie moguls retreated into assimilationism, marrying Gentile women and demanding scripts in which no Jew appeared save as a cultural neuter. Goldwyn, for example, fought to change the comedian Danny Kaye's nose and curly black hair in order to avoid a "sinister" look. And he chided Ring Lardner Jr. for his script of an assimilationist novel, Gwethlyn Graham's *Earth and High Heaven*, telling him he had been hired for his Gentile point of view, but "You betrayed me by writing like a Jew."

Every studio harbored such a legendary Jewish figure. Jack Warner was so aggrandizing that he bolted to the stage to snatch Hal Wallis's Oscar for *Casablanca* as his own. Laemmle and Zukor presided as though foxy grandpas over Universal and Paramount. Mayer tried to rule MGM as the patriarch who always found jobs for relatives, played "Jewish mother" to his stable of stars, and railed against unions as destroying his patriarchate. Together, these men provided the iron link between the Jewish American community and moviemaking, a link that, to the vexation of friend and foe alike, they half-hid behind assimilationism. For example, in the last generation of the classical era everyone knew that Edward G. Robinson had been Emanuel Goldenberg, Paul Muni had been Muni Weisenfreund of the Yiddish theater, Melvyn Douglas had been Melvyn Hesselberg, and Jack Benny had been Benny Kubelsky. Their sons broke with the ghetto culture of the first generation, attended eastern universities, and became "cultured." Budd Schulberg, son of the mogul B. P. Schulberg wrote the ur-satire of Hollywood moguls, *What Makes Sammy Run*. At MGM, Irving Thalberg, the son-in-law and heir to the throne, behaved as though polished by a finishing school but still had a learned colleague accompany him to his meetings to help him over blank spots in his education. Dore Schary married into Mayer's family and brought with him both an intellectual's breadth and an easterner's New Dealism. Above all, as Betty Lasky (Jesse Lasky's daughter) told Neal Gabler in *An Empire of Their Own* (1988), the trick was to avoid "animalistic types" who were "so ghetto ugly" as to seem "freaks."

How did this cross-purposed group manage to serve as a clearinghouse for American values? It is something of a feat when one considers that they were cut off from the main centers of American culture. Their legendary retinues of yes-men effectively sealed off even their lunchtimes from any outside idea. Many of them belonged to shuls, but few attended except on the highest of holidays. If they belonged to any group, it might be the Jewish Hillcrest Country Club. And they all read the same daily stuff: the trade papers, the *Hollywood Reporter*, and the *Hollywood Citizen-News*. They compensated for their insularity by hiring their middle managers from Gentile circles: Winnie Sheehan and Jason Joy at Fox, Eddie Mannix at MGM, and Steve Lynch and Y. Frank Freeman at Paramount. In addition, the production code was defined not only by Father Daniel Lord, Joseph Breen, Martin Quigley (its Catholic trinity), and the Presbyterian Will Hays, but also by Luigi Luraschi, Francis Harmon, Jason Joy, and other midlevel men in the Motion Picture Producers and Directors of America (MPPDA). The Americanist ideology that arose from these cadres had a loose imprecision that allowed for a fairly wide range of movie culture.

Reflective of this, total ticket sales for the Depression decade approached $1 billion. Moreover, moviegoers constituted a large, active group. As children, they averaged one movie per week, even if they were poor. As adults, mostly women, they remained undeterred in their moviegoing habits, with movies accounting for a quarter of every dollar spent on recreation. In 1936, the frequency of attendance approached three movies per week per family, sloughing off only when some event, such as a boxing championship, drew people to their radios.

This patterned behavior varied according to the tastes of age and class. If poor kids went to movies for escape, the middle-class kids, who read the fan mags, were drawn by a conscious identification with the stars or at least an emotional affinity for them. But hovering over the families' choices was, asserts Margaret Thorp in *America at the Movies* (1939), the "solid average citizen's wife who commands the respectful attention of the industry." To this aggregate of American moviegoers must be added European moviegoers, who had joined the clientele after World War I snuffed out their own cinemas. Thereafter, the Americans consolidated their foothold by capitalizing various foreign studios and theatrical chains, thereby undercutting every effort of European protectionism: Great Britain's quotas, Germany's proscriptions, France's censorship, and all countries' tariffs per foot of celluloid. Moreover, many of Europe's and England's finest, such as Billy Wilder, Fritz Lang, William Wyler, Karl Freund, Michael Curtiz, Fred Zinnemann, the

Siodmaks, and Alfred Hitchcock, emigrated to California. Some, such as Detlev Sierck (work name, Douglas Sirk), retooled their names to fit their new circumstances.

At the heart of this symbiosis of audience, journalism, star system, and communal company town was, of course, the studio, the economic engine that drove the system. Each studio had its own folkways and corporate ways, and all of them except RKO turned the Depression into a profitable decade. Honing their new tools of sound and color, they firmly consolidated their internal mores into what Tino Balio in *Grand Design* calls "aesthetic norms of Hollywood studio filming [that] as a whole constituted a group style." Indeed, throughout his analysis of the era, Balio resorts to a functionalist diction, as, for example, when he finds "social processes that translate filmmakers' goals and standards into new materials, equipment, and procedures"—in short, "institutions." This perspective recapitulates the work of a cadre of peers: Douglas Gomery's *The Hollywood Studio System* (1986), a compendium of studio "biographies"; Thomas Schatz's *The Genius of the System* (1988); and Ethan Mordden's *The Hollywood Studios* (1988).

Paramount, for example, began the 1930s in a style appropriate to the excesses of the late Republican era of Harding, Coolidge, and Hoover. It clutched at all sorts of assets: its Publix theaters; half of CBS; and, in the slough of the Great Crash, five hundred heavily mortgaged additional theaters. As if these were not enough, Paramount even fancied a merger with Warner Bros. and *its* one thousand theaters and musical publishing house. Only a stern warning from the Hoover administration of a possible antitrust suit headed off the union. Such a corporate urge could not help but result in a capital-intensive stretching of resources. The strain eventually so threatened the firm that John Hertz, eventual lessor of motorcars but at the time a partner in Lehman Brothers, took over the finance committee of Paramount's board, slashed costs, and sold off CBS, with the result that in 1933 Paramount just barely averted receivership. After bankers and creditors took a turn at the management of Paramount, a movie man returned to the helm in the form of Barney Balaban, the Chicago theater chain owner. By 1936, Balaban had returned a profit.

On the Paramount lot itself, the struggle between the accountants and the movie men resulted in a two-headed system: heading production was Y. Frank Freeman, a theater man from southern chains such as Saenger of New Orleans, and heading studio operations was Buddy DeSylva. Together they also built a Paramount style grounded in the urbane wit of Ernst Lubitsch but increasingly inclining toward the American brassiness of Bob Hope, Bing Crosby, William Bendix, and Betty Hutton, augmented by the beau ideal westerner, Gary Cooper, and eventually the sulky anomie of the film-noir star Alan Ladd. From time to time, they also briefly exploited presold stars from the stage and Europe, such as the Marx brothers, Mae West, Maurice Chevalier, and Marlene Dietrich. In addition, through a long-standing link to Cecil B. DeMille they underwrote or released his biblical and western epics that ranged from *Union Pacific* (1939) to *The Ten Commandments* (1956).

Down in Culver City, MGM took up a still more identifiable style, grounded in Louis B. Mayer's insistence on the family being its corporate as well as aesthetic image. With only a fraction of Paramount's houses, albeit among them a considerable number of elegant palaces, in addition to a piece of the French-Anglo Gaumont-British studio and theater chain that gave them access to Europe, MGM enjoyed such a low debt burden that it declared dividends throughout the Depression. Like Paramount, the firm drew its bosses from the theaters. Unlike Paramount, however, Mayer, Nicholas Schenck, and the producers went for classy features with a family orientation and preferred to distribute, rather than produce, shorts and ancillary material. Not until Dore Schary (a son-in-law of Mayer) took over in 1948 did the lot opt for a grittier style—"the dirty fingerprints on the wall" model, to use Mayer's words.

As the Tiffany's of the movie lots, MGM focused on the stylish imagery of their glittering stable of stars: Clark Gable, Greta Garbo, Spencer Tracy, Walter Pigeon, Greer Garson, Judy Garland, and Mickey Rooney. In the 1940s, it enhanced its image of classiness when Arthur Freed developed a string of realistically mounted musicals that departed from Busby Berkeley's cleverly edited but surreal production numbers. Freed's unit turned out, among others, *Cabin in the Sky* (1943), *Meet Me in St. Louis* (1944), *A Royal Wedding* (1951), *Singin' in the Rain* (1952), and *An American in Paris* (1951). In addition, the studio went for historical epics such as *Boomtown* (1940), a success myth of the oil fields; *San Francisco* (1936), which included a special-effects earthquake; and even an African adventure yarn shot in Uganda, *Trader Horn* (1931), not to mention the best of the Tarzan movies. Perhaps more than any other lot, MGM used the producer-unit system, described by Bordwell and his coauthors in *The Classical Hollywood Cinema* as a system that permitted deviations from the unit, so that a Freed movie differed from one of Hunt Stromberg's *The Thin Man* movies and MacDonald–Eddy duos or Sidney Franklin's elegant English stuff, such as *Mrs. Miniver* (1942) and *Waterloo Bridge* (1940).

Fox—after 1935, 20th Century-Fox—took a different tack, that of the historical epic or biography, a course that led a wit to brand the studio "19th Century-Fox." It embraced the producer-unit system even more than MGM did. The studio was such a creature of its energetic production boss, Darryl F. Zanuck, a rare Gentile in the colony, that wits referred to the firm as the "goy studio." The firm survived William Fox's financial and legal troubles after the Crash by selling off theaters, including the massive Roxy, and giving up its attempt to merge with MGM. Miraculously, at the end of the New Deal's first year, Fox had managed to earn a profit. Thereafter, an austere management style imposed by Sidney Kent in New York followed by Zanuck's entry after a decade at Warner Bros. as writer and production chief, trimmed the studio for a rough sail through the 1930s. Meanwhile, it lived off its bread-and-butter series: In 1934 and 1935, Will Rogers, often with Stepin Fetchit as a comic sidekick, played a string of wise rubes in *David Harum*, *Judge Priest*, and *The County Chairman*, and Shirley Temple along with *her* black sidekick, Bill Robinson, played a moppet in jeopardy in *The Little Colonel* and *The Littlest Rebel*; a few years later Temple starred with curmudgeonly Victor McLaglen in *Wee Willie Winkie* (1937). These movies helped keep the studio solvent until Zanuck could impose his iron will on the system (and on almost every movie and on history, particularly Anglo-Saxon variants of it), producing *Clive of India* (1936), a celebration of Britain's wresting control of India from France; *Cardinal Richelieu* (1935); *Stanley and Livingstone* (1939); nostalgic local color films such as *Kentucky* (1938) and *Maryland* (1940); sidebars to history such as *In Old Chicago* (1938), a tale of Mrs. O'Leary's cow and the Chicago fire, and *The Prisoner of Shark Island* (1936), about Samuel Mudd's imprisonment after setting John Wilkes Booth's leg; bio pics of Lincoln, Alexander Graham Bell, Lillian Russell, Jesse James, and, after the onset of war, Brigham Young and Woodrow Wilson; and renderings of literary classics like *Drums Along the Mohawk* (1939) and *The Grapes of Wrath* (1940). That Zanuck was the key may be seen in his longevity. Will Rogers died; Shirley Temple became a Republican; Stepin Fetchit became an anachronism; and Betty Grable, Alice Faye, and Sonja Henie came and went, while Zanuck took his tabloid style, high gloss, and classic form through World War II and the slump into the post-Hollywood era.

Warner Bros., though smaller and leaner than the other majors, played on the same field and used similar strategies, but it depended more on cheaply made genre films, serials, B movies, and styles that masked its limited resources. In *A New Deal for Entertainment* (1983), Nick Roddick analyzes this rational system by focusing on a film whose production is documented in the Warner Bros. archives, *Anthony Adverse* (1936), Hervey Allen's thousand-page novel that Warner Bros. characteristically trimmed to fewer than 100 minutes. From the assembling of the producer-unit, to the accountants' "costing," to the soundstages, to the sales department's search for a core of meaning that they might highlight in the ad copy, the result was a movie defined in form, mood, voice, and texture by "the genius of the system."

The system, in making its choices, such as the need for a classical hero, ended by almost willy-nilly making most movies into bearers of little nuggets of belief or faith, such as the centrality of the individual in American myth. For example, Warner Bros.'s *Bullets or Ballots* (1936), *The Charge of the Light Brigade* (1936), *Destination Tokyo* (1944), and *Angels with Dirty Faces* (1938) seem to be about urban crime, the British Army, submarine warfare, and juvenile penal codes, but in each plot, a maverick hero violates canons of law, practice, or loyalty, often clashing with a greying figure who lives by the book. Each movie teaches that the system needs both figures, working in creative tension: the maverick cop learns to live by the rules while solving the case; the sullen loner in a sub under Tokyo Bay learns teamwork; a dashing cavalryman dies in the famous charge at Balaclava, teaching priggish officers proper regard for individual heroism; and a crusading journalist exposes corruption in juvenile prisons, thereby revealing an institutional capacity for reform.

Conscious propagandizing on behalf of an establishment? Nonsense. Lone heroes allowed moviemakers to narrow their focus to courtrooms, submarine passageways, cadres of contentious officers, and such, thereby cutting costs while simultaneously tracing the trajectory of the loner, crusader, or winner to a pleasing denouement founded on familiar formulas. Formulas made for predictability, which made for ease of exploitation by the sales department.

At the same time, by then the studio crafts had grown specialized and applicable to any genre. For example, as Gomery reports in *The Hollywood Stu-*

dio System (1986), the cameraman Tony Gaudio shot the gangster film *High Sierra* (1941), the biopic *Juarez* (1939), the intrepid pilots' yarn *Dawn Patrol* (1938), and the B movie *Torchy Blane* (1937).

Thus the system itself embraced ways of doing that viewers received as ways of feeling and thinking, much like a ritual by means of which a tribe defines itself. A movie was the sum of intuitive marketing, cold accounting practice, the conventions of studio shop practice, and the MPPDA's code of censorship, all playing to moviegoers' "systems of memory," on which their expectations were based (the term is Bordwell and his coauthors').

The smaller lots, such as RKO, Columbia, Universal, Republic, and other poverty row studios, remained in play but often in narrower specialties, for lower stakes, and in venues limited by the smaller scale of their chains. This is not to minimize their often admired films, but rather to assert their jerry-built scaffolding, pinched bank accounts, and corner store retailing as defining factors of production. Many of the movies RKO produced are well known: *King Kong* (1933); *Top Hat* (1935), *Flying Down to Rio* (1933), and other Fred Astaire musicals; and Orson Welles's brazenly superb *Citizen Kane* (1941). It also put out a rich vein of somber film noir, including Val Lewton's famous *The Cat People* (1942) and *The Curse of the Cat People* (1944) and cheap detective movies, such as *Murder My Sweet* (1945), in which tenor Dick Powell found himself a second career. Almost all of the film noir was shot in low-key chiaroscuro lighting, as though on the cheap.

Less well known was RKO's struggle to achieve coherence out of its mixed pedigree, which went back to a B-movie fount, FBO; RCA and its sound technology; angels that included Rockefellers, David Sarnoff of RCA, Joseph Kennedy, and others; its chain cobbled from the old Keith-Albee vaudeville circuit plus the cavernous Radio City Music Hall; as well as European links through Pathe and Associated Talking Pictures in Great Britain. Despite these imposing resources, Gomery reckons only "the years 1943 to 1947 [as] a golden age for RKO," which crumbled after the energetically political Dore Schary's term as production chief gave way to a corrosive era under the ownership of the aviator-cum-roué Howard Hughes, who soon bled the firm's assets white.

The other small lots experienced roads that were just as rocky, if less corporately erratic. Universal saw not a dollar of profit until the eve of World War II; Columbia, not until 1944; and United Artists (ever a distributor of the work of others), never. For these lots, hits were like blades of grass in a compost heap. Universal had *All Quiet on the Western Front* (1930), *Dracula* (1931), *Frankenstein* (1931), B movies such as *The Wolf Man* (1941), and a spurt of Abbott and Costello comedies during the war. Columbia survived on its trimmed sails and light debt, not to mention the work of Frank Capra, whose *It Happened One Night* (1934) won five Oscars using borrowed actors. His streak included *Lost Horizon* (1937), *You Can't Take It with You* (1938), *Mr. Smith Goes to Washington* (1939), and other populist fables. Harry Cohn's annual cash crop at Columbia was his B-movie series: Charles Starrett's westerns and crossovers from other media, such as *Blondie* (1938) from a comic strip; *Boston Blackie* (1941), *The Whistler* (1944), and *Jungle Jim* (1939) from radio shows; and *The Lone Wolf* (1939) from a novel. Many of them featured fading stars dropped by the majors, Warner Baxter, Warren William, Richard Dix, and Arthur Lake among them.

Considering that the studios were a hierarchical system of rivals, working for East Coast masters to make products for worldwide consumers, the variety that they achieved was remarkable. Bordwell and his coauthors quote Schary as explaining that the system combined "hand-craft" and the "custom-job," both rooted in the economies of a factory system that yet allowed for "the picture's individuality." In part, also, the uniqueness and variety were accounted for by a creative tension between the studio bosses and their moviemakers, an endless contest between ego and id. The units and their creative spirits, writers, directors, and actors—all of whom considered themselves artists—fought to make movies as though they were trapped in the "putty knife factory" run by accountants and martinets.

Every movie buff knows a war story about a victory or defeat for one side or the other. MGM shortened Erich von Stroheim's *Greed* (1924) from hours to minutes, after which it smelted the film stock in order to recover its silver nitrate. In his last days, Thalberg hobbled the Marx brothers' zaniness by demanding seventeen rewrites of *A Day at the Races* (1937) after various previews. On the creators' side, certain directors earned the title of "auteur" (the term is Andrew Sarris's from *The American Cinema: Directors and Directions, 1929-1968*), imposing their style on their movies in spite of the system. John Ford, when on location, shot so little insurance footage that he seemed to edit in the camera. Alfred Hitchcock, as though to haze his masters as they sought to tether his macabre wit, slipped in fleeting bits of his own image. Douglas Sirk shot moody, color-saturated "women's pictures" laden with a melodramatic subtext that floated beneath the Technicolor gloss his producers requested. Sometimes writers achieved similar tiny victories, as when the Communist John Howard Lawson wrote the word "comrade" into *Action in the North Atlantic* (1943), the wartime epic of the Murmansk shipping run. I do not wish to make as much of this as Sarris does in his zeal to celebrate direction over other contributions to film art, but his auteur theory does have a ring to it, harkening to the antiauthoritarianism of schoolboys, prisoners, and lifers of all sorts who covertly get their way despite the rules set down by their keepers.

Occasionally, happenstance opened a fissure into which personal style might slip. For example, a script that was a homage to the Army's black engineers came to Dore Schary's desk just as he mused on warning Americans of the long war to come. By rewriting it and assigning it to Tay Garnett, a compliantly apolitical director, he turned out an atypically—for MGM—racially liberal movie, *Bataan*. Similarly, the fabled *Casablanca* (1942) grew from romantic yarn into voice of the Allied cause, this time with the writers as auteurs inventing the subtext. Sometimes, inept producers let slip little gems of directorial style, as when Mark Hellinger produced Abe Polonsky's *Brute Force* (1947) and Jules Dassin's *The Naked City* (1948) and George Jessel did Edmund Goulding's *Nightmare Alley* (1947). Hitchcock came from Great Britain, where he either had been left alone or had learned to lard his movies with identifying touches (including his own visage). Meanwhile, when his stuff crossed the Atlantic it earned rentals unmatched by any other British movies, winning Hitchcock the freedom to be "difficult." Ford combined Hitchcock's traits into an American version of prickliness that he put into his densely authentic westerns.

Moreover, certain journalist critics—James Agee in the *Nation* and *Time*, Philip Hartung in *Commonweal*, Bosley Crowther in the *Times*—often spotted the wisps of artistic freedom, the subtle slips of tethers, the inner men screaming to get out, and wrote about the resulting subversions of Hollywood convention. Much later, Sarris gathered his thoughts into his compendium, *The American Cinema*, in which he ranked directors with respect to their covert credentials for belonging in a "pantheon" or found in them "less than meets the eye."

If this seems a too romantic sketch of what free-thinking directors got away with, it must be remembered that although the system created its own tensions and fissures, only a few had the freedom to take advantage of them.

Hollywood, then, was not the monolithic state apparatus in which directors simply took orders, as some theorists argue it was. Rather, as Staiger writes in *The Classical Hollywood Cinema*, it merely "provided economic support for an ideological/signifying practice." Within this institutional framework that tolerated Hitchcock and Ford there was also another set of tensions. Students of a "managerial revolution" such as Thurman Arnold and Peter Drucker have pointed out the gulf between the untamed capitalism of stockholders and the New Dealish capitalism of Schary or Walter Wanger, a gulf at least as wide as that between Mayer and his son-in-law Schary. Thus for every Bryan Foy or Charles Schnee grinding out his B movies, or Henry King creating his paean to Americana, or B. Reeves Eason fashioning his action movies, or William Witney constructing his serials, there were lesser Hitchcocks and Fords within the system who worked their tastes and politics into movies—Budd Boetticher in his westerns, Edgar G. Ulmer and Jules Dassin in their film noir, and so on.

As we have seen, these trails through the maze of Hollywood history have been exposed to fresh scrutiny. One reason for this is that some studios have made their archives public, shedding new light onto Hollywood history. At the same time, historians have enlarged their toolkits to include concepts drawn from other disciplines. In effect, as Sarris made auteurs of some directors, so new theorists make auteurs of the moviegoers.

From a feminist angle, Laura Mulvey in *Visual and Other Pleasures* (1989) asserts that a "male gaze" is an unwitting adjunct to both viewing and making of movies. Similarly, in Whitney Museum program notes, James Snead argues the existence of a screen defined by white eyes; unwilling to give their attention to problematic black images, whites prefer a screen from which blacks have been "structured out." These views of movies as conveyors of deeply held sensibilities that only seldom flare into consciousness owe much to the extensions of Freud provided by Jacques Lacan, who found moviegoing a replication of humans' infantile gropings in mirrors for a sense of self. Some students have found class-based meanings in movies by inventing similar extensions of Marx, which allow them to see Hollywood as akin to a state apparatus retailing a seamless, pleasant image of the status quo that prohibits dissent. Or, borrowing from the Marxist revisionist Antonio Gramsci, they have found a less teleological sense of ongoing struggle in history. Some historians, Gomery among them, see politics as local and begin their analyses in the nabes.

Thus Hollywood has been seen as "a major ideological force," a force that, as mentioned earlier, Roddick examines in *A New Deal for Entertainment* by studying the production of *Anthony Adverse* (1936), a "prestige" rather than merely generic Hollywood picture, and one that required a hero who triumphs over adversity. Unlike the scholars who rely for insight on theoretical extensions of theories that themselves were extruded from sources who could not have ever seen an actual movie, in analyzing the production of this movie, Roddick refers to the documents in the Warner Bros. archives, in addition to borrowing what he needed from these scholars.

In memo after memo, Roddick shows, the bosses demanded a conventional hero, a DeMille-style epic on a Harry Warner nut, and a tight script of Allen's thousand-page picaresque novel. When shooting stopped and cutting began, the Breen office expected "enormous difficulty throughout the South" unless Warner Bros. cut *something* of the race angle, either an Africa sequence or Adverse's overt abolitionism. In the novel, there is a passing scene in which the hero bristles at the slavery he sees in Africa. Moreover, Allen himself granted that a miscegenation scene between Adverse and a mulatto maiden not only crossed a PCA line, but also allowed the inference that a black woman was, as Roddick writes, "the objective sign of [Adverse's] degradation."

The result of the PCA's obligatory cuts of such racial politics was a passable distillation of a bulky book that had a run good enough to inspire a cycle of costume dramas. More important, Roddick argues, the movie's conservative politics and meaning arose out of a debate documented in memoranda between countervailing forces in Hollywood, not only ex post facto inferences drawn by observers not part of the culture who actually saw the movie.

As for the resulting costume dramas, they too were embedded with politics of a sort, this time in the nature of heroic conventions. The cycle may be seen as starting with the swashbuckling career of Errol Flynn, beginning with a boys' book version of Tennyson's *The Charge of the Light Brigade* (1936) and running through *The Adventures of Robin Hood* (1938), a pair of Elizabethan court dramas, and a suite of Rafael Sabatini seafaring yarns. The ideological core of each movie was embodied in its maverick hero, who violates the king's peace, stands against a cabal of courtiers, or proves the equal of pirates.

No matter what the genre, scores of movie plots were driven by the idea of the lone hero taking a stand against a world he never made. Even "de Lawd," as the black preacher from the bayous calls the god of the Hebrews in Marc Connelly's *The Green Pastures* (1936), frees "de chillun" of Israel to make their own way in the world under the guidance of their soldier/leader Hezdrel. In *Taxi* (1932), Nolan the cabbie leads the "little guys" against Consolidated Cab. In *Night Flight* (1933), set before the advent of radar, the hero must fly the night mail in order to win a government contract. In *Yellow Jack* (1938), he gives up his life to cure yellow fever by allowing an anopheles mosquito to bite him. More rarely, women were given such heroic tasks, often signaled by a title role: In *Cleopatra* (1933), *Nurse Edith Cavell* (1939), and *Belle Starr* (1941), the heroines stand against the Roman Empire, the German invasion of Belgium, and the scalawags and carpetbaggers of Missouri. In one way or another, all of these movies obliged their heroes and heroines to struggle against oppression or revealed the limits of established authority to right the wrongs done by elites.

The trick, states Roddick, "rested upon individualizing of social issues," a device often garbled by the New Deal's ambiguity, embedded in its promise to tame and reform capitalism in order to save it. As Maltby writes in *Grand Design*, whereas the "reaffirmation" of American life meant an economic life on new terms for New Dealers, for the PCA it meant the possibility of introducing its production code into the National Recovery Administration (NRA) as a more conservative version of the revived nation.

Moviemakers managed to mingle the two mentalities congenially in scores of movies by using a two-pronged formula. Whenever the hard edge of Marxist, or merely leftist, politics threatened to upset the fragile balance, either the PCA code or the studio bosses themselves stiffened and called for a softer line in which living with the status quo seemed tolerable. How did the formula work? As we have already seen, *The Charge of the Light Brigade* shows that the rebel and martinet might coexist in a creative tension in which both seem essential to the well-being of the group. Another example is James Cagney's citizen soldier in *The Fighting 69th* (1940), who shows that by bonding with his comrades any doughboy can stiffen up and do his duty. Prison movies such as *20,000 Years in Sing Sing* (1933) and *Angels Wash Their Faces* (1939) indicated that the prison system was capable of reform, if only selfless wardens and crusading journalists would intervene. Could the New Deal save both America and individualism? Indeed, yes, said these movies, provided that lone heroes emerged, rallied the good folk, and proved that by acting on behalf of their own interests all of society was the better for it. In times of crisis, when the fainthearted demanded collectivization or even fascism, the individual hero invoked a sort of laissez-faire of popular art in which everyone acting out of self-interest contributed to the well-being of the whole, with only a smidgen of New Deal economic tinkering necessary as a backup.

What of those scripts that strayed too far from the politics of the status quo? We can best see the tension between reform and stasis in the scripts that Warner Bros. sent to the PCA, perhaps because of the leftist aroma that lingered in the studio after a steady stream of reformist melodramas. "Of all the studios," reports Roddick, "Warner Brothers was the one whose production programme most enthusiastically reflected the New Deal"—the studio even placed an NRA "blue eagle" logo on the screen along with the main titles. Its *Black Fury* (1935) had been intended as a movie version of a book about a Pennsylvania miner who had been murdered by company goons in 1929. Breen needed almost no prodding to compel a softening of the story (he had been a press agent for a mining firm). Moreover, he recalled the labor strife of 1929 as no more than "a Communist undertaking." Not only did the script that arrived at the PCA contain no specific violation of the code, but it portrayed labor strife precisely as almost any American would know it: as a failed negotiation that ended in a strike that the company countered by hiring scabs.

Breen's solution was a classic. Why not, he suggested, retain the excitement of conflict while removing its class-based dimension? To this end union organizers could be identified as "crooked agitators" rather than "labor leaders." In this way, "legitimate" unionists along with "humane" mine owners might be portrayed as allies on the side of social justice. According to Gregory Black in *Hollywood Censored* (1994), this was a pacifist formulation to which Jack Warner "was receptive," because of his own labor strife at the studio gates. In Breen's mind it then followed that each volatile precondition of violence might be neutered: bosses were "reasonable"; the miners had "little to complain about"; scabs were hired to fulfill a contract, not to take jobs away from strikers; and goons were meant to "protect his property, not to terrorize his men."

On the screen toward the end of 1935, *Black Fury* seemed almost Edenic, with its neat miners' houses, roomy well-lighted mine galleries, and its willing workers who sing their way to the pit head every morning. Only an infiltrator from a detective agency disrupts the tranquility. He serves as agent provocateur who uses a well-liked miner (Paul Muni) as a stooge to provoke a strike, which attracts national attention that ends in a settlement in which everyone wins—a new contract is negotiated, production resumes, and so on. Not bamboozled, censors in coal-mining states attacked the film, opening a fissure between the PCA and the producer, Hal Wallis, who had been promised that the changes would avoid trouble in the local boards.

As though grateful for the small favor, the nation's liberal center and left deemed the movie as good a politics as Hollywood politesse allowed. Black reports, for example, that the *Literary Digest* found fault only with its "oversimplification"; the *Nation* called it "half a loaf"; to the *New York Times* it was a "handsome defense of the status quo"; and the *New Republic* called it a tepid attempt that seemed "great," however, in light of Hollywood's past timidity, a view shared by John L. Lewis of the United Mine Workers. This sense of a national polity across class lines was used to dampen any hint of actual strife in American life. Thus even the Republicans among the moguls, such as Mayer, kept up the appearance of cooperating with the New Deal, often punctuating the denouements of their problem movies with magical cameo parts by actors playing FDR, complete with the infectious optimism symbolized in the jaunty angle of his cigarette holder or the upward tilt of his hat brim.

In *Stand Up and Cheer* (1934), for example, the entire country marches in a parade, singing "We're out of the red" (of both Communism and debtors' ink) in a production number ordered by a "secretary of entertainment" in FDR's cabinet. Roddick finds such enthusiasm for collective solutions in almost all early 1930s movies. Typically, in King Vidor's neglected *Our Daily Bread* (1934), "the people," drawn from "all walks of life," in an instinctively populist manner choose leaders from among themselves; abandon their decaying cities; and create a benign, bucolic, socialist commune. A dark stain sometimes streaked this collectivity, an example of which may be seen in *The President Vanishes* (1934), in which the presidency is momentarily suspended in favor of government by a cabal who resort to fascist measures, after which, improbably, "the secret six" restore the president to governing his newly stabilized country. In *Gabriel over the White House* (1933), the president is a rascal in the pocket of "interests" until a brush with death in a car crash turns him into a fascist version of Roosevelt.

By the mid-1930s confidence, if not prosperity, seemed to have returned, and Hollywood decided to return to its lone heroes—a sweetheart of a

judge; a crusading reporter; or, of course, in comic books, a Superman—
who exposed the odd malfunction. Thus the action is carried in conventionally heroic interventions into an essentially just social order in which the
state held only a limited place. In *Bullets or Ballots* (1936), for example, a lone
hero (Bogart) learns that mob rule in a city can end only when its citizens
make a personal choice to stand against it.

In a sense, all such movies were about the New Deal. Thus as the Marxists
feared, movies seemed to follow an establishment party line, but at the same
time they were a Gramscian negotiation between class interests, resulting in
a compromise that Americans and Hollywood writers loosely agreed on, a
"liberalism of the heart." Thus the "at liberty" performers in *The Gold Diggers of 1933* are driven to collaborate in producing their own revue when
Broadway is closed off to them as individual performers. In the bio pic
Voltaire, Louis XV is not merely a feckless monarch; he is also a caution to
Roosevelt that France suffered because of its flawed ruler rather than a
flawed system. The actor Paul Muni's bio pics came to a similar solution: his
Zola, Pasteur, and Juarez revealed him to be a Lon Chaney with a conscience,
an actor whose activist characters reinforced America's contemporary need
for an interventionist government. Indeed, Roddick reports that the director of *Juarez* (1939) insisted that Napoleon's adventure in Mexico must echo
"Mussolini plus Hitler in their adventure in Spain," a sentiment that the
right wing had already tried to undercut by branding it "pre-mature antifascism." Other bio pics made more general points: *The Charge of the Light
Brigade*, that individualism and authority must coexist in creative tension;
Knute Rockne (1940), that dedication to sport may precede the dedication to
work that makes for success; and the pre-Pearl Harbor *Sergeant York* (1941),
that there are "just wars" and intervention in them on the right side is a
vaguely expressed obligation of right-thinking peoples.

Obviously, on both the left and right such political burdens of movies
were taken for an official line of a ruling class, much as the pre-Nazi Frankfurt scribes had predicted. For example, the Marxist Harry Alan Potamkin
(quoted by Bohn and Stromgren in *Light & Shadows* [1975]) thought this re-
duction of Progressivism to the resources of a lone hero merely offered "a
fairy tale . . . as a compensatory mythology."

Yet, on the right, a palliative Progressivism had its place. A writer in the
MPPDA's annual report for 1939 was pleased with Hollywood's "succession
of pictures which dramatize present-day social conditions," presumably be-

cause progressive action might follow. But how to mediate this latter promise to combine "social themes and commercial genres," as Mervyn LeRoy put it (quoted by Alan Casty in *The Development of Film* [1973])? Easy. A producer urges a director to work certain images into a script written by a writer who already knows the ropes well enough to please his masters.

How to warn America of the rising "fascisti" of Europe? Winfield Shee-han, the producer, worked on a script with Reginald Berkeley with a view to linking America to Europe through bloodlines—this being Hollywood we're talking about, preferably blue bloodlines that extend to romantic Louisiana. Then crank out memoranda, the preferred prose form of the moguls, urging the director to lay in imagery that had worked in his previous movies. The American hero should possess an admirable and identifiably American trait that is the "source" of the drama; Sheehan's preferred trait was "drive." Of course, if a southerner was to be the quintessential American, there had to be the obligatory black foil, who, it followed, must be played by Fox's con-tract player, Stepin Fetchit. And if this political tract was to make money, its message had to float in a nutrient broth of "plenty of comedy and fun." Berkeley and his successive coauthors went all out: their hero echoed the Confederate General Pierre G. T. Beauregarde, part French seigneur, part American patriot whose ancestor had fought with Andrew Jackson at New Orleans in 1814. By the third draft of the script, the sinking of the Lusitania provided the magnet that drew the modern Franco-American to the trenches in France, with Fetchit in tow as a sort of batman. Fetchit, for his part, played it "colored," referring to his bayonet as his "razor" and mum-bling his lines so much that the stenographer taking them off the screen could not follow them.

These factors of production came together in the form of 20th Century-Fox's *The World Moves On* (1934), at once a romance of the Old South, a tribute to the renaissance of the New South, an early warning of the rise of European fascism, and another Hollywood certification that African Amer-icans enjoyed the life they had been dealt. The artifact had been hammered out by several scriptwriters, each of whom may not have known of his pre-decessor; shaped by a producer who knew what he wanted; and directed by John Ford, a man of often maudlin sentimentality as well as one who counted Fetchit as a trustworthy trouper who knew what was wanted. To-gether, not entirely consciously, they assembled a classical Hollywood movie that, clean of ambiguity, flowed to its place in the exhibition schedule. But of course there were ambiguities. Ford was an auteur and often slipped in his own sensibilities. Indeed, Sheehan knew this and played to it, suggesting, for example, that Ford introduce ethnic music into the soundtrack. Fetchit so thoroughly knew his stock role that Ford found him "undirectable" and, as though he were a prescient racehorse, gave him his head and let him run.

Backing their play was the MPPDA, who also responded to outside forces in dozens of cases. They kept profiles of regional censors and knew what nettled them, and they read their mail: the irate newspaperman in Shreveport, Louisiana, predicting a boycott if interracial dancing such as that done by Louis Armstrong and Martha Raye in *Artists and Models* (1937) recurred, the German consul in Los Angeles threatening worldwide trouble unless the MPPDA induced Chaplin to withhold from circulation his parody of Hitler, *The Great Dictator* (1940), and so on. In 1935, as gangster movies softened into the argument that environment caused crime, an MPPDA spokesperson promised an association of police chiefs that movies thereafter would treat them as "heroes of the law." Reflecting the trend, Andrew Bergman reports in *We're in the Money* (1972), is the ad for James Cagney in *G-Men* (1935): "Hollywood's most famous bad man joins the G-Men."

The result of the tension induced by the pulling and pushing of all of these forces, from movie lot to pressure group, was a cinema that was neither the monolith anticipated by leftist Cassandras nor the pristine work of artists alone in their garrets. The result was a tangle of ambiguity. Peter Roffman and Jim Purdy make this case in *The Hollywood Social Problem Film* (1981). They grant that "the central dramatic conflict revolve[d] around the interaction of the individual with social institutions" but argue that the movies' pat endings tended only "to inspire limited social change or reinforce the status quo." Thus, as Bergman observes, the movies of this "high" Hollywood era evolved from early gangster movies, such as *Scarface* (1932) and *Five Star Final* (1931), in which "shyster city" is ever in the hands of invincibly cynical rascals, to the late-Depression versions in which Cagney and Bogart change sides, criminality is explained by the environment, and the last reels hint of solutions. Apparently, as Paul Strand and Lewis Mumford's documentary *The City* (1939) and Vidor's *Our Daily Bread* show, the problems that the Great Depression brought could be solved by a "sentimental yearning for an idealized past."

If Roffman and Purdy are even half correct in their assertion that in the High Middle Ages of Hollywood's classical era the system ensured that "a coherent ideological vision of the world is acted out in every formula movie," then it must also be asserted that movies were released with fissures in their ideology that allowed a play in viewers' reception of them. As a result, the insistent portrayal of a dysfunctional society resulted in an ideology that remained resolutely reformist, rather than either revolutionary or royalist.

CHAPTER EIGHT

Genre Movies: Art from
a Putty Knife Factory

This irreverent chapter title is, as older readers will know, from H. Allen Smith's satire on Hollywood, *Life in a Putty Knife Factory* (1946), a book that echoed every New York writer's public contempt for the movies' company town. Their kvetching stemmed from the incongruity between Hollywood and their romantic notion of themselves as free spirits creating in noble solitude. In New York they were "authors," but in Hollywood they were mere "writers." In New York they sat alone in their apartments, lost in their private visions, pecking away at their novels. In Hollywood, they rewrote other people's stuff, sat in story conferences, trimmed their scripts to please the moguls and the Hays office, and punched in and out as though they were on the line at Lockheed (though at $2,500, their weekly paycheck was a good deal higher than an assembly line worker's). Worst of all, like all artists, they fancied themselves above the moil of the market, only to find that the moguls meant for them to cater to it.

This meant catering to an audience who did not have the same expectations of the movies that perhaps the writers had, an audience for whom going to the movies had become a habit and movies themselves "the flicks," rather than works of art. Perhaps genre movies were hammered into form by the symbiosis between these two forces, maker and consumer. After all, the "sure-seaters," as *Variety* called them, were the only moviegoers who knew what they wanted, and what they wanted was a variation on something they already knew, whether western or musical or film noir. By playing to this community, moviemakers arrived over time at a codification of movies' traits that became what Sloan calls "cultural signposts of paramount importance."

At issue in this formulation of genre movies is a politics of movies. Recent leftist critics have identified genre movies as palliatives designed to induce acceptance rather than action. John Cawelti, Robert Warshow, and Thomas Schatz have all analyzed the genre movie as a familiar but variable form that contributed to a cohesive, if not coherent, culture. In *American Film Genres* (1974), Stuart Kaminsky invokes the influential work of Northrop Frye in asserting that genre movies were universal in a way Frye meant when he said "archetypal," in that they were about the unremarkable lives and deaths of common folk. In this sense, they presented a system of symbols and conventions that endlessly rehashed—and rarely resolved—the problems of the common folk of American life and history. Indeed, the rehashing was the heart of the forging process. Robert Ray writes in *A Certain Tendency of the Hollywood Cinema* (1985) that genre movies' obvious redundancy arose in part from the irreconcilable issues they endlessly reiterated, such as the tension between the individual and society, between the Indian and the European, between the rural and urban. Owen Wister's Virginian in *The Virginian* (1929), Ernest Haycox's Ringo Kid in *Stage to Lordsburg* (which in 1939 became John Ford's *Stagecoach*), and Nicholas Ray's westerners are, like Huck Finn, both creatures of American culture and fugitives from it, a sensibility in conflict with itself and therefore endlessly worried over and picked at, in much the same way Henry Wirz picks at his wound in MacKinlay Kantor's *Andersonville*.

Hollywood seemed to be both temple and countinghouse and thus to represent an ethical conflict of interests. This play of conflicting interests made their relationship with moviegoers symbiotic: they released genre films that they liked, and hoped moviegoers would also like, and moviegoers voted with their feet and wallets whether each new movie was hot or not. Were the two sides behaving like John Kenneth Galbraith's "countervailing forces"? In a way, one critic, Rick Altman, argues this point when he writes that movies "respect . . . the play of contradictory forces." Not to see this play in the wheels of movie commerce is to fall in line with critics who have found Hollywood movies so good at what they did—providing a narrative that flowed compellingly toward its satisfying ending—that the viewer is all but powerless to challenge the ideology embedded in the story.

I suggest that although moviemakers were certainly precise in what they did to reach their audiences with fare they would find pleasing, they were not surgically so. They sometimes missed their mark, were off-putting in their art or politics, flopped miserably, or sent garbled messages. In addition, stories abound of auteurs deftly lacing movies with elements of their styles or politics, resulting in "rebel texts within the Hollywood empire," as Barbara Klinger calls them in "Cinema/Ideology/Criticism" in Barry Keith Grant's *Film Genre Reader* (1986). In *Shadow of a Doubt* (1943), for example, Alfred Hitchcock twitted America's idolatry of the virtues of the family by insinuating into it the same sort of nameless dread that colored Val Lewton's gothic *Curse of the Cat People* (1944). Also, perhaps because they were less thought out, genre movies were sometimes spiked with unconscious imagery. This usually happened in the B genre movies, but it could also happen in the A ones. In *Stagecoach* (1939), for example, we can see Ford's wry vision of life overriding his Catholic conservatism in the scene in which a lawman allows the Ringo Kid to light out for Mexico, suggesting that justice is done only when law officers violate their oaths. In Ernest Schoedsack and Merian Cooper's *King Kong* (1933), the hairy hero's death is attributed to his obsession with beauty, but the densely packed images of capitalist greed suggest otherwise.

The occasional insinuation of the auteur's true politics notwithstanding, genre movies dealt in well-worn conventions. That is, moviemakers behaved as artists in any other medium did. Canaletto could not have painted his *vedutas* of the Grand Canal or Jacques Callot his etchings of sprawling Spanish fairs without the conventions provided by the concept of perspective. The conventions of Dutch still-life painters obliged almost every canvas to contain broken bread and its crumbs, a half-peeled lemon, a goblet that has caught the light, and so on. Likewise, biographers have long shaped the raw data of their subjects' lives into conventional episodes of maturation, conversion, efforts made against the odds, and so forth in order to shape life into a source from which lessons and morals may be drawn. Movies drew deeply on this narrative form, mainly because of the considerable value Western culture places on heroism, particularly heroism in the name of a cause or quest.

This social angle gave both substance and meaning to genre movies. Indeed, their endless reassertion of familiar traits constituted a "contract" with the audience, the terms of which required what Schatz calls in *Hollywood Genres* (1981) "formal strategies for renegotiating and reinforcing American ideology." That this was so may be seen in the frequency with which genre movies came ready-made from other media. For example, the westerns *The*

Virginian (the movie and television show) and *The Spoilers* (1923), both remade frequently, came from Owen Wister's and Rex Beach's popular novels; the horror movie *The Phantom of the Opera* (1925), another frequent remake, was taken from Gaston Leroux's novel; the film noir *The Maltese Falcon* (1941) came from the most famous of Dashiell Hammett's hard-boiled detective novels; the musical *Oklahoma!* (1943) came from Lynn Riggs's drama *Green Grow the Lilacs*; and the boxing yarn *The Set Up* (1949) was based on a poem by Joseph Moncure March.

The genre that lasted the longest, surviving peaks and troughs of popularity, was the western. The first western, *The Great Train Robbery*, appeared in 1903, bringing to the screen conventions from the melodramatic stage and from Buffalo Bill Cody's Wild West shows. More than any other genre, the western possessed a capacity for touching the American soul, serving almost, James Agee claimed, as a "native ritual dance." As quoted by Jeremy Morton Paine in *The Simplification of American Life* (1988), the French critic Andre Bazin argues that the western taught an American culture "distilled from several myths into a pure state." It is in the purity of repetitive form (such as the ritual clash between civilization, represented by the sheriff and the schoolmarm, and savagery, represented by the lone gun) that Robert Ray, in *A Certain Tendency*, finds an inclination to repeat unresolved cultural ambiguities, endlessly worrying them, sometimes confronting them, but never resolving them.

As though to belie their political diffidence, westerns often adopted a dress code—almost a habit—to convey a sense of moral clarity: black hats for the bad guys, white hats for the good guys, as everyone knows. And, as everyone also knows, this distinction eventually became so overdrawn as to approach parody. Alan Ladd's doelike Shane against Jack Palance's hissing black heavy in *Shane* (1953) and James Stewart's stammering bumbler against Lee Marvin's cool, cruel heavy in *The Man Who Shot Liberty Valance* (1962) show an almost operatic excessiveness. Masters of the genre, in contrast, could take liberties with its conventions. For example, the famous gunfight at the OK Corral in Ford's *My Darling Clementine* (1947) pits Doc Holliday (Victor Mature), the black-clad, tubercular good guy, against Ike Clanton, played by Walter Brennan in his usual role as gimpy, amiable rummy suddenly gone cold and lethal.

Such black-and-white encounters notwithstanding, the ambiguities of the western (and of American attitudes) remained. The small town was presented as both idyllic and rife with scheming for water rights, railroad rights of way, and grazing (or farming) land. Life was portrayed as savage but softened by the kindnesses of schoolmarms and gold-hearted prostitutes. Indians were depicted as so blindly hostile as to seem a natural force no different from drought or a sudden blizzard in the high pass and yet at the same time as noble. Caught between civilization and savage, the lone hero embodied the choice between the two worlds. The drama of these ambiguities was enhanced by the natural beauty of the location, whether the familiar roadside rocks of some studio's own "ranch" or humbling Monument Valley, which Ford made use of during his entire career.

Westerns, then, were remarkably accessible and presented scenes that lived long lives in their fans' memories. The critic Pauline Kael has said that her father saw a western "every night of his life," no matter what. Binx, the protagonist in Walker Percy's novel *The Moviegoer*, always remembers the scene in *Stagecoach* after the Ringo Kid shoots Luke Plummer (off camera). The scenes I carry around are of Billy the Kid alone in a high-ceilinged cave, tending his small wisp of a fire, and Noah Beery Jr., standing at the chuck wagon, licking sugar off his finger in *Red River*. This latter memory always brings the sensation that I had at the time, along with every other kid in the theater, of waiting for the impending clatter of a tin pan that would set off the stampede.

To liken the actors' costumes to a habit is perhaps not an inspired simile, but it nonetheless conveys the sense of religious ritual with which westerns were imbued, not unlike traditional theater in any culture. A Stetson, its wide brim curled against the crown by daily riding in the wind; a sidearm, holstered and tied to the thigh by a thong; faded Levi's, rolled at the bottom; cheap, low-cut cowboy boots; and a rough shirt, often a blue or grey cavalryman's blouse, indicating which side had been taken in the Civil War—these articles of clothing made up the habit of a monkish order from which there was no apostasy.

Of course, over time the outsized neckerchiefs, leather cuffs, and work gloves that real cowboys found necessary were replaced with Hollywood trappings, such as horses' tack bedecked with hand-tooled silver, ten-gallon (or bigger) hats, shirts with piping on them, and hand-tooled boots that call to mind the tastes of Liberace or the later Elvis, rather than the austere aesthetics of the real cowboy. And they seemed to live off the air itself during their months on the Goodnight or Chisholm Trail: no blanket rolls stuffed with poncho, linen duster, and the staples of coffee, salt, fatback, dried beans, and canned peaches. There were no politics to be seen anywhere, either. Totally unconscious politically, they were concerned more with their principles, which were as clear to them as the air.

The bad guys, of course, had their own getups. Armed "road agents" wore masks, naturally; traveling gangs of bandits wore motley garb; shyster lawyers, cattle barons, and gamblers strode through the streets of the cattle towns in string ties and frock coats concealing two-shot Derringers. They connived to gain water and mineral rights, sold whiskey to Indians, drove out "nesters" and "sodbusters," and talked up the new railroads (in which they had secret holdings, of course). Indian heavies, much rarer than one might recall in the western canon, ranged from mindlessly murderous marauders to noble savages to hapless victims under the flawed protection of the cavalry or at the mercy of corrupt Indian agents.

In hundreds of westerns these dramatis personae were put in the service of dramatizing the unspoken enigmas of American culture. For example, the individual's right to his or her property was exalted in a society that eschewed hereditary aristocracy, but it also undermined the sense of community. The movies' unremitting emphasis on water, land, and mineral rights ritually dramatized the conflict between individual and social interests, without resolving it. During the 1920s no fewer than twenty-eight movies dramatized the issue of water rights. Two of them appeared within sixty days of each other in 1930: *Shadow Ranch* and *The Dawn Trail*. As was characteristic of the genre, *The Dawn Trail* evaded resolution by means of a tacked-on ending in which the boss of the cattlemen abandons his struggle against the sheep drovers after inadvertently killing his own son.

Class issues were similarly obliterated. Conflict was most often a matter of individual good and evil or of opposing interests, such as those of cattle drovers and shepherds. If class was brought in, it was by introducing various characters who by dress or manner represented the various social strata. *Stagecoach*, for example, is peopled by a whining whiskey salesman; an embezzling banker; a courtly (and thus southern, one knew) gambler; a prim eastern matron heading west to join her officer husband; another woman with a darker past; and, of course, poor but honest Ringo, being taken back to do time for avenging his father's murder. On the drivers' box are a good-hearted teamster and the equally good-hearted lawman who will let Ringo escape across the Rio Grande. In this way, the cinematically brilliant *Stage-*

coach introduced itself as portraying the clash of classes in the microcosm of the moving coach. But by reducing the scale to individual dramas it accomplished no more than did dozens of its cinematic inferiors—picking up the issue but in the last reel returning it unaltered to the very spot it had been found. The stagecoach riders' sole collective act is a running firefight against a war party of Indian cavalry.

The dramatic role of the U.S. cavalry in the American settling of the West most reveals the ambiguities of western American history, and moviemakers in the classical era used the cavalry more than any other entity to stand for the best and the worst in American culture. In every western command, it seemed, the officers lined up as either doctrinaires or mavericks, each type proving the value of the other to the Army. Consider Nathan Brittles in *She Wore a Yellow Ribbon* (1949) and George Custer in *They Died with Their Boots On* (1941). Both rashly violate orders in their last campaign, Brittles showing the value of independent command and Custer showing that Army doctrine has its uses. In addition, the yellow-kerchiefed soldiers almost always proclaim their respect for Indian foes or demonstrate it by learning "plainscraft," Walter Prescott Webb's word for the survival skills needed west of the 98th meridian. Or as Buffalo Bill Cody puts it in reply to a question as he surveys the fallen warriors after a skirmish in *Buffalo Bill* (1944): "They were all my friends."

Respect for American Indians extended throughout Euro-American culture. Almost coincident with the coming of movies, the Boy Scouts of America appeared, modeled in part on Lord Baden-Powell's British boys groups and in part on the plainscraft and woodcraft of Indians, which also served as the basis for the novels of the German author Karl Mays, who wrote western novels in German. The Boy Scout movement paralleled trends such as the Campfire Girls and literary fads such as Dan Beard's *Buckskin Book for Boys* and Ernest Thompson Seton's *Wild Animals I Have Known*. As early as 1909, D. W. Griffith's *Broken Doll* suggested that Indians had similar regard for European culture, symbolized by a broken doll that a white girl gives to an Indian girl, who clutches it to her breast in her last-reel death scene. Later, during the New Deal, such movies formed a prestigious, if not smashing, cycle of A movies. Included were *Laughing Boy* (1934), MGM's film of Oliver LaFarge's Pulitzer Prize–winning novel, and Fox's thrice-made *Ramona* (1916, 1928, 1936), the movie version of Helen Hunt Jackson's novel of struggle among Spanish Californios and Indians, and *Massacre* (1934), a tale of cross-cultural conflict in which an Indian briefly trades traditional culture for an empty life in a white man's school and on the road with a black valet in a Wild West show.

During World War II, the nation's propaganda against Hitler's racism helped revive the movement. Fox brought to the screen its biopic of Buffalo Bill Cody, along with *Devil's Doorway* (1950) and *Broken Arrow* (1949), in which Indians take a stand against European culture not merely as nameless warriors but as members of a free-standing, indigenous culture. The conservative Ford even dipped a toe into the debate in *She Wore a Yellow Ribbon* (1949), having Nathan Brittles and Chief John Big Tree mourn the old days of peace with honor that threatened to be shattered by the warmongers of each group.

In contrast to their portrayal of the military conquest of the West, the moviemakers' portrayal of the exploitation of the West for its agricultural and mineral wealth was unreflective, even blind. Without exception, *The Iron Horse* (1924), *Covered Wagon* (1923), *Cimarron* (1931), *Western Union* (1941), *Boom Town* (1940), *Union Pacific* (1939), and a half-dozen later epics of the railroad frontier celebrated manifest destiny as though it were the Gospel. Only rarely was the struggle for the frontier presented as a mosaic of complex issues, as it was in Ford's "eastern" western, *Drums along the Mohawk* (1939), set in the Mohawk Valley of New York during the Revolution. Even less frequently was the struggle between cattlemen and railroaders portrayed as a conflict in which there were losers as well as winners. *Duel in the Sun* (1946) is one example.

No American trait so engaged the writers of westerns as the linkage of manhood to private violence and the private bearing of arms. Countless westerns climaxed in a violent duel between two adversaries. Conflict was distilled down to its dramatic essentials: men in individual combat meant to settle a moral or personal (the two are coequal in westerns) argument. The decay of the western, as Hemingway predicted of any art form in which personal courage under pressure is the core of the dramatic conflict, began precisely at its high point. With the release of several superb so-called adult westerns—William Wellman's *The Ox-Bow Incident* (1943), Ford's *My Darling Clementine* (1947), and Stanley Kramer and Fred Zinnemann's *High Noon* (1952)—signs of rot were beginning to be evident, and the genre bottomed out in the stark, iconic, Freudian westerns of the 1950s.

B movies, in which form mattered even more because the sure-seaters' tastes were more ossified than those of the art house crowd, persisted as a genre during World War II, even surviving later in their pristine form as television series. However, it was during the war that they begin to garble their own codes by trotting in one too many gimmicks, such as "Lash" Larue and his animated whip; Roy Rogers and "the smartest horse in the movies"; and Sammy Baugh, the Washington Redskins' quarterback who played a Texas Ranger who threw football-like missiles at the bad guys; and ever so many crooning cowboys costumed in fancy piped shirts, tailored pants, and hand-tooled boots instead of work clothes.

As for A westerns, *The Ox-Bow Incident* broke with the unspoken Lockean individualist politics of the genre by consciously offering itself as a warning of the rise of fascism. It also differed from other westerns in that it was shot on the 20th Century-Fox lot amidst overly gnarled trees that offended James Agee with their artiness. *My Darling Clementine* actually started out not as a western, but as Wendell Willkie's plea for a world order under the aegis of the United Nations. After this pet project of Zanuck's died in surgery, its parts were exhumed by the Oscar-winning writer Lamar Trotti for Ford's western, and the horrors of war that it had inveighed against became the gunfight at the OK Corral. Local color was painted in with a too-heavy hand—Doc Holliday with his cough, Wyatt Earp with his laconic manner in the lank body of Henry Fonda, the manic hatreds carried in the breast of Ike Clanton as played against type by Walter Brennan. Five years later, in 1952, Carl Foreman, a wartime lefty on his way to being blacklisted for his politics, wrote *High Noon* to sound an alarm against the rising tide of political intolerance that carried the name of its instigator, Joseph McCarthy. In this movie, Gary Cooper, in a twist on his roles as loner in *The Virginian* and DeMille's version of Wild Bill Hickok in *The Plainsman*, played a marshal who aches for a sense of community and acts out his moral solitude reluctantly, only because the town council will not join him in a fight against vengeful bandits.

Of them all, George Stevens's *Shane* (1953) most showed the overripeness of the genre. Alan Ladd as Shane is Everyman, wearing a hodgepodge of gear from all types of westerners: the high-heeled boots of a drover; the low-slung, pearl-handled weapon of a gunslinger; the split-seamed pants of a vaquero; the fringed buckskin shirt from the northern high plains; and the too perfect Stetson that sits back on his head as if he were a chorus boy in *Oklahoma!* He is so airily remote from civilization he seems spectral. His rival

(Jack Palance) is also stylized (predictably, in black) to the extent that he seems a caricature. Indeed, when he polishes off his first innocent townsperson (Elisha Cook Jr., veteran of dozens of roles as feckless, whiny loser), Palance is so oily, hissing, and sneering as to draw cheers of appreciation from audiences enthralled by his bold flirtation with campiness. The sets are equally mannerist, with three gnarled trees looking suspiciously like the ones that appeared in *The Ox-Bow Incident*.

One of the marvelous accomplishments of the moviemakers who worked in the genre as it was waning was their prescience in capturing the pain of decline in the lives of the saddle tramps, who realized, often after seeing their first airplane or car, that they were on the rim of the dust bin of history. *Butch Cassidy and the Sundance Kid* (1969) and *The Wild Bunch* (1969) did it best, in last-reel confrontations that pit their heroes against entire armies who pursue them in motorcars and gun them down in orgies of overkill. Their almost operatic excesses iconically signaled the end of the genre.

As adept as they were at worrying the moral dilemmas of individualism versus community, the rights of Indians versus westward expansion, and the like, whenever westerns tried for a conscious politics they were quite inept, either garbling their intentions or alienating their intended communicants. The exception to this rule was the cycle of post–World War II movies that advocated a "conscience liberalism." Their particular brand of racial integration within a white circle may have anticipated the nonviolent civil rights movement of 1955 through 1965. Other overtly political movies rarely made clear their preferred reading. It is said that after Kramer and Zinnemann's putatively anti-McCarthy *High Noon* appeared, Howard Hawks made *Rio Bravo* (1959) as a rebuttal, but most reviewers perceived both movies simply as expressions of the heroism in the peace officers' professionalism. In another case of bipolar readings of movies, Robert Sklar, in *Movie-Made America* (1975), vividly recalls John Wayne coolly shooting a Mexican whose land he covets in *Red River*, whereas Alan Casty, in *Development of the Film* (1973), misses this assertion of manifest destiny and writes only of "the sweep of the cattle drive across the prairies and the truly felt and rendered wonders of their vastness."

The fans were more interested in scanning the horizon than in looking for political messages in their westerns, anyway. Most would have agreed with Pauline Kael's father, who was of the opinion that "if you're going for a western, it doesn't matter which one you see." Schatz may mean something akin to this when he describes westerns' "formal strategies for renegotiating and reinforcing American ideology," as mentioned earlier. Robert Ray sees in them, if not this mediating quality, at least an endless redundancy of theme. In *Showdown: Confronting Modern America in the Western Film* (1980), John Lenihan extends this endlessly replayed ambiguity in the cycle of interracial movies, such as *Broken Arrow* (1950), that recapitulated Du Bois's notion of blacks' "twoness" as "both Negro and American." In the end, westerns may have actually wished to have it both ways, resulting, Lenihan writes, in an "individualism [that] has become . . . tempered with the social sensitivity," a cowboy version of the puritans' "collective individualism."

Not that this cowboy centrism eliminated politics entirely from the genre; however, the filmmakers who attempted consciously political westerns were few. On the left, Henry King's *Jesse James* (1940) spoke for many westerns in asserting a populist resistance to the railroad as the ruinous "machine in the garden" of the West and the populist belief that "there's no law for poor folks except at the end of a gun." On the right, writes Lenihan, were fans who exclaimed, "I don't want them changed!" and producers like Nat Holt, who insisted on "having no truck with any social ideas."

Discussion of the western has consumed so much of this chapter because, of all the movie forms, the western most accessibly played out its role as tribal legend. Other genres—screwball comedy, film noir, the musical—all owed debts to older, often European, forms, and all succumbed to numerous pressures to dilute their substance and tame their impulses.

This was particularly true of comedy. Except for Chaplin, almost every comedic actor in Hollywood's preclassical era felt reined in by the emerging system. Frenetic and physical; rife with class antagonisms; hostile to authority; driven by elemental emotions such as spite and revenge; and rooted in the Italian commedia dell'arte, burlesque, and the circus, silent comedy not only gave the world a rich legacy, but also, as David Cook writes in *A History of Narrative Film* (1990), "contributed substantially to America's commercial dominance of world cinema."

Yet the intricately choreographed anarchy and energy of silent comedy lasted only fifteen years, and Laurel and Hardy were the only practitioners to survive in the more controlled era of soundfilm. Mack Sennett, inventor of Keystone comedies and mentor to a generation of slapstick comedians, lapsed into idleness and bankruptcy. Chaplin struggled to maintain his independence, first by cofounding United Artists with D. W. Griffith, Douglas

Fairbanks, and Mary Pickford; then by creating the Chaplin Studio; and finally by withholding his product except under almost fiercely defended
terms. Keaton, unable either to translate a stone-faced manner into sound
imagery or to adapt his style to the emerging system, became an idle "consultant" in Thalberg's MGM. Harry Langdon and others found that a fragile, fey, impishness seemed out of place in the hard times that followed the
Great Crash of 1929.

Thereafter, comedy took the form of the wisecracking shtick, the tightly
timed, polished verbal routines that often drew on Jewish childhoods. Dialogue tricks came to be sources of identity. Mae West had her earthy purr,
W. C. Fields delivered wisecracks under his breath while shooting pool or
juggling, the Marx brothers brought playfully surreal "business" and dialogue from their zany Broadway revues. However, these too would be toned
down at the insistence of studio bosses in need of control over sometimes
expensive spontaneity. In time, West's breathy erotica fell victim to the Hays
office, Fields replaced the bite of his wit with a more benign nibble, and the
Marx brothers were tethered by MGM's insistence on retakes after each preview. Thus the spontaneity of their pioneering sound comedies, *Cocoanuts*
(1929), *Horse Feathers* (1932), and *Duck Soup* (1933) gave way to the likes of
The Big Store (1941) and *Go West* (1940), each with its nonsequitur boy-girl
singing interludes that detract from the business at hand. Their imitators
burned out like Roman candles, either quickly lapsing into B movies (the
Ritz brothers, Olsen and Johnson, and Abbott and Costello) or two-reelers
(Ted Healy's Three Stooges) or, like Martin and Lewis, breaking up and trying their luck as singles.

The burden of satirizing American life and puncturing its pieties fell to
the writers of screwball comedy. Indeed, writing was the backbone of these
movies, and they succeeded only when directors and actors allowed the dialogue to reign. At its best, screwball comedy transformed the inspired vulgarity and lowlife of W. C. Fields and the Marx brothers into a literary form
that played out in plots, which the spontaneity of these forerunners had precluded. In any case, a frothy raffishness became the benchmark of the genre.

Screwball comedies played off the contrasts between elites and masses,
stuffed shirts and rebels, and the bourgeoisie and bohemians, effectively
raising up the contradictions in American myths. They had a sly, wry way of
tweaking the status quo on the nose and holding out prospects for its
change, but they rarely suggested ways to bring about that change. Because

plot twists and phrases were elusive and more difficult to snip than images, within the limits of the Production Code Administration (PCA) screwball comedians played a game of moral and aesthetic croquet that was meant to end in a tie, with the Breen office certain that primness had been saved and the writers fairly certain they had preserved their movie's puckish spirit. The resulting formula began with a merciless kidding of, for example, old money, and ended by finding a nugget of decency at its core.

Not all historians, of course, have approved of these pulled punches. Robert Ray, for example, in *A Certain Tendency* points out the contrast between biting European movies such as *Der Blaue Engel* (1930), in which a teacher's infatuation with a slatternly dancer ends with his losing every shred of his dignity, and American movies in which skirmishes between classes were reduced to cute trivia, such as whether donuts should be dunked or nibbled dry. Yet Bazin (quoted by James Harvey in *Romantic Comedy in Hollywood from Lubitsch to Sturges* [1987]) has argued that screwball comedy was America's "most serious genre" because it took up "the deepest moral and social beliefs of American life." The contradiction in Bazin's argument lies in the fact that institutional intervention clipped the wings of Hollywood comedy while the result stood as American "cultural myth making." If screwball comedy was mythic, part of its myth included throttling, as Sklar writes in *Movie-Made America*, "those dangerous levers of social change."

A few comic movies promoted the notion that hardworking little people can triumph over adversity without resorting to class warfare. Frank Capra's fables of the well-meaning outsider who shakes the establishment—*Mr. Smith Goes to Washington* (1939), *Mr. Deeds Goes to Town* (1936), and *Meet John Doe* (1941)—all ended with individual heroes winning against external threats by the powerful. Walt Disney's animated cartoon *The Three Little Pigs* (1933) also celebrated the Calvinist effort against misfortune. It is only the hard-working pig who builds his house with brick who prevails against the wolf at the door (the Great Depression, to be sure) confirming the bourgeois values of hard work, thrift, and investment as bulwarks against hard times.

For producers, such as Ernst Lubitsch, who came from a continental tradition of sidelong, dry, drawing room humor, sly indirection and double entendre became part of the game they played with the PCA watchdogs. But the point was the same: to maximize humor or politics within institutional limits. Obviously, this indirection induced by the marathon game with the

PCA was at the heart of a quarrel between the left and the movies. Robert Ray, for example, finds *The Philadelphia Story* (1940) an illustration of how Hollywood shifted focus from class difference to morals. A mainline Philadelphia woman is divorced by her rakish aristocratic husband, who finds her too prim. Later her planned marriage to another man, a journalist who is hardly of her class, fizzles when she has an innocent late-night escapade with her ex-husband. Her newly revealed streak of impishness offends her sober, hard-working intended groom and draws her into remarriage with her former husband, who sees in her a now charmingly reformed puritan. This final moral choice, writes Ray, diverts attention from the class issues with which the movie opens.

Waggish critics took special aim at Frank Capra's fables of warmhearted naifs, calling them "Capra-corn." In *We're in the Money* (1972), Andrew Bergman calls Capra's work "Saturday Evening Post socialism" that gave fans "a glow of satisfaction." However, after World War II, those fans made it clear that the war had transformed them and that movies must follow. Capra's *It's a Wonderful Life* (1946) replayed the old story of the good soul, filled with self-doubt and beset by devious heavies (flinty bankers, in this case), but able, in the end, to restore an old-fashioned moral order. This time the fans stayed home, as though preparing to stand in line for 1948's *The Snake Pit* and *The Naked City* and the other realist movies soon to come.

The musical comedy strummed similar emotional chords. Like movies in general, the musical grew out of loosely linked vaudeville turns presented in revue form, such as Earl Carroll's *Vanities* or *The Ziegfeld Follies*. At the same time, the romantic Italian and Viennese operetta came to America, giving a narrative line to the handiwork of composers such as Victor Herbert. In the late 1920s, the form added a dramatic dimension wrapped in a more highly developed plotline; Jerome Kern and Oscar Hammerstein's *Show Boat* (1927, 1936, 1951) and Marc Connelly's *The Green Pastures* (1929 as drama, then 1936) are prime examples of this. In the hands of innovators like Busby Berkeley and Fred Astaire (who choreographed his own RKO musicals), new tools gave the musical a new sense of vibrant motion; optical effects; and, in its narrative parts, a heightened drama that itself was carried by the songs and music. At the height of its powers, in the hands of the Arthur Freed unit at MGM, the musical achieved a distinctive American voice, at once romantic, driven by the high energy of syncopated music, and rooted in the myth of individual aspiration. From 1943, when *Cabin in the Sky* came out, through 1952, which brought *Singin' in the Rain*, MGM polished the genre into a unique art form that survives in the occasional attempts of today's moviemakers to imitate it and to match its elusive charm.

Of all the genres, the most insistently political was film noir, with its despairing portrayal of America as John Kenneth Galbraith described it—a civilization marked by private excess and public squalor. Equal parts old-time gangster movie and social problem movie, film noir sketched an America down at the heels, wheedlingly corrupt, despondent over the unexpectedly mixed results of victory after World War II, and, far from the New Deal optimism with which it had entered the war, consumed by a vague dread. Gangster movies had portrayed a similar aspect, but they had always ended on a social workerish upbeat. Both genres depicted a moody streetscape marked by darkened doorways occupied by darker versions of Capra's little people. But the difference between 1936 and 1946 was that whereas in 1936 such streets had caused remediable crime, in 1946 they merely provided a nutrient milieu for it.

Both the gangster film and the film noir lent themselves to the needs of the system. The characters were "the same, only different," and thus adaptive to the routine of the movie lots, particularly those with a darkened, tightly focused style that kept costs down, such as Warner Bros. and RKO. Even the actors came cheap, "the Cagney role" readily filled by either a promising underachiever, such as Dick Purcell, or a fading star, such as Ricardo Cortez. Moreover, both genres enjoyed the cooperation of civilians, whose contributions helped cut costs. Reformist judges and wardens lent their images and institutions to the cause of gangster movies, and on-location shooting, once rare, became common as urban governments lent aid to film noir projects. Their differences appeared only in the last reel, when, in gangster movies, society learned to reform and thereby remedy the causes of crime, whereas in the film noir outcomes were more ominously ambiguous.

Not that the two forms were polar opposites in their politics; after all, one was the ideological parent of the other. Both genres often evaded the implications of their premises. In the older genre, the first-reel general problem was solved as the singular case that engaged the hero. Or, lacking the special pleading given it by the hero's attention, the problem was often quietly dropped or even recast in a surprise turn of the plot in the last reel. In *Black Fury* (1935), for example, the union-busting capitalists presented in the first reel are made to look relatively good in the end, when renegade goons are revealed to be the real heavies. "If anything," observed a reviewer in *Variety*, capitalism was "given a subtle boost." Thus gangster movies wore their conservative politics not on their sleeves but up them.

Postwar film noir often opened on a bleak world in which all rules seemed to have been written in disappearing ink. The hero was a loner, and denouement derived from liberating revenge, rather than social redemption. Clearly, the worst sort of disillusionment—that of victors—clouded postwar morale and helped prepare Americans for film noir. The light of victory and its accompanying prosperity was shadowed as society's ills, patriotically censored during the war, were gradually revealed. War profiteering, slacking, and draft dodging all merged with a postwar slump; a burst of inflation; the scent of corruption in Washington; and, worst of all, a profound change in the posture of our wartime ally, the Soviet Union. Accompanying the Soviet Union's defection from Churchill's Grand Alliance against Nazism was a sense of intrigue, betrayal, and a chill that would eventually become the Cold War. Finally, there came the revelations of the Nazis' anti-Semitic genocide and, at home, a rise in juvenile delinquency, long-suppressed racial antipathy, and labor strife in the coal and steel industries and indeed in Hollywood itself. Heady victory? More like Cornwallis's band at Yorktown in 1781 when it played "The World Turned Upside Down."

Because it challenged the facile narrative style of prewar Hollywood, film noir made possible a new politics of the movies. Certainly, Abraham Polonsky must have thought so when he wrote *Body and Soul* (1947), a dark movie in which the boxing arena was used as an allegory for the meanness of capitalism. So must have Harry Belafonte, whose firm later engaged Polonsky to transform a suspense novel set in the milieu of small-time bankrobbers into an allegory of racism and its nasty fruits, his *Odds against Tomorrow* (1959). Directed by Robert Wise, who had begun by directing one of Val Lewton's gothic noir movies of the midwar era, *Curse of the Cat People* (1944), *Odds against Tomorrow* combined the dark cityscape of film noir with the politics of the racial left that had carried over from the war.

In any case, the evocative combination of realism and studio gloss eloquently sketched a once stable society turned on its end. Killers seemed adolescently attractive, and the actors who portrayed them, like Alan Ladd, were so good at what they did that they quickly lost whatever range they once possessed.

Cops were not so much forces for good as simply gruff harness bulls, cynics on the take, or merely burnt-out gumshoes. The bad guys often came from a sleekly groomed elite with an eye for a chance to fence a stash of hot ice. Their women were pouty, tipsy debutantes or good–bad women who seemed too at home on the chrome stools of dark saloons. In these movies, fatalism thwarted every quest and revealed every grail to be tarnished or empty. In *The Glass Key* (1942), *This Gun for Hire* (1942), *In a Lonely Place* (1940), and *Somewhere in the Night* (1946), the story was the same: dark forces, forlorn hopes, a world in disarray.

The Maltese Falcon (1941) attained a beautiful, almost too neatly turned style that its creator, Dashiell Hammett, must have liked for its streetwise, witty cynicism. Its young director, John Huston, turned the quest for a holy grail—actually a jewel-encrusted black bird once given by the Holy Roman Emperor Charles V to the Knights Templar who had settled on Malta after the Crusades—into a descent through the lower life of San Francisco. Everyone is either larcenous or murderous, with the exception of Sam Spade, who lives by a simple code of personal ethics that neither of his adversaries—cops or crooks—understands. Spade, played by Humphrey Bogart, tells Mary Astor, the girlish, stammering, and nonetheless lethal killer, that he will lose sleep over turning her in but will remember, even "wait for," her. He probably means it. Because despite the dram of cynicism that flavors his every coolly wise line, Spade's (and our) upended world holds together only because of the privately held codes of a few lone men of integrity.

The genre took form during the war, cobbled from the remains of gangster movies and gothic fiction. Val Lewton's RKO gems, *Cat People* (1942) and later *Curse of the Cat People*; Fritz Lang's movie of Graham Greene's novel *Ministry of Fear* (1945); and other midwar suspense movies rested on character-driven plots. But while still in prototype, the genre also was wasted on the seriocomic *All through the Night* (1943), which was meant to fold the gangster movie into the war effort by reworking Lang's *M* (1931), his Universum Film Aktiengesellschaft film in which criminals, not cops, catch a Berlin child killer. In *All through the Night,* the child killer is replaced by sneering German spies.

Perhaps the most polished gem in the evolving genre was Michael Curtiz's *Casablanca* (1942). Its setting, a shakily neutral country during World War II, was perfect for inventing a closed world in which nothing is what it seems and where spies, refugees, and men on the run contend for documents that will allow them passage to America. The script, by Howard Koch and Julius and Philip Epstein, worked because it allows Bogart as Rick, the owner of the fabled Cafe Americain, his cynicism (rooted in an unspoken past) and yet develops him into the anti-Nazi warrior that Americans had become. The movie possessed all the elements for success: the cynical but principled lone hero, the woman in need of rescue from shadowy bad guys, the closed society without rules.

After the war, the mood was right to stir into these ingredients a few legacies from other sources: newly arrived Italian neorealism movies, echoes of German expressionism, and a revival of interest in Freud that followed from the use of psychoanalysis in the treatment of "combat fatigue." Roberto Rossellini's antifascist street movies *Open City* (1946) and *Paisan* (1948) portrayed outsiders (partisans and even, in *Paisan*, a black man) taking a stand against the German occupiers, who had little to fear from the army and police. Casty in *Development of the Film* also finds film noir's sources in the frayed despair, raffishness, and romantic moodiness of French gangster films such as *Pepe Le Moko* (1941) and the dark streetscapes of Lang's legendary *M*. In America, the emerging genre cast doubt on established institutions, such as the police (*The Maltese Falcon* [1941]) and hospitals (*Murder My Sweet* [1945]); even rare book dealers were not exempt (*The Big Sleep* [1946]). As Cook points out in *A History of Narrative Film*, all of it was shot in chiaroscuro tones befitting the "postwar disenchantment with American life."

The tour de force of the genre was *The Fallen Sparrow*, which Warner Bros. released in 1943. This movie anticipated the cultural paranoia that would impel the Cold War, and it did so by portraying not a shadowy Soviet menace breaching America's defenses, but rather a nameless Spanish fascist demimonde, attired in formal dinner jackets and gowns. Covert and seemingly purposeless in their hounding of a panicking, battle-shattered American veteran of the Spanish Civil War, they hope to drive him mad in an effort to recover Falangist battle flags without which Franco cannot have complete victory. Driven to night sweats by the memory of the sound of a crippled foot being dragged at night along a hallway, a sound that preceded torture sessions in a Spanish jail, the hero cannot persuade his woman, the police, or anyone else that his fears are a response to a real threat. Every stick of furniture, every shadow conspires to heighten this dread against which there is no defense, an anticipatory allegory of the mood of the early Cold War: even victory did not guarantee freedom from fear.

Dozens of such movies introduced film noir to American audiences.

Eventually, their psychological center shifted away from the war to return to conventional (and now threatening) urban settings. Their varied sources seemed bottomless wells of inventions designed to exploit Americans' postwar angst. Alfred Hitchcock's *Spellbound* (1945), George Cukor's *Gaslight* (1944), and Vincent Minnelli's *The Clock* (1945) exploited the fad for Freud. Hitchcock's *Shadow of a Doubt* (1943) and Otto Preminger's *Laura* (1944) introduced the threat of violence into even the tightest circles of family and friends. Jules Dassin's *The Naked City* and Henry Hathaway's *Call Northside 777* (1948) drew on the rhetoric of prewar social problem movies. *The Red Menace* (1949) and its B-movie clones were alarmist versions designed to make a quick buck while playing sycophant to the House Un-American Activities Committee. Even westerns drew on the form, for example, in Nicholas Ray's *Johnny Guitar* (1954), in which the urge to toughen women's roles in the West resulted in a mise-en-scène that exuded sadomasochism.

The High Middle Ages of the genre started when Raymond Chandler's seamy, down-at-the-heels Los Angeles and his cynical but ethical detective Philip Marlowe appeared on the screen. In contrast with Hammett's San Francisco, whose smarminess was relieved by a touch of whimsy, Chandler's Los Angeles was irredeemably sleazy. His *Murder My Sweet* (1945), starring Dick Powell, and *The Big Sleep* (1946), written for the screen by William Faulkner and starring Bogart, came to the screen a year apart. In these tales of lawlessness and decaying elites, not one police officer makes an appearance. Los Angeles is like rotted fruit, its institutions inert, its civic life dying, its nights alive only with the activities of crooks. At least in Hammett's San Francisco there are some safe havens, such as the brightly lit John's Grill. In both movies, Marlowe is beaten senseless and learns how close to the edge even the most knowing private eye can be and how high the price is for a lone man to cling to his private code.

Perhaps the apogee of the genre was John Huston's film of W. R. Burnett's *The Asphalt Jungle* (1950). The cast is stratified according to its distance from the scavengers who feed on the bottom of their fetid pool, this time a squalid eastern city. All of the principals in a jewelry theft fall victim to their own weaknesses, not because the PCA obliged them to but because Burnett aimed for a classical tragedy rooted in hubris and human failings. With oily eagerness, Emmerich, the elegant aristocrat (Louis Calhern), agrees to bankroll the caper; Riemenschneider, "the Doc" just freed from "the walls," has a plan for a last big score before retiring; Cobby, the cheap gambler, likes the action and the association with the elites of his world; and Dix, a vile-tempered petty crook who plays the horses, is to be "the mechanic," the hired gun and driver. But the wheels soon come off their job: Emmerich wants too much and is willing to betray them to get it; the Doc has an eye for the nubile feminine form, takes too long to ogle a dancer at a jukebox, and is nabbed; and Dix's impulsiveness gets him mortally wounded (he is able to flee only as far as Kentucky, where he dies in the grass at the feet of a curious thoroughbred). Although every character is given his defining scene, two of them with their women, who are sidebars to the main plotline, the movie's real star is the corrupt city. Indeed, Burnett's story is unrelieved by either a Marlowe or a Spade.

Thereafter, few movies in the genre managed to hold to the encoded values at their centers. Even those that offered richly noir moments suffered for want of the little engines at the core of Chandler's and Hammett's stories, that is, the protagonists' abiding wish to embrace an unyielding ethical code. Edgar Ulmer's *Gun Crazy* (1950) was perhaps the first "road movie" that followed a youthful duo to their deaths after a shooting spree. In *Rope* (1948), Hitchcock not only mocked the genre by making murder a game, filming the whole movie on a claustrophobic single set, and making sly use of an incredibly lengthy shot, but also turned the tables and allowed a coolheaded cop to solve the murder.

As any reader might guess, film noir, like the musical and the western, declined less as a result of the loss of some inner value or the addition of some rococo conceit or mannerist excess than as a result of changes in the circumstances of its production and in its audience's taste-culture. Movies and their audiences both changed after World War II. Movies changed because the Supreme Court's ruling in the Paramount case (1948) obliged the studios to divorce themselves from the oligopoly that their chains of theaters had given them. The audience changed because the postwar burst of private wealth provided a centrifugal force that, along with a racist wish to preserve social distance between blacks and whites, impelled urbanites toward their cultural doom in the green-lawned suburbs far from the broadways and rialtos and downtowns that had once provided them with a densely cultured experience, of which movies had been a big part.

If these genre films were no more than the visual equivalent of the die-stamped products of an assembly line, we would study the line much more than we would study the grommets or O-rings or countersunk wood screws that the line spat out. But as we have seen, genre movies, despite their status as a product of a rationalized system, were also somewhat like the individualized output of an atelier. Though they cleaved to their specific traits, they offered a range of quality (and a range of readings to their fans) that never would have been tolerated by the Pass/Reject gauges of the grommet-making assembly line. Each movie was meant to be different, even if "the same, only different." By achieving this, genre movies in all their forms—western, musical, and film noir—became the cash earners that made the whole Hollywood system possible between the two world wars. As cash earners, they played out the game of the marketplace: customers sought the satisfaction of having their old, familiar expectations fulfilled by a new product that manufacturers had assembled and distributors had retailed on the basis of a template provided by past box office returns. Admittedly, because good genre movies were much like Victorien Sardou's or Arthur Wing Pinero's well-made plays in their familiar situations, climaxes, and denouements, they could be considered advocates of a changeless status quo, voices of the center. But who knew them as such? Certainly not their fans, who went to see them for their images of a fast-drawing cowboy, an elegant woman seated beside her white telephone, a lithe dancer swirling through "Puttin' on the Ritz," and a lisping Bogart slickly disarming Wilmer, the little killer.

CHAPTER NINE

Hollywood Goes
to War

Roger Dooley ends *From Scarface to Scarlett* (1981), his celebration of the movies of Hollywood's classical era, with the ur-year 1939, and Clayton Koppes and Gregory Black begin their *Hollywood Goes to War* (1987) with a sketch of the same year. Independently of each other, the authors of these two books were taking the same point of view: that crises alter circumstances in ways that starkly break off one era from another. In this case, it was an era of fragile peace from an era of international war. Much as the year 1500 has come to stand for the end of the Middle Ages and the beginning of the Italian Renaissance, so 1939 has come to be seen as a watershed. Just as Botticelli's humanist *The Birth of Venus* followed Fra Angelico's medievalism, and Fra Filippo Lippi's virgin/madonna exuded a holy spiritualism whereas those of Ghirlandaio seemed at home in a secular Florentine apartment, so the movies made before and after 1939 seem as though they are from different cultures.

Moreover, in both instances the makers of their arts played to what Peter Burke in *The Italian Renaissance* (1987) calls an "art world" of, in the first instance, a clientele of popes, doges, and *condottieri* and, in the second, a clientele of fans and moviegoers. The point, of course, is that changed circumstances resulted in newly creative ideas by new artists who offered their work to a changed "art world." Moreover, in both Hollywood and Florence, but Hollywood especially, the last days of the old culture somehow brought forth a canon of works that reached a zenith of critical and popular success.

The year brought John Ford's softened version of Steinbeck's populist novel *The Grapes of Wrath* (actually released in January of 1940) and his beau ideal western, *Stagecoach*; George Stevens's colonialist romp *Gunga Din*;

Greta Garbo as a screwball Marxist in *Ninotchka*; Laurence Olivier in Sam Goldwyn's *Wuthering Heights*; Juarez and Ford's bio pic *Young Mr. Lincoln;* Rouben Mamoulian's faithful rendering of Odets's social drama of the fight game, *Golden Boy*; Claire Booth Luce and George Cukor's catty screwball comedy *The Women*; Frank Capra's *Mr. Smith Goes to Washington*; Raoul Walsh's recapitulation of an old-time gangster movie in *The Roaring Twenties*; Marlene Dietrich's comeback in *Destry Rides Again*; yet another Ford, this time a film of Walter Edmonds's saga of the New York frontier, *Drums along the Mohawk*; *Idiot's Delight*, Robert Sherwood's antiwar play, which kept its wry bite despite being bowdlerized out of fear of congressional inquiry into Hollywood warmongering; Selznick's classily mounted *Intermezzo*, with its elegantly frail Leslie Howard and its ingenue Ingrid Bergman; and, finally, the impossibly high benchmark attained by Victor Fleming, who directed *The Wizard of Oz* and *Gone with the Wind* in the same year.

The difference between early modern Florence and late modern Hollywood is to be found in outcomes. Italianate painting spread and influenced the French mannerist painting of Watteau, Fragonard, and Hubert Robert; the northern Renaissance of Steen, Claesz, Rembrandt, and other observers of Netherlandish light; and the British Hanoverian set—Gainsborough, Reynolds, and Hogarth. Hollywood, on the other hand, fell victim to forces brought to bear by a second world war, an American society transformed by it, and a European cinema revivified rather than enervated by it. Moreover, as though in battle against the omnipotent "trusts" of the Progressive era, the federal judiciary struck down the practices that had allowed Hollywood to become HOLLYWOOD: blockbooking, blindbooking, and vertical integration from studio to picture palace. Worst of all, World War II brought with it paradoxical forces that thrust Hollywood into a disequilibrium from which it never recovered. Instead of the loose array of contending forces— East Coast leftist writers tweaking the politics of Republican bosses, auteurs slyly slipping their style and politics into movies under the noses of both production bosses and the Breen office, and audiences wishing for more than the moguls seemed ready to risk giving them—the war brought with it an exaggerated urge for an Americanist consensus directed at foreign enemies.

Unavoidably, every genre of movies narrowed its focus to the common cause of the war effort. To "persuade" any balking studios, the government not only created the Office of War Information (OWI), an agency devoted to shaping a national propaganda, but also gave it a West Coast office in the fabled heart of the movie colony, the Taft Building at Hollywood and Vine. Drawing these antagonists into cooperation fell to two veteran journalists: Lowell Mellett, late of Scripps-Howard but seconded to Roosevelt's White House, and Nelson Poynter, of the *St. Petersburg Times*, whom Roosevelt appointed to the Washington and Hollywood directorates of the movie activities of the OWI.

At first the moguls blanched at the prospect of the OWI, seeing it as another East Coast keeper joining with their Wall Street masters in snooping around and making trouble. "Mellett To Read Scripts," blared the *Hollywood Reporter*. Yet, early on, the OWI revealed an abiding respect for the movie men, and this combined with their awareness that their European Jewish heritage was one of the stakes in the war put the movie men in a cooperative frame of mind. Indeed, in *Movie-Made America* (1975), Robert Sklar quotes a Signal Corps colonel as telling a Senate committee that in their role vis-à-vis the Army, the moviemakers were "wholehearted, willing, patriotic people." Higher praise, to be sure, than Thornton Delahanty's report in the *Herald Tribune* that the OWI had a tepid opinion of Hollywood's cooperation on racial propaganda, conceding only that "by slow . . . degrees the film industry is coming around." Obviously, it was a touchy love affair. Nonetheless, the OWI found itself struggling to limit strident portrayals of enemies with whom the United States would have to treat after its presumptive victory over its Axis enemies. The European enemies suffered the least, save for the occasional "Eyetie" (but never "wop"), "Hun," and "Boche," but the movie men, perhaps because they were Californians caught up in the local panic that had led to the "relocation" of West Coast Japanese, seldom found an alternative to cant words like "Jap." Frank Capra particularly exercised the OWI because of his cartoonish enemy gargoyles in the famous *Why We Fight* series of theatrical documentaries, particularly in *Know Your Enemy: Japan*. But, in the main, both feature films and the government's own propaganda films succeeded in portraying the enemies as both formidable, often creepily cruel warriors and victims of fascist ruling cliques.

Historians have not given Hollywood the benefit of the doubt for this ambiguous achievement and have regarded its entry into the war as timid and driven by fear of congressional investigations of its putative "warmongering" in such potboilers as *Lancer Spy* (1937) and tocsins as *Confessions of a Nazi Spy* (1938), a charge that allowed anti-Semites to imagine a Hollywood Jewish plot to drag the nation into Europe's war. In general, historians have followed Dorothy Jones's reckoning of the achievement of wartime Hollywood. As head of the OWI's in-house reviewers, Jones concluded that the moviemakers had offered a "poor diet for a nation striving to become fully united," had allowed patriotism to become a veneer over a trite plumping of "things-as-they-are," had mishandled "actual social problems" brought on by the war, and in general had "lacked real understanding of the war." In *A Certain Tendency of the Hollywoood Cinema* (1985), Robert Ray quotes the British filmmaker Basil Wright in describing Hollywood's wartime canon as empty of all but "instant simplification." And Koppes and Black begin their chapter on Hollywood's entry into internationalism by quoting a Production Code Administration (PCA) staffer as asking, "Are we ready to depart from the pleasant and profitable course of entertainment, to engage in propaganda?" If anything, writes David Cook in *A History of Narrative Film* (1990), the movies provided only their "perennial therapeutic function that films assume in time of stress." Among recent historians, only Sklar finds the Hollywood apparatus so devoted in its prosecution of the war as to underbill federal agencies for the costs of making training films.

The truth of the matter lies ambivalently between. During the late New Deal, as Hitler pressed his still fragile luck in Sudetenland, the Rhineland, and Austria and the pitch of Nazi anti-Semitism rose, Hollywood vacillated between internationalism and isolationism. As early as 1936, Jack Warner urged other moguls to join him in a Hollywood Anti-Nazi League. Chaplin not only made his anti-Nazi fable *The Great Dictator*, but the PCA parried pressure from the German consul in Los Angeles to quash it. The resulting worldwide distribution of its parody of Hitler so shook *der Führer* that he ceased doing his Chaplin imitation at parties. A cycle of comic-book style Nazi spy movies ran its course. Veiled references to anti-Semitism peered out from several movies. And in Washington the moguls gave as good as they got from a committee headed by Senators Gerald Nye and Burton Wheeler that conducted an inquiry into "warmongering." They engaged Wendell Willkie as counsel and refused to let pass unanswered the committee's often patently anti-Semitic asides.

Moreover, the English colony of actors and actresses in Hollywood, including Clive Brook, who played the elegant gentleman; Arthur Treacher, who played the butler; Flora Robson and Florence Bates, who played Elizabeth I and aristocratic ladies, lobbied to draw Hollywood up to full soldierly height. They were joined in this work by American Anglophiles such as Douglas Fairbanks Jr. and the scriptwriter John L. Balderston. No less compelling a factor in drawing the moguls toward a war footing was the studios' lost overseas investment in both production and theatrical realty, particularly because of German anti-Semitic confiscation.

Balderston, an American expatriate in London who had returned to write such scripts as *Frankenstein*, was one of the most devoted of the Hollywood Anglophiles. As early as 1939, on the eve of war, Balderston wrote to his friend Air Minister Sir Archibald Sinclair that California was a "black spot" in Britain's campaign to win over Americans. In view of "an almost lamentable swing of opinion . . . against you," he wrote, "you need active help." Later, the OWI itself thanked him for pressing for an early release of *Mrs. Miniver* (1942), MGM's hymn to the pluck of the British gentry, one of several Anglophilic movies that also included *Goodbye, Mr. Chips* (1939) and *A Yank at Oxford* (1938). Such movies had been the goal of the producer Walter Wanger, who had called for "strong pictures" in an essay in *Foreign Affairs* in 1939.

Thus World War II set in motion forces that prodded Hollywood's vertically integrated oligopoly into service as the state apparatus Marxists had always thought it was. The change toward an overt patriotism turned up in subtly effective ways. As we have seen, in 1938 Wanger's *Blockade*, a warning that the Spanish Civil War was a dress rehearsal for an international war, was gutted by the heavily pressured PCA. Yet, from its purchase in early 1941 through its release in December 1941 his *Sundown* evolved from a garden-variety African yarn into a script whose "blue" (rewrite) pages echoed the shifting fortunes of British and German forces and warned Americans against Axis ambitions in North Africa while promising a postwar liberal racial order. A Canadian character in the movie bristles at racial "discrimination" directed against an Arab woman, to whom he promises that "the England that's going to win this war is going to do away with that nonsense."

Meanwhile, movies inched toward antifascism. *The Mortal Storm* (1940), although coyly avoiding the word "Jew," managed to dramatize the impact of Nazi anti-Semitism on one family. Closer to home, as early as the summer of 1941 *Sergeant York* used a hero of World War I to personify the American drift from ambivalence toward the notion of a "just war."

Surely meant to ratify America's plunge into belligerence after Pearl Harbor, *Casablanca* (1942) was a marvelous blend of film noir, romance, propaganda, and Oscar-caliber éclat. "Everybody comes to Rick's," says a habitué of Rick's Cafe Americain, a saloon in North Africa that serves as a mecca for Europe's antifascists on the run from Nazi pursuers. In the course of the movie, Rick, whom the viewer knows as a disillusioned fighter against fascism in Spain and Ethiopia, drifts from callousness (insisting, "I stick my neck out for nobody") to a reverie in which he wonders, "What time is it in New York?" and concludes, ominously, that "they" (meaning Americans) are "asleep," to a last-reel departure in which he and the defecting Vichyite police chief of Casablanca go off to join a "free French garrison" as the onset of "a beautiful friendship." As though to underscore the impact of the teeming war on American conventions, "Sam," a black piano player, enjoys an uncommonly egalitarian friendship with Rick.

Even before this spate of movies that put the question of American interventionism on the table, a cycle of "preparedness" movies, often shot on location at a military academy, anticipated the need for expanded American military action. Typically, they established a dramatic conflict between the martinet who lived by the rule book and the maverick who did not. In the last reel, after a tangled plot that tests each hero's values, both learn that the individual and society must coexist. Sometimes the arena in which this conflict is fought is the "sham battle" that ends every training cycle in a test of the recruits' mettle; sometimes it is in flight school, where the rebel who was washed out returns as a wisecracking test pilot who proves the worth of an experimental divebomber. With the onset of actual war, the conflict between maverick and martinet played out as a subplot rivalry, often over a woman, and ended with the death of the rebellious soldier in an escapade that demonstrated the virtue of the symbiosis between rules and exceptions to them. *Air Force* (1943), *Destination Tokyo* (1944), *Wake Island* (1942), and *Bataan* (1943) are examples.

A star's well-worn persona could be enlisted time after time in the war effort. For example, only forty days after the attack on Pearl Harbor, Bogart led a motley company of New York crooks against a cadre of Nazi saboteurs in *All through the Night*; eight months later, he starred in *Across the Pacific*, a tale of Japanese intrigue in the Panama Canal Zone; a couple of months later, he turned up in *Casablanca*; in 1943 he sailed to Murmansk in *Action in the North Atlantic*; in that same year he commanded a polyethnic tank crew in *Sahara*; and, finally, in 1944, he played another loner with a past in *Passage to Marseille* and in Howard Hawks's (and William Faulkner's) retooling of

Hemingway's *To Have and Have Not* into an anti-Nazi yarn set in the West Indies. Much as James Cagney did in *Yankee Doodle Dandy* (1942) and *Blood on the Sun* (1945), as John Garfield did in *Destination Tokyo* (1944) and *Air Force* (1943), and as Errol Flynn did in *Objective Burma* (1945), Bogart managed to commit his outlaw outsider to the Allied cause.

Curiously, Hollywood's leap into the war effort coupled with the government's abiding gratitude for the gesture combined to alter profoundly the future of American moviemaking. The various tensions between the movie moguls and their audiences, their workers, their critics (in journalism and in the Congress), and their masters in New York that had shaped Hollywood into its classical era ceased to generate a creative energy that had often driven moviemakers. Instead, Hollywood began to act like the state apparatus the Marxists had always taken it for. Eager to conform to the restraints imposed by their movies' taste-culture and its attitude toward the war and by the re-doubling of censorship that resulted from having to answer to the OWI as well as the PCA, the studios produced increasingly stylized movies. By speaking for the government's war policies through their products, the studios had indeed become an official voice of the nation's rulers. Much as some studios during the Great Depression had inserted the NRA blue eagle logotype in their main titles, so a "V" for victory appeared at the end of each movie, accompanied by the first four notes of Beethoven's Fifth Symphony, which also happened to be Morse code for the letter "V." This trope had the further effect of calling to mind the "V" Churchill was perpetually making with upraised fingers to symbolize doughty Britain. Never had movies so willingly surrendered themselves to national war aims.

Moreover, as Koppes and Black argue in *Hollywood Goes to War*, after a few early pangs of fear of eastern meddling, the moguls, who had spent their business lives pleasing their masters in New York, found knuckling under to Washington a relatively easy matter. They readily formed private agencies such as the War Activities Council, the Hollywood Writers Mobilization, and the Hollywood Victory Committee to augment the bureaucrats' drive to create a homegrown "propaganda of truth." Sometimes the poles of political opinion formed partisan patriotic groups such as the Hollywood Citizens Committee on the Arts, Sciences, and Professions on the left and the Alliance for the Preservation of American Values on the right.

On balance, despite occasional scare headlines in the trade papers, such as *Variety*'s "US Will 'Cue' Hollywood," the moguls felt unexpectedly at ease in their new role as agents of the government. Partly this was so because they knew that Poynter's muscle was limited to appeals to conscience and partly because they knew a hostile Congress was itching to find an excuse to cut the OWI's budget, anyway. Appropriately, the OWI manual for the industry merely urged good thoughts upon the moguls: a concern for "the common man," an anticipation of a postwar United Nations, an avoidance of mere escapism and profiteering, and a hope that movies might contribute to the "understanding" of "current" events.

If any issue proved beyond quick resolution, it was racism. Americans needed to redefine blacks in the nation's life both as a repudiation of Nazi racism and to show blacks that small favors were omens of a better future, not merely wartime necessities.

In a startling enactment of the Italian Marxist Antonio Gramsci's theory that in times of crisis oppressed minorities might find fleeting moments of opportunity, when the aims of their rulers and themselves coincide, World War II provided a window of opportunity for Washington politicians and black organic leaders to propose a sort of antagonistic cooperation on behalf of the momentarily shared goal. When blacks heard in the government's propaganda the nonce words "brotherhood," "tolerance," and "unity," they knew they had to seize the opportunity to return racial issues to the federal level from the state level, where they had languished ever since the *Plessy v. Ferguson* Supreme Court decision of 1896, which had effectively overturned a generation of post–Civil War civil rights legislation and amendments.

They began by insisting on the increased national presence anticipated by Roosevelt's gestures in this direction, such as appointing the first black governor general of the Virgin Islands and seeking counsel from an informal "black cabinet" who consisted of a circle of black federal officers. With the onset of World War II, William Nunn of the black *Pittsburgh Courier* promoted the idea of a "Double Victory," a suggestion offered by a black worker at a Cessna plant in Wichita, Kansas. A. Philip Randolph, founder of the Brotherhood of Sleeping Car Porters, had already provided a public link between the war and black fortunes when in 1940 he had threatened a "march on Washington" to demand greater black participation in the war industry. In response to Randolph, Roosevelt, acting on advice from liberals in the cabinet and his wife Eleanor, a known "friend of the Negro" who had resigned from the Daughters of the American Revolution to rebuke them for denying their auditorium to the black singer Marian Anderson, had issued

Executive Order 8802, which provided blacks equal access to jobs, pay, and opportunities in war industries. Adding to this mood was the increasing presence within the OWI of yet another, more racially liberal OWI. The most ideologically grounded of these individuals were the anthropologist Philleo Nash and a staff of movie reviewers led by Dorothy B. Jones. There were liberal moles in other federal agencies as well, such as the historian Saul Padover in the Department of Agriculture. Even the Army included in its ranks a few of these leftists, among them the civilian consultants Charles Dollard and Donald Young; the senior officers Frederick C. Osborne, son of the director of the Museum of Natural History, and Samuel Stouffer of the University of Chicago; and General Lyman Munson, a strong advocate of making movie propaganda aimed at solving the problem of racism.

Thrust together with these amenable, even activist, figures in Washington were various allies within Hollywood and the National Association for the Advancement of Colored People (NAACP). The person who brought them together was an organic leader of the very sort anticipated by Gramsci (though in his prison notebooks he discussed not blacks but Sardinians). Walter White, the executive secretary of the NAACP and a devoted follower of celebrities, combined his interests as activist with those of his other self, the movie star hound, by persuading the NAACP to hold its annual convention in Los Angeles, virtually at the doorstep of the studios. Moreover, he booked the defeated presidential candidate Wendell Willkie as keynote speaker and prevailed upon the Office of Defense Transportation to waive its ban on needless travel so that delegates could flock to the coast. Willkie spoke not only as a friend of the cause, but also as chair of the board of 20th Century-Fox. As for the moguls, White and Willkie induced them to attend a luncheon at which they urged the moguls to pledge to award "citizenship" to African Americans in their movie roles, meaning that roles would no longer be limited to menial stereotypes but rather would include bourgeois extras. This liberal coalition of the OWI, the NAACP, and movie studio bosses interwove the government's goals with those of African Americans, just as Gramsci predicted oppressed groups' needs would be addressed in times of crisis.

Eventually, now that studio archives have become more accessible to the public, we shall know how much influence each of the parties in the alliance had on specific movies. For the moment, we can know only that the war created a mood of "conscience liberalism," or what Philip Dunne called a "liberalism of the heart," as opposed to a programmatic movement, and that the mood not only resulted in short-term gains for African Americans, gains rooted in the wartime propaganda and its merely necessitarian aims, but also held out the promise of permanent changes in racial arrangements. This was the "Double Victory" for which so many African Americans and their liberal allies struggled.

In Hollywood, some of these liberalized movies went into release as unadulterated products of this leftist sensibility, others as bargains arrived at between moguls and activists, and still others as signs of Walter White's "fine Italian hand," as he called it. One film that presented its leftist mood undiluted was the young John Huston's film of Ellen Glasgow's Pulitzer Prize–winning novel *In This Our Life* (1941). Unbidden by pressure groups, Huston included a powerfully wrought black student falsely charged with manslaughter, a role so compelling to black audiences that the actor (Ernest Anderson) heard stories of black soldiers in camp theaters stopping the film to demand reruns of his scenes. Things were not usually this simple, though. More typically, the liberal movie was the product of a tug-of-war between activists, agencies, and studios. For example, a summer's debate in 1942 among White's NAACP, Howard Dietz and Mayer himself at MGM, Poynter and Mellett at the OWI, Balderston (who claimed to "know Mellett"), and David Platt (a film critic for *The Worker*) contributed to a bowdlerized reworking of *Tennessee Johnson* (1943) that satisfied no one. However, it *was* useful in revealing how much movie politics had come to matter in the making of a movie. White insisted that this bio pic of the "misunderstood" President Andrew Johnson remain faithful to new Reconstruction-era scholarship, such as W.E.B. Du Bois's *Black Reconstruction*, but Balderston wrote of a Johnson maligned by various allies of black freedmen. Predictably, the result aimed down the middle. In *Casablanca* (1942), the role of Sam the piano player was strengthened and given to Dooley Wilson rather than a familiar (and typed) black actor, again without obvious pressure. Wanger's *Sundown* (1941), on the other hand, grew from a mere yarn into a story of Allied war aims as a result of the producer's acquaintance with White and his decision to do rewrites in parallel with the campaigns of the Afrika Korps and the British 8th Army. Thereafter, combat movies had their racial politics sharpened by the intervention of activists, as in the case of *Sahara* (1943), a platoon-scaled tale of the African campaign written by the Communist writer John Howard Lawson, and *Bataan* (1943), a tale of a polyethnic platoon of stragglers in the last days of the Philippine campaign (yet another movie in which White had a hand). In still other films, such as Selznick's *Since You Went Away* (1944), producers reshaped their racial material by heeding the advice of preview-card writers. Although Selznick succumbed to arguments by Ulric Bell of the OWI for "possible retakes," he also heeded the advice of recruits in the black Women's Army Corps, who had written irate preview cards.

Usually, the moguls hoped to avoid direct confrontation with pressure groups or the OWI, but the OWI's reviewers kept a log of screenings, testing "progress" against previous releases and its own manual of practice. The smallest deviation from the manual caught their eyes. Preston Sturges's *The Palm Beach Story* (1942), despite, or because of, its rollicking Sturges touches, seemed to Jones and her staff "a fine example of what should not be made" because of the "unseemly luxury [and] childish irresponsibility" portrayed. Mellett saw *Pittsburgh* (1942), a saga of the steel mills, and thought its "propaganda sticks out disturbingly." But in general, the agency credited Hollywood with effective (and profitable) cheerleading of the war effort—although the moguls never ceased watching their backs for signs of encroaching censorship by OWI snoops.

Selznick's *Since You Went Away* stands out as an example of a prestigious Hollywood movie that also gave the OWI everything on its lengthy wish list. Mrs. Hilton and her daughters are at the center of a plot meant to celebrate the idea of individual sacrifice for the good of all. Mr. Hilton is off serving in the Navy and clearly in harm's way. Their diminished income obliges them to do without their black maid, who in turn makes her own sacrifice by offering to work only for room and board. Together the women make do, team up against the burden of work, weep over incoming letters written at sea, volunteer to help in hospitals, and yet plug away at work and school. Ethnic harmony is affirmed by a number of sequences. As a hospital aide, one of the daughters feeds ice cream to veterans, one of whom is black. A farewell sequence in a railroad station includes a pan of scores of typical Americans, including an uncommonly dignified black couple. An immigrant woman having lunch at the aircraft plant where she works just happens to recite in its entirety the Emma Lazarus poem at the foot of the Statue of Liberty—"Give me your tired, your poor, your huddled masses yearning to breathe free . . . " A naval officer named Solomon turns up at a party, conveniently providing an example of a Jew who has been awarded the Navy Cross. Moreover, not only did Selznick heed the wishes of the OWI, but he used his preview cards as cues for rewrites and retakes that added to the ethnically harmonious ambience.

Yet even prestigious pictures, including those that enjoyed the government's blessing, sometimes stumbled over their own complexities, which did not lend themselves to the cross-purposed needs of propaganda. *Mission to Moscow* (1943), for example, began life as an assured success, arising from, as the producer Robert Buckner describes it to the historian David Culbert in the introduction to the published script (1980), Roosevelt's own wish "to show American mothers and fathers that if their sons are killed in fighting alongside Russians . . . the Russians are worthy allies." The movie snagged on its own ambiguities, however. Were "reds" in Hollywood exploiting Roosevelt's wish or Ambassador Joseph E. Davies's ghostwritten and by turns disingenuous and credulous memoir of his service in the Soviet Union? Was there yet another gaggle of congressional snoops waiting on the sidelines for another headline-grabbing foray into Hollywood, this time in search of not "warmongers," but Bolsheviks? Would the Roosevelt government stand by its wish for Stalin to become a benign "Uncle Joe," or would Buckner and his unit be left to hang alone? Warner Bros. called on Howard Koch, who had written Orson Welles's radio thriller *The War of the Worlds* (1938), *In This Our Life*, and, in part, the multi-Oscar winner *Casablanca*, to concoct a movie from Davies's concocted book. In the end, Hollywood's worst nightmare recurred. Although an OWI synopsis concluded that *Mission to Moscow* "pulls no punches [as] . . . the most powerful propaganda of all: the truth," a number of voices on the left, particularly those of lapsed Communists, called attention to the already emerging tales of Stalin's crimes against dissenters among his own people. Culbert quotes the educator John Dewey as calling the movie "totalitarian propaganda for mass consumption" and the film critic Dwight Macdonald as saying it "falsifies history and glorifies dictatorship."

Difficult as it is to find a clearly delineated genre here, a few traits can be identified. The most sharply defined form was the platoon movie, in which, usually, a martinet was humanized, a maverick learned that discipline was as vital to an army as his own rebelliousness, and, together with the polyethnic members of the unit, the two enlisted in the war against fascism. Seven movies released in 1943 were the best of the platoon genre: *Bataan*, *Crash Dive*, *Sahara*, *Lifeboat*, *Gung Ho!*, *Guadalcanal Diary*, and *Air Force*.

Then there were the movies about quietly valiant civilians who learned to sacrifice and to stand up to adversity in the name of their own "Double Victory," their own future stake in the outcome of the war. The England of *Mrs. Miniver* unifies across class lines and expects democratization at war's end, much like the America of *Since You Went Away*, the China of *Dragon Seed* (1944), and other national sagas of conversion to a war footing dramatized. In other movies, civilians were as sanguine toward the future but were made to suffer directly, as though the movies were warning that decent life would end if the Nazis won. *This Land Is Mine* (1943) in France and *The Moon Is Down* (1943) in Norway made the point. Whenever the OWI saw a slackening of effort, a letter from Poynter was sure to arrive, pleading "give us a *Mrs. Miniver* for China."

B movies often achieved a similar level of entertaining propaganda. The Blondie series, drawn from Chic Young's comic strip, often teased around the constraints imposed by wartime regulations and shortages; Tarzan fought Nazi interlopers, rather than ivory poachers; and even cowboys found German saboteurs on the prairie. When movies failed in the OWI's view, it was because they overstated their case. The two biting homefront satires Sturges made in 1944, *The Miracle of Morgan's Creek* and *Hail the Conquering Hero*; B movies that overdid the beastliness of the enemy, such as *Little Tokio USA* (1942); and almost any musical (a genre stubbornly out of step with the war effort) all drew bristling letters from Poynter and snappish reviews from OWI staff.

Documentaries faced similar scrutiny and mixed responses. Ford's *The Battle of Midway* and William Wellman's *Memphis Belle*, for example, earned Oscars in 1944. Moreover, in the case of *Memphis Belle*, Wellman turned out a documentary that revealed probably the worst aspect of aerial combat: the high anxiety that stemmed from the inadequate defenses of American bombers against the *Luftwaffe*'s nimble pursuit planes, particularly on the lengthy (and thus largely unescorted) flights over Eastern Europe. The trick for the crews was to outlast their mounting anxiety for a total of twenty-five flights over heavily defended targets, after which they were rotated out of the combat pool and often sent home.

Other documentary makers were less successful in steering their work into eventual circulation. John Huston's *The Battle of San Pietro* (1945), for example, suffered heavy censorship of its harsh sequences of a nasty, ongoing firefight with German defenders of a rugged mountain village in Italy. His *Let There Be Light* (1945), a late-war attempt to show how the Army used psychotherapy to restore minds shattered by the stress of combat, was so realistic in its portrayal of the inner suffering of these emotionally wounded soldiers that the Army prohibited its exhibition to any audience.

Finally, of course, wartime movies included the work of Frank Capra ("Colonel" Capra, actually), whose introductory segment in *Why We Fight* won an Oscar in 1942, leading the Army to hope for eventual civilian release of some of its better films. Capra's work stirred acrimonious debate, however. Mellett and others found his portrayals of the enemies' prosecution of the war extreme, breeding a "nervous hysteria" among civilians that they believed would preclude cultivating "a saner world . . . after the armistice." In addition, the fetid odor of racism hung over Capra's work, particularly *Prelude to War* (1942), which portrayed military aggression as an ethnic trait of Germans.

Despite the mixed reception given Hollywood's documentary output, which ranged from the awarding of Oscars and good audience response to outright banning of too truthful films and agency attempts to dampen the racial bases of hazing enemies, World War II did wonders for the documentary film as a cinematic movement. For the first time, moviemakers believed not only that movies might have an affectively persuasive role in the war, but also that they had a duty to make movies persuasive. Moreover, Dorothy Jones, as the OWI's chief reviewer, lamented "the poor diet" that Hollywood feature movies provided and their "exaggerated" attention to the nonexistent threats of domestic spying and sabotage; she called for a more journalistic documentary cinema.

In contrast, between the two world wars documentarists had surrendered every ambition in their striving for an absolute neutrality that enhanced their movies' "educational" value while offending no one. The few films that had taken up race issues had addressed not political issues, such as racial discrimination and antiunionism, but safe matters such as reducing the incidence of pellagra, hookworm, and malnutrition among blacks through "practical" solutions such as better flyscreens, deeper privies, and better food-canning methods. Even Pare Lorentz's New Deal films, *The River* (1937) and *The Plow That Broke the Plains* (1936), had been epics of humans' struggle with nature, rather than calls for political solutions to events such as the Dust Bowl and rural poverty. And with good reason: lacking a foreign enemy to blame for the social dysfunctions of the Great Depression and fearing that Congress's southern contingent would seek revenge on the Farm

Security Administration and other agencies that had sponsored these films, filmmakers had remained circumspect and fearful.

With the onset of World War II, however, the mood changed. As a matter of necessity, the movies were enlisted as a weapon. Moreover, Hollywood's early feature film efforts, aside from their utility as either propaganda or commercial art, often reflected an authentically flavored mise-en-scène, usually as a result of willing cooperation between the studios and the commanders of military posts in southern California. *Sahara*, for example, achieved much of its documentary "reality" by borrowing a Sherman tank from the Army. *Wake Island* acquired its flavor of the early, daunting, but not defeatist weeks of the war by its use of authentic Grumman Wildcat aircraft. *Bataan* owed its last-ditch bravura to the prominent role it gave to a water-cooled Browning machine gun, complete with its muzzle flash and jumpy recoil. Hollywood's feature film success in replicating the war obliged documentarists to strive not only for authenticity, but also for classical Hollywood forms of heroism and conventions of pacing and denouement. Not to do so risked the contempt of the ever sharper-eyed audience, especially the young, who, bored by their classroom films, had taken to the Hollywood version of the war with zeal.

The few foreign movies that reached America from their sources in belligerent Europe also reflected a high level of documentary authenticity. In Britain, for example, the socialist tradition of John Grierson, Basil Wright, Humphrey Jennings, and the London Film Society produced marvels of immediacy and classless pluck in the face of adversity in such films as *Fires Were Started* (1943) and *London Can Take It* (1940) and in the documentary-like feature films *One of Our Aircraft Is Missing* (1942) and Noel Coward's own *In Which We Serve* (1942).

The odd German film that turned up confirmed the wisdom of American documentarists' decision to avoid pomp and circumstance and eschew bald-faced lying. Although it is true that in a few sequences, German filmmakers celebrated Germanness (its half-timbered villages, its gemütlichkeit, the *Kameradschaft* of its soldiers, and the particularism of each region), they also reached for a ponderous ceremonial mood. By the time the Nazi Party made her its white goddess of moviemaking, Leni Riefenstahl already had access to ceremonial sorts of movie magic in such films as *Für Uns* (1937), the first movie in which Hitler pulled out all the stops, laying wreaths on the Greek-revival monuments to the dead of early putsches and chucking little girls under the chin and mouthing thanks to their mothers for bearing the dead sons being apotheosized by a calling of the roll. In her own career in "mountain movies," a western-like genre in which blond Teutons tested themselves against challenging mountain faces, she had found the idealized figure that linked sport with nation. It remained only for her to make a test swatch, a party congress film called *Sieg des Glaubens* (1934). Her nascent skill in handling crowds and ceremony on the grand scale earned her the chance to make what would become her landmark films: *Olympia* (1938), a celebration of national life and sport on the occasion of the 1936 Olympic Games in Berlin, and *Triumph des Willens* (1935), the party congress film in which folkishness, localism, sacrifice, drums, roll calls, bombastic oratory, uniforms, and summer camp *Kameradschaft* all come together in a sort of Nazi high mass. Parallel to Riefenstahl's work, Fritz Hippler made *Der Ewige Jude* ("The Eternal Jew") (1940), which invoked every hoary stereotype of Jews and in which Hippler at every opportunity dissolved from scenes of Jewish perfidity to shots of plump rats gnawing away at the grain sacks of Europe.

The resulting ideological overkill must have touched only the already converted, an inference that American moviemakers made along the way toward arriving at their "strategy of truth," a policy of celebrating good news and glossing over the bad. They chose a self-effacing mode that emphasized "teamwork," a cant word that they used to mean a wish for a collective effort while not surrendering the ideal of individualism. Certainly, this ideal was at the heart of *Memphis Belle* and *The Battle of Midway*. The pilot in the Boeing B-17 in *Memphis Belle* could not have survived his twenty-fifth mission had he not flown in tight formation with his wingmen and had not every crewman carried out his duty. Likewise, in *The Battle of Midway* the task force sent to fight the Japanese Navy in the first major counterattack of the war could not have succeeded without the unitary dedication of all hands, from blackgang to bridge.

I do not mean to suggest that the American product was a work of cinematic genius; far from it. Most American movies were either training films—how to strip and clean a Garand rifle, how to avoid venereal disease, and so on—or plodding tributes to the plodding life of the citizen soldier. Among the tributes were *Welcome to Britain* (ca. 1943), a primer on how to adapt to life in Britain; *Westward Is Bataan* (ca. 1943), a boring account of the boring life of an assault force on a troopship; and *Henry Browne, Farmer* (1942), about a black peanut farmer whose son is training in the all-black

99th Pursuit Squadron, an "insipid" piece in the view of Claude Barnett of the Associated Negro Press.

Of all the films the federal government contracted for during World War II, two, *The Negro Soldier* (1944) and *Teamwork* (1946), proved to be the most exemplary expressions of the notion that the wartime confluence of black and mainstream war aims might flow into the peacetime future. Both were Signal Corps products intended only to address the troops' anxieties toward "other" races in the ranks. Yet, each also served to give enough thrust to the propaganda nonce words "unity," "tolerance," and "brotherhood" that they were conveyed as wartime values that would persist after the war.

Each movie spoke for the "conscience liberals" in the OWI and their black allies, and each went incrementally beyond the necessitarianism of the Army's short-term use of it. Moreover, in a broader sense, the Signal Corps and other agencies taught the next generation of Hollywood moviemakers, who would bring to their civilian lives not only their skills, but also their racial politics. In this way, far from merely promoting the status quo, these two movies anticipated stark changes in postwar racial arrangements. Indeed, *Teamwork* integrated the ranks long before the Army itself would.

The black leadership, particularly Walter White and Roy Wilkins of the NAACP, lobbied the Roosevelt government not only simply to make prints of the movies available for civilian use, but also to give away surplus prints to any civilian agencies that asked for them after the war. The result, thought one liberal activist, would be "a permanent front," and Wilkins saw this front as moving forward "both now and for the future." Of course, radical change invited reaction, and George Roeder reports in *The Censored War* that among whites it was "universally" predicted that "when the war is over, we are going to have to fight another one against the Negroes."

That these social goals of African Americans had also become part of the intellectual baggage of the mainstream could be seen in the ways in which blacks carried their message to the political left-center. Both they and the OWI imagined a future in which their sort of activism had a place. At the same time, unbidden by either, audiovisual librarians and filmmakers in every corner of the nation imagined their own activist futures. While black activists pressed the Army to release *The Negro Soldier* "in full to audiences of both races," librarians gathered at their annual conferences spoke of their own "great boom" in using the "military films after the war" to act as a "corrective democratic force." One OWI staffer believed the result would be "a permanent chance for improvement under democracy" for black citizens.

Thus by the war's end the government's need for propaganda of the most utilitarian sort had led to a documentary film movement that was animated at its core by "the liberalism of the heart" that had begun to color Hollywood movies. Therefore, by the time the OWI eventually fell victim to the budget slashing of conservatives in Congress, the new generation of filmmakers had already entered a thriving East Coast documentary film culture or had been picked up by Hollywood studios. To both camps they brought change, snuffing out the last of the breed of "educational" filmmakers and becoming part of the late-1940s message movie era.

This change did not come easily, mind you. It says a great deal that in *Hollywood Goes to War*, Koppes and Black devote a full six pages to the struggle to make Paramount's *So Proudly We Hail* (1943) into a stirring hit that combined entertainment with a strong dose of American will to fight. Into this story of the grinding defeat of the Philippine campaign, the moviemakers, with Poynter's prodding, found ways of introducing many of the OWI's most treasured devices for promoting national unity without surrendering traits that Americans considered their most endearingly "American." A company of nurses sent to the islands behaves heroically, with one of them even sacrificing her life for the group. They also behave according to the female conventions of the day: they carry on romances under the worst of combat conditions, strive to keep every hair in place, and sometimes react hysterically to the rigors of combat. Poynter wanted still more: he told the producer that "the girls" should act more like nurses than like petulant children who fold under pressure. He also rewrote a sermon into a ponderous soliloquy that turned out to be unusable. He wanted the causes of the war to be worked in with such attention to detail that some scenes seemed like foreign policy briefings. After the making of this movie, Poynter felt obliged to provide directors with a tutorial on how to portray the Japanese enemy (cunning but not beastly), our Chinese allies (folkish but rapidly modernizing), and our British allies (quaint in their use of proper English but eager to learn how to say "okay" and almost as eager to dismantle their class system). He and the agency's manuals also set forth—too leftishly for Congress's taste—the failure of isolationism to face up to the rise of fascism and thus the need for postwar collective security to be provided by a United Nations. And so on.

In any case, although the sea anchors that kept Hollywood on the course of conservatism remained—that is, the Breen office, the studio establishment, and the well-worn studio practices—the war gave moviemakers an unprecedented opportunity to rock the boat. Moreover, Hollywood looked to enter the postwar marketplace with its eye on a more jaded, sophisticated audience and one with the wealth that provided for more education, a greater variety of leisure-time choices, and a suburbanization movement that would scatter audiences and sector them according to income. In place in this new Hollywood were the Hollywood lefties who had matured politically during the war: Carl Foreman, who wrote *Home of the Brave* (1949), the antiracism message movie; Dore Schary, an activist on behalf of Roosevelt, an Oscar-winning screenwriter, and, ultimately, production boss at MGM; and Stanley Kramer, who moved from the Signal Corps studio in Queens to the mailroom at Columbia and finally to his own independent firm that made movies that the war's impact anticipated. Already in 1946 the major studios sensed that change was in the air and that things would never be the same. For example, George Norford, drama critic of the *Amsterdam News*, recalled that Hitchcock's polyethnic *Lifeboat* (1943) had done "wonders for the morale of the Negro GI" and predicted that after the war Hollywood "would go even further in terms of film content." However, worrisome changes were also afoot, with Spyros Skouras of 20th Century-Fox pointing out the soaring labor costs and thinning crowds and warning his demi-moguls that unless they broke free of old, classical ways of doing business, they "will face inevitable ruin." It was 1946, and the postwar future had already arrived.

CHAPTER TEN

The Long Good-Bye

Is there a central theme in movie history? The question matters as we approach the end of this look at Hollywood's classical era. Among American historians, a struggle has ensued between those who take a centrist, consensus view of history, often grounded in a central theme, and those with a multicultural perspective on history, who view the absence of a central theme as a national virtue. Some of the themes that the consensus historians have offered as guiding the course of American history have been the frontier experience, an uncommon amount of shared material wealth, and even the "troublesome presence" of African Americans in the nation's life. Since the countercultural movement of the 1960s and 1970s, however, many historians have replaced the search for consensus with the search for difference, applying to history theories they have borrowed from disciplines such as psychology and anthropology. Interestingly, as this multicultural movement in general history has emerged, movie history has drifted toward a monist, centrist model founded on "the mode of production," "the genius of the system," and other conceptualizations that assert a common economic basis for the politics of movie art. This socioeconomic model has been advanced by David Bordwell, Janet Staiger, Kristin Thompson, Douglas Gomery, Richard C. Allen, Russell Merritt, Thomas Schatz, and many others, including a school of academic Marxists who have provided much rigorous work.

I bring up these open issues to call attention to their relevance to "the long good-bye," the breakup of classical Hollywood and its eventual displacement by today's transnational corporate system in which moviemaking is merely part of larger production and marketing strategies. The classical era of Hollywood was based on a less impregnable system, in which various interest groups, however unequal in power, "countervailed" (to use John Kenneth Galbraith's term) in an endless dance of adversaries in search of place, privilege, and pelf.

As the circumstances of production and consumption changed after World War II, so did the movies, but almost never in the ways Hollywoodians wished them to change. The socioeconomic forces that caused these changes came from all over—the movie lot craft guilds, the hearing rooms of federal regulators, and the television dens of the growing ranks of suburbanites in the 1940s. Like most disputes that pitted workers against bosses, labor tensions in Hollywood abated until the end of the war, much as new houses awaited the transformation from blueprint to green lawn until after the war.

Suburbs and television—the twin imps of narcissism in postwar America, they induced a diminution of gemeinschaft, or community, in favor of a sterile gesellschaft, or corporate mentality, and an atomization of society into cells of self-interest bounded by a patch of green lawn and lit by a flickering blue screen that reduced human affiliations to a sort of electronic onanism. The beauty of this scenario, said its advocates, was that it averted the need for public space in the noisome and noisy cities; families now had their own insular spaces. The arrival of suburbs and television paralleled institutional and economic changes in Hollywood, and no doubt other industries as well, and may eventually be shown by sociologists to have constituted a contrasocial, hypercommercial narrowing of engagement. Surely the eponymous Levittowns that dotted (and eventually blotted out) the green expanses around American cities seemed almost a war prize to which returning veterans were entitled. Television appeared somewhat later, after technological advances allowed the creation of networks of stations that broadcast "free" programs supported by commercial messages, and it reduced movies to its own small-scale screen.

Shocked into stasis by these postwar changes, the once rustproof Hollywood system began to corrode. Declining revenues intersected with rising labor strife and costs, and in 1945 Spyros Skouras told his producers at 20th Century-Fox that ruination would be the result unless they found a way to stop the alarming declines of grosses that were being seen even during formerly surefire times, such as the Christmas season. However, the moguls had become so accustomed to the delights of easy profits at the wartime pinnacle of their industry that they could not act resourcefully on their own behalf. "This wasn't the way it was supposed to be with the war over," writes Nancy Lynn Schwartz in *The Hollywood Writers' Wars* (1982). "There was supposed to be harmony, unity, joy," not scrapping over shrinking revenues.

Their craft guilds provided the moguls with their most disjunctive break with prewar practice. Before the war, the guilds had rumbled with discontent, and during the war, even though they were slowly growing into a countervailing power, they had remained quiescent, in deference to the needs of either the nation or the Communist Party. When the war ended, though, labor strife came to the looming gatehouses that had become the logotypes that accompanied the main titles of America's movies. The revivified unions not only fought the management, but, in wasteful jurisdictional disputes, also took on rival unions. The disputes shattered the decorum that had defined labor relations before the war, when various sweetheart deals that the Motion Picture Producers and Directors of America (MPPDA) had made with the guilds—with the MPPDA agreeing to recognize the unions as bargaining agents and the unions agreeing to forego the demand for union shops—had muted the guilds' mounting discontent. In fact, the famous Academy of Motion Picture Arts and Sciences was far more a company union than a genuine academy, Robert Sklar writes in *Movie-Made America* (1975). In such a structured system, the studios, in a series of agreements in the 1920s, had recognized five crafts that loosely served either construction or production needs.

In exchange for their sweetheart deals with the studios, which effectively not only protected jobs, but allowed them to be handed on within families, the guilds did little to form alliances within the labor movement or to enlarge their ranks. Under this arrangement, competition for individual credits mattered more than collective action, so that the Screen Writers Guild, for example, and the MPPDA itself emphasized allocating credits and awarding prizes on the basis of individual achievement. Thus movie stars such as the flamboyant Tom Mix earned $1 million a year, while at the bottom of the scale his brothers in arms in the labor movement worked as casual laborers paid at daily rates. It also meant that each worker, by acting as a free agent rather than a union member, lived in fear of lost roles; feared gossip columnists whose "blind items" (unattributed pieces of damaging gossip) might blight a career; fretted over the possibility that the National Recovery Administration or the National Labor Relations Board (NLRB) might recognize the MPPDA as a bargaining agent; or, as was the case among the craft workers, faced the divisive squabbling of jurisdictional strikes of one union against another. In one such strike in the 1930s, the International Association of Theatrical and Stage Employees (IATSE) and electrical workers guilds fought over which group was eligible to recruit electricians, while Columbia and the other lots stood cohesively together and brought in strikebreakers. When labor scored a point, the moguls presented themselves as innocent victims, as when the IATSE, having been defeated, brought in George Brown and Willie Bioff, two veterans of the Chicago gang wars whose shakedowns, sweetheart deals, and other forms of racketeering discolored Hollywood labor relations all the way to the eve of World War II.

On the Disney lot in 1941, such a labor dispute grew even more divisive when the Cartoonists Guild was distracted from, as the Marxists say, its objective class enemies. The striking guild not only feared that the conservative Disney would couple them to Bioff, but seemed tainted by an affiliation with the Painters Guild, which was led by Herbert Sorrell, whom the moguls branded a Communist agitator at a time when congressional investigation of "un-American" activities was underway. In what had become typical Hollywood labor practice, the strike and Disney's ensuing lockout in the spring of 1941 pitted the Cartoonists Guild and a "company union" against each other. Although the cartoonists eventually won recognition, the outcome of the bitter struggle gave Disney a platform from which to rail at Communists and to brand as malcontents the despairing cartoonists—among them Walt Kelly and Stephen Bosustow—who had left the strife-torn lot.

Disney's tarnishing of the issue by introducing the idea that Stalinist goons were infiltrating Hollywood was a harbinger of things to come after the war. By then, the Grand Alliance that had defeated the Axis powers had opened acrid fissures between the East and West and Stalinism had emerged as a species of totalitarian thuggery second only to Nazism. Liberals of all sorts who had searched for what Philip Dunne calls a "liberalism of the heart," rather than a liberalism grounded in Marxist cant, drifted into more New Dealish cells of activism. From doctrinaire Communists on the left they suffered charges of "deviationism," and from the right they were threatened by revived congressional snoops who ransacked wartime scripts in search of words such as "comrade" or appeals to postwar collective security that they could use to smear writers as "red" or at the very least fellow travelers in the van of Communism.

Thus, by 1945 the studios had been transformed from the workplaces of

stalwart soldiers in the war against fascism into scenes of strife and squabbling. Moreover, Jack Tenney, a conservative member of the California legis-
lature, set in motion an "investigation" of Hollywood figures such as Sorrell,
whom Tenney accused of following "the Communist line," and thereby portrayed labor's militancy as not the predictable result of wartime quietude but
a sign that Hollywood had been infiltrated by "reds."

In any case, the Hollywood that had been a coherent movie colony, a self-
satisfied company town bonded by gemeinschaft, had come to an end. With
World War II all but over, Sorrell drew together as many as nine guilds that
had been affiliated with IATSE into a Conference of Studio Unions. On October 5, 1945, he assembled a sort of Wobblies of the San Fernando Valley,
one big industrial union that began massive picketing of the Warner Bros.
lot. As though scripted from the Ford Motor Company strife of 1937, the Los
Angeles County Sheriffs and the Burbank Police played their roles as defenders of the studio and its property. Within days, the tense standoff at the
studio gates broke into violence between the police and strikers. Red goons
or bad cops? In the end, what mattered was that the political right had been
able to portray the event as Communist inspired, bringing to a close the legend of Hollywood as lotusland. Within the year, this perception was confirmed as Sorrell's group struck most of the major studios while the moguls
aligned with IATSE, thereby allowing the right to portray the left as reds and
the left to portray the right as fascists. Each side declared the other the enemy of America.

Thereafter, it was an easy matter for rightists to coalesce into such groups
as the Motion Picture Alliance for the Preservation of American Ideals
(MPAPAI) and to characterize the entire left, including the "conscience liberals," who had begun to distance themselves from Stalinists, as a deep Communist infiltration of the movie industry. The House Un-American Activities Committee (HUAC), searching for some Cold War role for itself, saw a
headline-grabbing opportunity to investigate "reds" in the movie colony.
"The strike nourished the Motion Picture Alliance and made it more powerful," recalls the writer Ben Margolis in Schwartz's *The Hollywood Writers'
Wars.* "It was a stimulant to [the] HUAC."

While the right solidified itself by adopting as its base this official arm of
Congress, the liberal left stood by helplessly as each new agency it formed or
joined—the Hollywood Writers Mobilization, the Hollywood Democratic
Committee, and the Hollywood Independent Citizens for the Arts, Sciences,

and Professions—was infiltrated or coopted by the Marxist left. For its part, the Marxist (actually, mostly Stalinist) left was crumbling under the pressure of not only the HUAC, but also leftist industrial unions in search of a pragmatic rather than ideological leftist identity. Its erosion also derived from its sectarianism, the result of endless spats over doctrine, demands for mindless discipline on the part of intellectuals who had tired of it, and obligatory defenses of Stalin's increasingly exposed murderous paranoia.

The result was that at a time when Hollywood needed a friendly press, it was characterized as a creature of a foreign power. Except for the mainly Marxist "Hollywood Ten," who decided to exercise their constitutional right to speak freely yet eschew self-incrimination, Hollywoodians caved into the pressure that was coming from all sides: their own gossip columnists, Hedda Hopper and Louella Parsons; Congress; groups such as the MPAPAI; and the right-wing press. Every studio made one or more "quickies" that played to the political paranoia of the moment—*The Iron Curtain* (1948), *The Red Menace* (1949), *I Was a Communist for the FBI* (1951), and so on—while at the same time issuing ambiguous documents such as their famous "Waldorf Statement," in which they invoked the freedom of thought that they purported to treasure while at the same time promising to fire any Communists on their various lots. Wambling still further, they explained that the firings would not be because of these individuals' politics, God forbid, but because of the loss of marketability that presumedly would be a result of their politics.

Although labor strife marred 1946, it was still the most prosperous year in Hollywood history, and the studios' expectations remained high, fueled by the heaps of dollars Americans had earned by working overtime during the war and the postwar boom in leisure time that was everywhere apparent. They presumed that old-time Hollywood movies would resume their place in the hearts of moviegoers.

They soon learned, however, that Americans had been changed by the war. It had inured them to hardship and hardened them against the attractions of movie sentimentality. Moreover, although leisure had always seemed its most rewarding when linked to consumption of goods, with the war's end the link became a weld. Having won the war to defend FDR's "four freedoms"—of speech and religion and from want and fear—Americans stood in line for their spoils. Heady with the scent of peace, they were particularly interested in exercising their "freedom from want." Even as inflation soared on the updrafts of their war-deferred indulgences, they took advantage of everything that conversion to a peacetime economy made available: not only more leisure time, but also more cars, boats, lawnmowers, radios, and newfangled television receivers.

Moreover, some forms of passive leisure adapted to changing social patterns. The stale, small-time traveling vaudeville and burlesque shows gave way to well-mounted road companies of Broadway shows. Professional sports grew more appealing and teams located in ever larger population centers. Intercollegiate athletics ranging from basketball tournaments in Madison Square Garden to postseason football "bowl" games on New Year's Day became national events. Mock sports such as professional wrestling and roller derby prospered, partly because of their pioneering slots in television schedules. Professional football and basketball moved from marginality to central places in the annual round of sports seasons. With almost startling speed, basketball moved out of towns like Anderson, Iowa, and Rochester, New York, to the big cities. Of them all, baseball made the boldest steps, taking advantage of the conscience liberalism of the war years to bring blacks into the major leagues and moving to teeming population centers formerly underserved by professional athletics.

At first, the impact of these changes on movies was masked by the short-term profits brought by inflated ticket prices. But swollen labor costs and the myriad new leisure-time options soon began edging the movies out of their privileged place in American psyches. The GI Bill, a congressionally mandated means of making up for veterans' interrupted educations and careers, contributed to yet another factor in refining tastes already made sophisticated, not to say jaded, by the experience of war. As a result of their taking advantage of the free education the GI Bill provided, as well as their overseas experiences, America's veterans became more cosmopolitan in their tastes. The enterprising importation policies of Joseph Burstyn; Walter Reade Sterling; and other independent, urban theater men drew the increasingly sophisticated audience away from the Hollywood product and toward literary British features; earthy, neorealistic Italian films; and ponderously Stalinist Soviet movies.

Even people's taste in movie venues changed. Audiences abandoned the first-run palaces in favor of the "art house," where they could take in an art exhibit in the lobby and could sip their coffee from china cups during the feature. Thereafter, the downtown palaces proved to be most unliquid assets, not unlike an aging cow in Calcutta. Simultaneously, automobiles and the

Veterans Administration's cheap housing loans for veterans combined to drive the populace to the suburbs, far from the downtown rialtos where the faithful had worshiped. Not only were the suburbs remote from the real-estate holdings of the movie house chains, but new house owners learned to view maintenance work as leisure, devoting time and income to lawns in want of mowing, cellars in need of finishing, and furnishings that required dedicated shopping before purchase.

In Hollywood, the moguls did what they could to halt the downward turn after the banner year of 1946. They trimmed the marginal units that made B movies, newsreels, and shorts. They hired George Gallup and other students of public opinion to try to predict the fickle audience's every change of mind. They rid their stables of high-priced, fading, and often idle stars, tightened the numbers of producer-units (whose bosses had begun to form independent firms, anyway), laid off crews, and sealed off unused sound-stages. Eventually, they even auctioned off their props to memorabilia collectors.

Still the studios' grosses kept falling, until, in 1962, they were half the 1946 figure. The studios with the biggest chains suffered the most as their real estate fell ever deeper into disuse. MGM and 20th Century-Fox suffered retrenchment. Universal survived only by merging with the conglomerate Music Corporation of America (MCA) and Technicolor. RKO bled to death during its ownership by Howard Hughes, and its corpse was bought by Desilu, a television production firm. The lesser lots, such as Columbia, stayed afloat only by forming television divisions and selling their inventories of old movies to local stations, which were insatiable in their appetite for anything to fill dead air. One by one, the "poverty row" studios such as Republic fell into idleness and oblivion. The old moguls died off or, like Louis Mayer, were ousted from their own studios. Foreign markets dried up as a result of both protectionist tariffs and the magnetism of Europe's own postwar cinemas. Exhibitors more than ever lived off their popcorn sales. Only the chimera of inflated dollars and the growth in drive-in movies eased the slide into second-rate earnings and vulnerability to threats from federal antitrust investigators, congressional snoops, and audience fickleness.

The audiences may have known what they liked, but the studios, seeming to have lost touch with them, did not know what it was. At every turn, they astonished the moviemakers with their almost alien shifts in taste. They went to see *Since You Went Away* (1944) and *The Best Years of Our Lives*

(1946), prestigious movies about postwar readjustment, but they snubbed *Gangway for Tomorrow* (1944) and even RKO's ensemble of budding stars, *Till the End of Time* (1946). For racial message movies, they liked *Home of the Brave* and *Intruder in the Dust* but not *Lost Boundaries*. They liked the grit of foreign realism in Rossellini's *Paisan* (1948) and Guiseppe de Santis's *Bitter Rice* (1949), but they went for realism in American movies only if it was given a studio-shot gloss of film noir. In 1946–48, *The Naked City, Crossfire, Somewhere in the Night, The Big Sleep*, and *Kiss of Death* all won audiences in sectored batches (a pattern that soon would become typical of all movies except a few biblical boomers, such as *The Robe* [1953]), yet some noir movies, such as Nicholas Ray's *In a Lonely Place* (1950), attracted only the faithful few. With this "dissolution of the homogeneous audience," as Robert Ray calls it in *A Certain Tendency of Hollywood Cinema* (1985), the day of the "sure-seater" came to an end.

One new thing that did catch on was the movie with a "social consciousness" that David Cook in *A History of Narrative Film* (1990) links to "postwar disenchantment with American life." This was the fabled "thinking picture" that the historian James Shotwell had anticipated in 1945 would be an outcome of the war. This newly Europeanized American who had won the war soon felt the drive of the victor's rising expectations. It was as though a "victory culture" arose to challenge the authority of classical Hollywood in providing an ethical and aesthetic core for the postwar audience. Quoting William Manchester, Ray asserts that "a common lore" allowed total strangers to become friends as soon as they mentioned *The Philadelphia Story* or *Mutiny on the Bounty* or some other movie that had defined them.

The old movie formulas decayed into what Ray calls "stylistic conspicuousness," a prime example being David O. Selznick's plump, imperialistic western *Duel in the Sun* (1946). Meanwhile, relative newcomers, such as Elia Kazan, who began with *A Tree Grows in Brooklyn* (1945) and ran off a decade-long string of hits that grew ever more politically challenging, gave the old forms new spins that seemed to fulfill Shotwell's hope for a thinking picture. In *On the Waterfront* (1954), for example, Kazan retooled the outlaw-reluctantly-turned-hero from westerns to fit a plot that required him to break the code of the crime-ridden waterfront, choose to stand by his own code, and inform on the crooks who run the unions of the oppressed stevedores. Like John Garfield's boxer in *Body and Soul* (1947), the hero stands up to the mob because an inner conviction requires it, even though evil men will exact retribution. "What are you gonna do, kill me?" asks Garfield's character. "Everybody dies." Indeed, as we have seen, both the style and substance of film noir fed on these upended ambiguities.

Less successfully, but still profitably, the angst generated by postwar social dysfunction also appeared in the form of the message movie, with its dual heritage in prewar social problem films and the wartime propaganda of unity. Perhaps the message movie and the film noir were two sides of the same political coin. The former took pains to expose some social dysfunction, such as racism, and then often too stridently (too much "on the nose," as the scriptwriters said) called attention to the need for reform. The latter, with its narrow, darkened focus and the unremitting despair at its core, took a conservative point of view, insisting that the status quo, complete with crooked cops and fatcat criminals, was inevitable and only the lone hero who followed his own private code could remain pure of heart in a dirty world.

Both genres emerged in response to the disillusion brought about by war. Message movies called attention to the paltry gains that had been made toward war-borne hopes for "a better world." Film noir shrugged its shoulders and lived with what had been dealt. Unavoidably, it had an easier time of formulating a politics of its art. Its moody style, its hero who showed no mercy and asked none, and its fatalism all corresponded to the cool, deadpan manner of the increasing audience of self-consciously, even willfully, alienated youth. Bogart's Spade, Dick Powell's Marlowe, and Alan Ladd's Raven all spoke to the blues that late adolescents felt.

Message movies seemed to speak for a liberal wing, but only if, like any good propaganda, they avoided preachiness. Moreover, sometimes they fell short of the flip, urban, liberal political attitudes of the kids who learned hipster lingo, dug folksingers, went to Roseland and Bop City for their jazz, and sometimes wore modified zoot suits. At the same time, they failed to impress the surviving conscience liberals of World War II, who had moved to the buttoned-down suburbs. Predictably, the message movie became a genre of prestige event that dramatized its homilies, received awards during Brotherhood Week, and earned profits enough to persist with its exposure of social dysfunction. Yet a gulf yawned between these movies' promise and their attainment. However politically acute the audience had become, it had also become a moving target of hard-to-reach sectors.

Moreover, with no Office of War Information (OWI) looking over their shoulders, the moguls wambled. Selznick's *Till the End of Time* (1946) is a case in point. It began as a purchased property: Niven Busch's *They Dream of Home* (1945), a novella of a black soldier, his family, and their adjustment to peacetime (and his missing legs). But by its release, the movie had become lily-white, almost certainly because RKO wanted to use its more bankable white stars. Or consider Selznick's story department's decision to reject Ann Petry's *The Street* (1946), a novel of the black urban poor. Although, ironically, it had been bought by *Reader's Digest*, this novel was deemed too hot to handle by Selznick's story editors, as well as by every other studio that read it. Unfortunately for the cause of conscience liberalism, the historian Garth Jowett reckons that "movie themes were ahead of domestic [racial] practices."

The gap between Jowett's estimate of Hollywood liberalism and the apparent timidity of Selznick's story department lay in the changing nature of postwar Hollywood. The habitual audience of prewar America was fractured by its postwar drift to the suburbs, the loose cash it had earned during the war and was now sinking into lawn care, trips in new cars, and other new leisure-time options, and its pursuit of education and careers paid for by the GI Bill. Moreover, its new aesthetic sophistication, born of a cultural relativism that the war had induced, made it no longer the surefire audience for which Hollywood used to grind out fifty films per year, per studio, because it was able to count on fifty weeks of solid bookings. Predictably, caution hung in the air during story conferences and over budgeting desks.

The exception to this industrywide circumspection was a gradual decision to take up social and political issues that could be portrayed in personal terms, that is, in message movies. This had been done in prewar social dramas, but now the verisimilitude of such movies could be heightened by on-location shooting. This decision was prompted by the moguls' anxiety over the incursion of Italian neorealist films into the American marketplace and their presumption that wartime documentary film had trained audiences to appreciate the textures of realism. Thus Hollywood entered the peacetime era with a new genre on its hands: the film that portrayed a social problem in personal heroic terms, presented it in a realistic setting, often shot on location, and sometimes offered a more ambiguous denouement than the Production Code Administration would have allowed before the war and yet used a glossy, freely flowing narrative that was so certain in its resolutions that we might call it "Hollywood social realism."

At any rate, these were the angles that earned praise from critics of the day and have been praised by recent historians. "Shatteringly realistic," Bosley Crowther wrote in 1945 of Billy Wilder's *The Lost Weekend*, based on Charles Jackson's novel of the blurred seaminess of the life of an alcoholic. Alcoholism was an easy target, of course, not unlike the boll weevil in prewar documentaries. Nonetheless, many recent historians have concurred with Sklar's view in *Movie-Made America* that these movies were "laudable" in beginning "to tackle fundamental human issues." The success of such movies in tackling unjust court decisions *(Call Northside 777* [1948]), anti-Semitism *(Gentlemen's Agreement* and *Crossfire* [both in 1947]), the haplessness of the emotionally disturbed *(The Snake Pit* [1948]), and the blight of southern white poverty *(The Southerner* in 1945) eventually freed the majors to entertainingly, and even boldly in spots, dramatize the injustice of American racial arrangements. Among the best (all made in 1949–50) were Darryl F. Zanuck's *Pinky*, Dore Schary's movie version of Faulkner's *Intruder in the Dust*, the newcomer Stanley Kramer's *Home of the Brave*, Joseph Mankiewicz's *No Way Out*, and Louis DeRochemont's documentary-style *Lost Boundaries*, each of which borrowed from wartime genres by lowering a single black man into an otherwise white circle, with the result that the whites become better for the experience.

However, the studios' circumstances were still too uncertain for the moguls to take too great a risk with stockholders' money. The times were still too uncertain for the movie business. In fact, Gerald Mast argues in *A Short History of the Movies* (1971), postwar movies were liberated only in their ad copy. Though the studios would herald each new Kramer or Otto Preminger movie as "explosive" or "controversial," the movie itself coyly took care to "offend almost no one." Mast makes a good point. It was an easy matter for ad copy to reflect the collective mood and "expose" the underside of every easy target. Movies such as *I Was a Communist for the FBI* (1951), *The Phenix City Story* (1955), and *High School Confidential* (1958) played to the same collective suspicions targeted by the books of Jack Lait and Lee Mortimer, who "ripped the lid off" some sin, or of John Gunther, who, in his *Inside* series purported to reveal the "real" story behind some social problem but avoided actual politics.

At the same time Hollywood was trying to get to know its new, selective, and sectored audience, changes were taking place in the nation's halls of government. As we have seen, Congress had already used its investigatory, not to say inquisitorial, powers to drag the moguls to Washington to testify as to their warmongering, harboring of "reds" in their writers' bungalows, and the deleterious effect of movies on, as Henry James Forman titled his 1933 book, "our movie-made children." And yet, the moguls also had much to thank the government for, being beholden for much of their prewar and wartime profit to government agencies that had represented their interests to foreign governments; to the Pentagon, which had provided consultation and props for war movies; and to the OWI and other agencies that had commissioned training and propaganda films.

The love-hate relationship continued after the war, as Hollywood alternately found itself in the embrace or stranglehold of the countervailing cultural and political centers of Washington. The rising hysteria of the Cold War all but obliged the congressional right-wingers to seek more "reds" than it ever found, but at the same time almost every social or political agency joined with Hollywood in mapping the new territory opened up by the federal court that allowed Burstyn to show *The Miracle* in Manhattan in 1951. When, on the basis of this case, the National Association for the Advancement of Colored People (NAACP) sought for southern exhibitors the right to show racial material, everyone lent a hand. Louella Parsons branded a southern censor "Un-American." Gradwell Sears of RKO invoked the "four freedoms" speech in defense of an open screen. And Eric Johnston himself, the former chair of the U.S. Chamber of Commerce and Hays's successor at the Motion Picture Association of America, perhaps feeling boxed in by events, took the same tack.

The kiss of death came when the Department of Justice revived its stetted antitrust cases. Once again, at issue was the vertical integration that linked movie lots with theaters. This time, only a year after their most profitable year ever, the movie firms were charged with restraint of trade through their practices of blockbooking and blindbooking.

Even before the war, the Department of Justice had pressed the studios to restrain these practices, which shut out independent houses entirely and which denied the owners of their chain houses a free choice, forcing them to play turkeys, stuff their schedules with studio-made shorts and trailers, book movies even before they were released, and wait out a "clearance" between the first and second runs of a movie. Effectively, the practices funneled moviegoers into a small number of plush downtown houses, such as the Century and Valencia in Baltimore, where the faithful passed a bas relief of the founder, Marcus Loew himself, as the usher walked them to their seats.

In 1948 the adjudication that had begun in 1938—*U.S. v. Paramount*—was reopened, charging the studios with violating the Sherman Antitrust Act. The majors had already inched toward accommodation by trimming production schedules; promoting movies as "better than ever," that is, on their merits, rather than relying on blockbooking; playing angel to some of the independents in return for a share of rentals; and making cuts in staff all the way from gaffers (electricians) to stars. However, this was all too late to head off the court-ordered "divorcement," as the dis-integration was called. The resulting separation of production from retailing altered the essential nature of moviemaking, perhaps for the better for both consumers and makers. Moviegoers now saw movies that exhibitors had competitively bid for rather than merely bought off the rack and were given a chance to see their old favorites on television, as the studios sold movies to the television networks in an effort to find new sources of operating capital. For their part, the moviemakers cut their fixed realty obligations, thereby getting a little relief from the postwar slump.

Parallel to these institutional changes, the surviving studios also embraced technologies that television could not emulate. First among them were various forms of the wide screen: Cinerama, CinemaScope, and VistaVision. Cinerama, never more than a plotless spectacle that its proprietors (the journalist Lowell Thomas, RKO producer Merian Cooper, and its inventor Fred Waller) played in only a few disused palaces that had been adapted to the complex technology, could never compete with familiar narrative-style movies. But the other "anamorphic" systems accomplished precisely what their backers had hoped: they provided a broad sweep to the frame that lent itself both to biblical spectacles and westerns. Indeed, for 20th Century-Fox, which owned CinemaScope, the new wrinkle brought millions to see *The Robe* (1953), a fable of Christ's crucifixion drawn from Lloyd C. Douglas's novel. This was a visual experience that television could not match. Soon epics of many eras found their way onto the wide screen: *The Ten Commandments* (1956), *Ben Hur* (1959), *El Cid* (1961), *Spartacus* (1960), *Mutiny on the Bounty* (1962), and twentieth-century epics such as *Lawrence of Arabia* (1962).

In like fashion, Technicolor, the process that had won an Oscar in 1934 but had been used sparingly because its costs had been prohibitive during the Great Depression and then materials shortages had prevented its production during the war, soon became the preferred medium in which to make musicals; westerns; and, eventually, even film noir. Even so, Bordwell, along the lines of Gomery's essays on the reception of soundfilm, argues that Technicolor became the norm only as culturally based market forces intervened—in this case, the threat of television.

Since 1916, Herbert Kalmus, who was joined later by his daughter, Natalie, had been researching a means of reducing the complex color process to a single strip of film, while keeping the Kalmus firm's name in the engineering trade papers for other achievements. Gradually, in the decade after the Kalmuses won an Oscar for their Technicolor process, they convinced the majors to use it occasionally in features (or segments of them), notably, *Gone with the Wind* (1939) and *A Midsummer Night's Dream* (1935), and in a couple of Oscar-winning documentaries of World War II released in 1944, *Memphis Belle* and *The Battle of Midway*. With its proliferation after the war, the Kalmuses' invention gave the movie industry a respite from its head-to-head competition with television. "During its two decades of hegemony," reckons Bordwell, "Technicolor demonstrated that an engineering firm could flourish by shaping technological innovation to the economic and stylistic needs of its customers." The role technology played in the coming of sound and Technicolor illustrates the complex links between art, commerce, and technology. It gave movies a decade of relief from competition with television, which was still in black and white.

This is not to suggest that after the Paramount "divorcement" order, the studios clung to life only by using new technologies. In fact, not all new technologies were accepted. Old practices persisted, if for no other reason than moviegoers mostly stuck with what they liked, craft guilds knew how to deliver it, and directors already knew its artistic uses, and any new technology that intervened in this symbiosis was rejected. For example, the introduction of 3-D technology to the movies in the 1950s failed not because of the fun journalists and comedians had hazing the silly-looking spectacles audiences had to wear to experience the illusion of 3-D, but a reason more organic to moviemaking. To adapt to and exploit the technology, the camera operators, and thus the director, the writers, and even the actors, were obliged to alter the visual emphasis of their work, its perspective, framing, and cutting of the images. In so doing, they found themselves warping the familiar conventions of movies that had brought moviegoers to their movies—all as a means of calling attention to a gimmick. In *Bwana Devil* (1952), for example, the producer, the radio writer Arch Oboler, refocused viewers' expectations of the stock African adventure yarn by cutting to close-ups of spears hurled at the audience as though they would break through the picture plane. So distracting was the result that a few classy 3-D movies, such as *Kiss Me Kate* (1953) and *Dial M for Murder* (1954), were also run in conventional format.

Other technical devices proved themselves capable of augmenting classical movie conventions and thus survived: Dolby technology cleared surface sound from recordings, and eight-track recording allowed more sophisticated mixing. In addition, as David Cook reports in *A History of Narrative Film* (1990), the wide screen encouraged longer takes that wove cause and effect into the same shot. The French critic Andre Bazin has described this as a politics of technique: by integrating time, space, foreground, and background, the long take restored the dominance of shooting over cutting, thereby providing a "democratic" alternative to the manipulation of mass audiences that, say, Sergei Eisenstein's montage theories had provided his totalitarian masters.

Some technological advances, such as the Cinemobile, altered not the image on the screen, but production processes. Fouad Said, who had been a gofer on the set of Sam Spiegel's *Lawrence of Arabia*, came to California to attend film school, worked on Bill Cosby's sitcom, and eventually developed the idea of the Cinemobile, a studio-on-wheels that freed filmmakers from the aesthetic strictures of the soundstage, got them around Hollywood work rules, and even got them out of the bosses' sight. Thus it allowed independent producers to crawl out from under costly studio overhead costs, the last tether that allowed the old-line studios to dominate the form and substance of post-Hollywood movies. Entire companies could be based in a Cinemobile while on location, and by 1967 nearly half of all movies were shot away from the back lots. At the end of the 1960s, makers of "blaxploitation" movies all but lived in Cinemobiles in their rush to shoot films in black ghettos and to speak in a politics remote from the safe Hollywood model.

But such devices, along with the Steadicam, Minicam, portable battery pack, videotaped sequences that allowed immediate appraisal of the "rushes" (the day's output of a filmmaking unit) that once had required overnight processing, and even the use of videotape as an alternative to film, all served television production at least as much as they helped film production. As early as 1977 the consulting firm Arthur D. Little predicted that by 1985 videotape in the home "will be almost the only way to see film."

Thus the competition between television and film became moot. Hollywoodians simply bought into the new technology whenever they could. As we have seen, Paramount acquired a piece of CBS as early as 1929. Early in the 1950s, Columbia formed its own television arm, Screen Gems; MCA invested in a video system through its subsidiary; Westinghouse broadened from its Group W into seeking to purchase the equipment producer TelePrompter as an avenue into cable television; and studios without access to broadcasting routinely dumped their unpromising movies directly into video stores. The effect was that Hollywood moviemakers offered A movies to the national distributors; B movies metamorphosed into the stock prime-time series that studios supplied to the television networks; and trash movies went directly to the video stores, in much the same way the "poverty row" lots before the war had provided exploitation fare to the grind houses.

At this point it is helpful to recall that different historians may arrive at different conclusions on the basis of the same data. For example, in *The Decline and Fall of the Roman Empire*, Edward Gibbon portrays the end of the classical era of human history as a fall precipitated by internal decay, not the least evidence of which, in his view, was the acceptance of Christianity. In contrast, in *The End of the Ancient World*, William Bark depicts the same time period as a transformation revivified by dynamic Germans who adopted Roman traits even as they changed them. Similarly, we may regard the end of classical Hollywood as either a decline or a transformation to a new thing. For the most part, historians have unwittingly likened Hollywood to Gibbon's Rome: in decline ever since the breakup of the studios and their chains in 1948. However, we might take a Barkian position and argue that external forces such as suburbanization and television transformed Hollywood into a different, rather than declining, force. The Gibbon analysis is by far the more poignant, romantic one, invoking phrases like "Hollywood at Sunset." But a broader Barkian inquiry into multiple forces will probably eventually prove more fruitful an analysis.

We may begin a Barkian analysis by returning to the moviegoers and the movies they liked after their exodus to the suburbs. As we have seen, after World War II, the ranks of moviegoers thinned, either because, living in the suburbs as they now were, they were too far away from the downtown theaters or because they were busy waxing their skis or mulching their forsythia or had surrendered to soporific television.

At least some new moviegoing patterns were driven by new social factors, such as the fact that the aggregate age of moviegoers was declining. Jowett, for example, points out that summer replaced the Christmas season as a boom time for moviegoing and attributes the shift partly to "the growing importance" of the drive-in theater, one of the temples of the expanding youth market—both the dating crowd and families in need of babysitting. The summer grosses also rose in part because kids on vacation from school were free to make use of the almost universally air-conditioned theaters in the shopping malls. Moreover, university students were marginally more likely to watch movies regularly and in the social packs for which they had become famous in the sociological literature.

Accompanying this drift of the young toward movies—a drift also toward the shopping mall and away from the downtown—were new cyclical patterns of boom and bust for the movies. Conventionally realistic musicals such as *Star!* (1968) and *Paint Your Wagon* (1969) flopped with this audience, as did old-fashioned star vehicles such as Richard Burton and Elizabeth Taylor's *Boom* (1968), a Hollywoodized Tennessee Williams play. These movie-goers preferred low-budget, truculently leftist agitprop such as *Medium Cool*, *Easy Rider*, *Goodbye Columbus*, and *Alice's Restaurant*, all of which came out in 1969, and they stayed away in droves from pop-up-book versions of the new politics, such as Stanley Kramer's *RPM* (1970). They also liked movies that floated on a wry or somber mood rather than movies that churned along on a well-made plot, such as *Slaughterhouse Five* (1972), Kurt Vonnegut's bitter indictment of the raid on Dresden in World War II; *A Clockwork Orange* (1971), Stanley Kubrick's portrayal of mindless barbarians; and Thomas Mann's *Death in Venice* (1971), with its wistfully perverse idealism. Indeed, any empathetic portrayal of outsiders in "buddy pictures" such as *Butch Cassidy and the Sundance Kid* (1969), "road pictures" such as *Five Easy Pieces* (1970), and rock documentaries such as *Monterey Pop* (1968) drew flocks of young audiences to otherwise underused theaters. The ultimate outsider movie was the martial arts product imported from the shops of Run Run Shaw and other Hong Kong or Singapore cineastes. Occasionally, an American moviemaker might weave the Asian traits depicted in the heroes of these movies—coolness under stress, rigorous discipline, and monkish self-denial—into a succinct, young-focused, American movie, such as Tom Laughlin did with *Billy Jack* (1971). Featuring a part-Indian hero who is not only a western loner, an Indian outcast, and an effortlessly skilled warrior, but also the sensitive husband of a woman who organizes a school for waifs in which the folkish values of the American New Left were taught, this was a sweetheart of a youth movie.

For those with a yen for the familiar, major studios annually turned out outsized, sleekly conventional epics of gangster life (*The Godfather*), outer space combats that echoed World War II wing-camera footage (*Star Wars*), long vanished white working-class life (*Grease*), and disaster films that reminded young moderns of human frailty (*Airport*). These movies also showed both mature adults and sobersided youth facing adversity, thereby offering a common ground on which Aquarian youth and square adults met to restore a common faith in Hollywood's genius for celebrating both heroism and convention. In turn, faith led to booming production budgets and even larger advertising campaigns. As any horseplayer might have told them, betting the day's wad on one highly touted horse invariably limits the total number of bets, transforming the delicate business of planning a day's betting over the full card into a hit-or-miss strategy that, in the case of movies, sometimes reduced a year's play into a half-dozen films, the bust of any one of which could shut the studio.

Everyone in the business seemed to be infected with this elephantiasis. Otto Preminger, who had been at his best in such neat chiaroscuro films noir as *Laura* in 1944, filled the genre with puffery in *Anatomy of a Murder* in 1959. To Ben Gazzara's overacting, James Stewart's foxy grandpa shtick, and the casting of Joseph Welch, the actual counsel for the Pentagon during the McCarthy hearings, as a wry old judge in a rural courthouse were added Franz Klein–like main titles by Saul Bass and a score by Duke Ellington.

Stanley Kramer followed a similar course from the light touch he showed in *Home of the Brave*, the tight little racial message movie he made in 1949, to the heavy hand he used in 1961 to make *Judgement at Nuremberg*, his recreation of the Nazi war crimes tribunals, which came complete with more stars playing against type, Judy Garland and Montgomery Clift as concentration camp survivors and Spencer Tracy over the top as the judge. Kramer, pleased as ever with himself, had used the process on other themes, such as race relations (*The Defiant Ones* [1958] and *Guess Who's Coming to Dinner* [1967]) and the threat of nuclear holocaust (*On the Beach* [1959]).

The work of Robert Rossen, a leftist neorealist, grew from a tabloid look at boxing in *Body and Soul* (1947) to solid but overlarge efforts such as a

Huey Longish *All the King's Men* (1949) and an anatomy of the demimonde of pool shooters, *The Hustler* (1961).

At the same time, as Mast points out in *A Short History of the Movies,* "the limits of American Realism" were also being extended by directors migrating from television. Martin Ritt made *Hud* (1963), the story of an antihero in the contemporary West. Sidney Lumet offered *The Pawnbroker* (1965), a realist movie that violated realist conventions by using flash frames of the Holocaust in portraying a Harlem Jew who had survived the camps, but at the terrible price of cauterizing his emotions. Arthur Penn made the era-defining movie with *Bonnie and Clyde* (1967), his ambivalent portrayal of two offspring of mid-America turned legendary bankrobbers.

Realism was also becoming superrealism, in the shiny style of the painters who did tromp l'oeil images of 1960s American cars. Douglas Sirk's "women's melodramas," such as *Imitation of Life* (1959) and *The Magnificent Obsession* (1954), attained a visual pitch in which realistic tone and texture were so saturated in color and so overripe with focused clarity and interior meanings as to abuse the memory of the Italian realism from which they descended. A good example of the shift from real to superreal may be seen in two extremes of the work of Nicholas Ray. His *In a Lonely Place* (1950) was a spare, dark, almost one-set melodrama of the anomic emptiness of postwar life that only film noir could portray. Less than a decade later, Ray had another opportunity to work in the same style. Columbia had picked up *The Fifty-Minute Hour,* Robert Lindner's collection of gemlike short stories based on the lives of the patients he treated as a psychotherapist in Baltimore. Ray's *Rebel without a Cause* (1955), considerably overwritten from Lindner's book and puffed into a melodramatic star vehicle for James Dean, the idol of teenagers and romantic rebels, was a paean to teenage angst and self-absorption.

Accompanying Lindner's psychoanalytic vista was a spate of movies drawn from the revived rage for Freud on Broadway: *Picnic* (1956), *Middle of the Night* (1959), and *Come Back Little Sheba* (1952). B-movie knockoffs were teenage movies set in prisons, dragstrips, beaches, and, finally, the plots of old movies, as in *I was a Teenage Frankenstein* (or *Werewolf* or . . .).

Curiously, moviemakers were rarely able to predict the ingredients necessary to keep a cycle rolling or to anticipate the next cycle. In the postclassical era, they knew only that audiences had scattered to the suburbs, saw movies in fickle, sectored taste-cultures, leapt from one fad to the next, and had begun to lose the anchoring they had once gleaned from the nuclear family. One year they would turn against *Cleopatra* (1963) or *Thoroughly Modern Millie* (1967); the next they might embrace the socialist grime of England's "angry young men" movies, *Room at the Top* (1959), *This Sporting Life* (1963), and *Look Back in Anger* (1958); and finally, they might take up their own version of leftist politics, not so much class based as generationally defined, in movies like *Easy Rider* (1969), *Alice's Restaurant* (1969), and the sad trail of flops that followed in search of access to a cycle, such as *The Strawberry Statement* and *Getting Straight*, both released in 1970, and *RPM*.

Moviemakers knew they needed to win a loyal audience of the young, but no one had found the secret to continuity among moviegoers who, though young, also soon grew older. Furthermore, some movie patrons, as they grew more sophisticated and even began to take film studies courses, became so discriminating as to see only the "rare" movie. Thus these post–classical era movies became almost adolescent in their erratic, pouty, precious politics, alighting on this or that issue or theme and quickly dropping it. Only documentary records of rock concerts—1970's *Woodstock* and *Gimme Shelter*—seemed aptly cohesive as "social metaphors."

The only theme to survive from former times was alienation from the city. In the few westerns made at the time, the loner heroes, who had been cast by modernism into the dustbin of history, not only despaired of the city and its technologies, but, indeed, were killed off by them. In the last reel, the heroes either chose to "die game" in a shootout or were pursued to their deaths by the law in trains or automobiles, as in *Tell Them Willie Boy Is Here* (1969), *The Wild Bunch* (1969), *The Magnificent Seven* (1960), *Butch Cassidy and the Sundance Kid*, and, in its way, *Easy Rider*. In the last reel of *Chinatown* (1974), a movie that presents layer after layer of urbane deception and moral rot, a cynical detective who has known his beat for a lifetime can only explain life in an empty mockery of a moral: "It's Chinatown, Jake."

A superficial look at this renaissance in moviegoing, rooted as it was in the unfocused rages of youth and the theatrical politics of the hippie counterculture and dominated by film school brats and other filmmakers from outside Hollywood, would tell one that it was an assault on the conventions of Hollywood and suburbia. But deeply embedded in many movies was also a vein of opprobrium of America. *The Godfather*, for example, was a textbook case of aspiration up Robert Merton's "alternative ladder of success"—

crime—by those who had been denied access to the establishment's ladder. Thus it was a subcultural icon of the nation's openness. In much the same way, the youth movies celebrated an America ruined by those "over thirty." This accounts for the westerns that ended with their free-spirit heroes destroyed (Butch Cassidy, Bonnie and Clyde, and Billy Jack and the other veterans of Vietnam), the nostalgia movies that sketched the painless days of yore (*American Graffiti* and *The Way We Were* in 1973 and *The Great Gatsby* the following year), and even the occasional ironic retrospective of *Casablanca* at the Brattle Theatre near Harvard Square. Of course, this shameless playing to the new audience smelled a little like the old Hollywood doing its duty to the stockholders by giving its fans the classical cinema that they demanded. The only difference was the segmental quality of the audience that allowed both the rebellious *Cool Hand Luke* (1967) and the dutiful *Dirty Harry* (1971) to be hits.

Of all the postclassical films, the most startling in its assault on convention was the "blaxploitation" movie. The movies' ideological echo of the civil rights movement and the riots that followed the frustration of the rising expectations the movement had given hope to, the genre of blaxploitation movies was created at a time when sexual mores, particularly as they related to promiscuity, were relaxing. Both of these breaches with convention—political violence and permissive sex—filled the nightly news on television, challenging the legitimacy of the ratings system by demonstrating that sex and violence were normative. In addition, white Americans' exodus to the suburbs freed scores of disused downtown theaters to be filled by black ghetto kids in search of the truculent politics of their new genre.

At the same time, in the mid-1960s Herbert Hill, the labor secretary of the NAACP, followed the path of Walter White, the former head of the organization, to Hollywood to assail the segregated craft guilds in the movie business and the studios' hiring practices. Hill brought against the unions the threat of decertification by the NLRB by charging that they violated the terms of the Economic Opportunity Act of 1964.

A final, unforeseen event that helped loosen the institutional bonds that defined Hollywood occurred in 1957, when the New York judge hearing *Excelsior Pictures v. New York Regents* overruled the denial of a license to a "nudie" movie, citing the free-speech aspects of *Burstyn v. Wilson*, better known as "the *Miracle* case" (see chapter 4). Two years later, Russ Meyer took nudity out of nudist camps and brought it into daily life, much as

Claude Manet had done in painting *Dejeuner sur l'Herbe*. Meyer's *The Immoral Mr. Teas* (1959) and other movies inched away from mere voyeurism toward plot-driven erotica and violence. His success encouraged others, such as Herschell Lewis, whose *Blood Feast* (1963) mingled sex, bloodletting, and racial politics and earned more than $1 million on a $20,000 nut. We cannot know how many black kids saw these movies, but the unrestrained revanchism as a motive for bloodletting certainly anticipated one of the traits they soon would expect of their blaxploitation movies.

As for black moviegoers, they had long since withheld their loyalty from the integrationist successors to the conscience-liberal movies inspired by World War II, the platoon movies such as *Sahara* and *Bataan* in 1943 and their successors in 1949, *Pinky* and *Intruder in the Dust*. The movies of Sidney Poitier that marked the next quarter century seemed merely to repeat the theme of the war movies and message movies that a lone black descending into an all-white circle can, by his presence, win over the whites and make them feel the better for the experience. *No Way Out* (1950), *The Slender Thread* (1965), *Patch of Blue* (1965), *To Sir with Love* (1967), and Poitier's Oscar-winning *Lilies of the Field* (1963) had all been the same movie. The enthusiasm that once had greeted almost any black attempt to test American racial arrangements had chilled, and black critics had begun wryly asking, "Why does white America love Sidney Poitier so?" Only Harry Belafonte's own *Odds Against Tomorrow* (1959) and Ivan Dixon's *Nothing But a Man* (1964) seemed to build on Poitier's early advances.

Besides which, television had entered the equation as never before. Its documentary footage, particularly of the Montgomery bus boycott of 1955, the Greensboro sit-in movement of 1960, and the marches in Washington, Selma, and other southern racial battlegrounds, carried the medium to such heights of advocacy of the black cause that the producer William Monroe called television "the chosen instrument of the civil rights movement." The networks had found their authoritative documentary voice in the 1950s and 1960s with such series as *See It Now*, *20th Century*, and *Project XX*. All of them brought into every home images of a violent resistance to racial change and the quiet dignity of the black leadership. Conventional Hollywood movies, with respect to racial angles, at least, could not keep up.

The waning censorship, the rising violence linked to racial strife, the loss of thrust in the racial material released by Hollywood, the daily television portrayal of African Americans bravely acting on their own behalf in the face of violent threats, and Herbert Hill's incursion into the lily-white labor system of Hollywood with the weight of the Economic Opportunity Act behind him all coalesced into a national mood that drove radicals forward. Whether a Swedish team's trailing of a Harlem cabbie *(Walk in My Shoes)*, Armand Schoendorfer's similarly framed film that followed a black West Point cadet to Vietnam *(The Anderson Platoon)*, William Jersey's abrasive reportage of a tense meeting of black and white minds in a Lutheran church, or merely the visualized news from Birmingham or Selma, the television films of the 1960s forced viewers to encounter their nation's shabby racial arrangements. Taken by surprise, Hollywood could only repeat itself in Poitier's movies or strive for strident sexual or violent exploitations such as *Drum* (1976), *Mandingo* (1975), *Free, White, and 21* (1962), and *I Passed for White* (1960).

At the end of the violent 1960s, even comedies turned bitter and contentious. Leading the new wave was Melvin Van Peebles, an American expatriate in France who had written some novels in French and thereby earned a director's card. He began to formulate his movie politics slowly, beginning with *The Story of a Three Day Pass* (1968), a neatly turned comedy of racial manners involving a black GI and his French girlfriend and their racial adventures during his weekend pass. A neat dram of wry, the movie became a cause célèbre when it was chosen as a French entry in the San Francisco film festival. What followed might have amounted to nothing had Van Peebles merely played the humble black aesthete. Instead, he came across in the press as truculent, prickly, too smart for his own good. Doors opened for him in Hollywood. His next movie was *Watermelon Man* (1970), a creditable Hollywood racial comedy that outreached anything the studios had ever risked, featuring the black comedian Godfrey Cambridge playing a white man whose life is wrenched from its moorings when his skin mysteriously darkens.

But it was his next movie, *Sweet Sweetback's Baad Asssss Song* (1970), that revealed the possibilities of exploiting the postclassical Hollywood order. Van Peebles worked around the guilds, pulled in front money on the basis of his newfound reputation, threatened white men and cajoled black men into giving him whatever he needed—more money or freer access to editing rooms, for example—and always allowed himself to be portrayed in the media as a heavy-lidded, simperingly dangerous outlaw with no fixed address. Indeed, his public persona and the protagonist he played—with not a little star quality—in *Sweet Sweetback's* meshed into one character. Never mind that this movie that called explicitly for black insurrection lost its way and became a black road movie with not a rebel but a fugitive as its hero. His example so inspired the next generation, the generation of Spike Lee, that when the director of a documentary on the making of Lee's *Do the Right Thing* (1989) shot on Lee's Brooklyn locations he focused much on Van Peebles, who even gave a little speech in which he pointed out the continuity between his own era and Lee's.

In between Van Peebles and Lee was a string of blaxploitation movies that followed the master's example. They were truculent in tone, vengeful in motive, and paced by hard-driving, percussive soundtracks. Often dismissed as a contemptible lot, they in fact were a mixed bag that provided a template for success in the new Hollywood. Many white independents had found their way onto the screen after the Paramount decree, but few had found the magic formula that included artful moviemaking and the chutzpa that drove up ticket sales. Shirley Clark's *The Cool World* (1964), Anthony Harvey and Gene Persson's movie of LeRoi Jones's *Dutchman* (1967), the entire canon of John Cassavetes, and even the outsized but prestigious pictures of Samuel Goldwyn, who managed to be in Hollywood while not quite of it, were among the scores of independent movies that were successful but largely lacked the flair that Van Peebles displayed.

Blaxploitation movies thus contributed to the creation of a new system in which independently accomplished work might be financed from the start in exchange for a right to distribute, financed by a line of credit established on behalf of a prospective distributor, or financed independently, either by a bank or by a firm such as Mattel, *Reader's Digest*, or one of the conglomerates (Gulf & Western, Warner Communications, Coca-Cola, or Sony) that had just entered Hollywood as the new owners of what had been the old-line major studios.

It is for this reason that as part of the cycle of blaxploitation movies we find MGM, an old-line studio on its last legs, engaging the black photographer Gordon Parks to make Ernest Tidyman's *Shaft* (1971), a conventional, if more violent and erotic, private-eye movie starring Richard Roundtree (a black cosmetics model); Mattel financing *Sounder* (1972), a black movie drawn from a novel of a Depression-era family in which the family's race was never mentioned; and classics such as Liam O'Flaherty's *The Informer* (1935) and W. R. Burnett and John Huston's *The Asphalt Jungle* (1950) (one of the last classic films noir) reappearing in black versions.

In tandem came previously unthinkable movies from black sources, such as *Cotton Comes to Harlem* (1970), Chester Himes's outrageously comic police-procedural set in Harlem, and *Five on the Black Hand Side* (1973), Oscar Williams's fable of a black family experiencing crises induced by facing up to black nationalism and feminism. In the classical Hollywood style, there were message movies against the proliferation of drugs, such as *Gordon's War* (1973) and *A Hero Ain't Nothin' But a Sandwich* (1978). And, always, there were the revanchist legends spun out in the style of Van Peebles, the movies in which "whitey gets his," such as Sam Greenlee's *The Spook Who Sat by the Door* (1973) and D'Urville Martin's *The Final Comedown* (1972).

Then, as suddenly as the cycle had turned into a genre, it dried up, a victim of its own redundancy and its unfocused racial politics. Blaxploitation movies had squandered the loyalty of their often vocal fans by playing only to their shallowest feelings of being victims. Except those movies that urged a sort of black guerrilla warfare against oppressors, which represented a distinct break with the increasing, almost Gramscian, pragmatism of African American leadership, they lacked a focused communal politics. They portrayed heroism in the old-hat terms of the Hollywood western, presented group cohesion only in the smallest of circles (family and neighborhood), and lashed out only at operatically overdrawn heavies, such as a sneering Mafioso.

Unavoidably, as the genre emptied itself of political content the audience looked elsewhere, mainly to Chinese martial arts movies that turned revenge into an art form. In 1968, after the death of Martin Luther King took away the civil rights movement's national focus, *Variety* reviewed Run Run Shaw's *The Golden Swallow* (1968), granting that it adhered to "unusually high standards" for such a low-budget movie but panning its strident revenge motif and predicting it would find a market only in residents of poor neighborhoods, whose simmering rage was easily aroused. The very movie that disaffiliated black, urban youth seemed ready for! Then came Bruce Lee, a minor player in a television series, *The Green Hornet*, whose exuberant style and earnest manner caught Americans' attention and who transformed the genre into a vibrant replacement for the flagging blaxploitation movies. A half-dozen factors fell into place to produce a retailing phenomenon: Shaw enlisted the help of Raymond Chow, former agent of the U.S. Information Agency and English teacher who knew American culture; Lee quickly revealed his star quality; the movies gave black kids a guilt-free revanchist politics, in which the bad guys were not white Americans but decadent mandarins; each movie centered on fast-paced action, rather than nuance; the moviemakers worked from tight budgets, shooting silent footage whenever possible and dubbing to fit various linguistic markets; and in America, whites had fled the nation's downtowns and their rialtos just as Hollywood's black-angled movies had lost their ideological thrust. The result was the last original genre that caught the fancy of a coherent market, a phenomenon that echoed classical Hollywood but in fact had been born in the cities on the rim of the South China Sea.

Thereafter, most genre films paid homage to the older forms, as did Clint Eastwood's and Sergio Leone's spaghetti westerns, shot in Spain and Italy, and their stylized heirs, such as Eastwood's *Unforgiven* (1992) and Mario Van Peebles's *Posse* (1993). The film noir work of Roman Polanski in *Chinatown* and Stephen Frears in *The Grifters* (1990) celebrated their 1940s forebears. Musicals, even though usurped by frequent tours by Broadway shows and live concerts, persisted in a few titles, such as in musical interludes in Robert Altman's *Nashville* (1975) and Spike Lee's *School Daze* (1988). In rhythm and trajectory, bio pics also reprised the bio pics of Hollywood's classical era. In Lee's *Malcolm X* (1992), for example, one sees the life of the black nationalist ideologue presented in the same cadenced narrative—the progression from humble roots through coming of age, self-knowledge, assumption of the mantle of leadership, death in the cause of the group's redemption, and, finally, admission into the hagiography of leaders who revealed the common humanity of their people—that moviegoers in Hollywood's classical era viewed in *Abraham Lincoln* (1930), *Juarez* (1939), and *Pride of the Marines* (1945), the story of the blinded Marine Al Schmid.

The point is, of course, that Hollywood's integral politics of art had passed on to other cultural centers, ranging from black ghettos to Asian capitals to, finally, small, independent studios, such as Hal Roach, Screen Gems, and Ziv, that served television's hunger for cheap thirty-minute shows. That is, the older, classical forms had passed onto "others": whether blacks in search of redemptive movies or television watchers. For the insular television viewers of the suburbs, sitcoms, prestigious dramas such as the Philco Playhouse, the US Steel Hour, and *Twilight Zone*, and weekly westerns such as *Gunsmoke*, *The Rebel*, and *Sugarfoot* reenacted the old Hollywood rituals, presenting easily digested, unproblematic resolutions of uncomplicated issues—surely bringing approving smiles to the faces of Hays and Breen, watching from their heaven.

These shifts in the circumstances of production and exhibition were, in turn, induced by the heat and pressure generated by larger external forces. That is, Hollywood at its sunset paralleled Bark's Rome more than Gibbon's Rome: It was being changed by alien, inexorable forces, rather than declining as a result of internal rot. Changes were even induced by foreign invaders. Not Goths and Vandals, to be sure, but Italy's Rossellini and Leone and China's Shaw and Chow. No longer an arbiter of a national taste-culture, no longer an "imperial" capital, Hollywood was adrift, pandering to each new segment of a market, seeking rather than defining art, having to answer to increasingly remote masters in other industries. Like the suburbs to which most of its patrons had moved, it grew characterless, dependent on commodities (whether popcorn or tie-in goods such as tee-shirts), and addicted to huge "hits" and their sequels—*Die Hard, Die Hard II*, and so on.

Bibliographical Essay

The reader should know that historians of film often come to their subject having only a generation or so of historical literature upon which to draw. This scholarly scaffolding is, as one historian once wrote of the ladder of social mobility in colonial America, "short and shaky." And yet, in recent years, the newest crop of historians of movies has reached for theories of historiography that often seem so confidently nebulous as to float free of everything that has come before. I hope this brief note captures some of the creative chaos that both drives and defines the state of movie history at this writing.

A glance at both the literature and the accessibility to the movies that have made writing it possible reveals the dynamism that impels this state of flux. I believe that more than thirty years ago, in May 1963, an essay of mine, "The Negro Reaction to the Motion Picture, *The Birth of a Nation*," was the first piece about the social history of movies to appear in an American historical quarterly. For a contrast with more recent trends, we need only turn to the June 1995 issue of *Journal of American History*. The cover illustration is a cropped movie "still" of Walt Disney's Mickey Mouse in his 1928 debut in *Steamboat Willie*, a "teaser" to Steven Watts's essay on the coming together of art and politics in the work of Disney. On the inside pages are bibliographical rubrics, such as "Visual and Performing Arts" and "Popular Culture," that embrace movies, along with more conventional subsections, such as "African Americans," that include movie topics. Other indicators of the trend may be found in specialized journals edited by historians, such as *Film & History* and the *Historical Journal of Film, Radio, and Television*.

With this broadening of academic attention to the social history of mass media has come an openhanded access to the primary documents of movie history. Today the most isolated student of movie history can borrow hundreds of historically significant titles from the corner Blockbuster or purchase them for extended study. Moreover, every metropolis seems to be served by a historically minded shop such as Baltimore's Video Americain. The available titles are rendered accessible not only by the stores' own catalogs but also by Tom Weiner's *The Book of Video Lists* (1988), the anonymous *The Video Tape and Disc Guide to Home Entertainment* (1986, 7th ed.), and other indexes. In former times, a prospective viewer of historical movies counted on the "audiovisual" section of the municipal library or, if affiliated with a "film society," consulted James L. Limbacher's famous guide, *Feature Films on 8 mm and 16 mm, Available for Rental . . . in the United States* (1967, *et seq.*), a daunting source at best because of its focus on "rental" films.

At present, an energetic reader might have the good fortune to live near the growing number of (usually) university-based film study centers as well as genuine archives devoted to both research and preservation. Harvard, Yale, UCLA, and other major universities offer both study centers and archives—UCLA's being the best by virtue of its link to the American Film Institute.

Less accessible to all but the most resourceful amateur scholars are the members of the Federation International des Archivs du Films (FIAF). Formerly a tight, closehanded group of archives in fear of studio snoops in search of misappropriated property in the archives' collections, they have since blossomed into relatively open "cinematheques" complete with Rene Beauclair's *The International Directory of Film and TV Documentation Centers* (1988). Of them all, the most accessible are the Library of Congress, the Museum of Modern Art (New York), the George Eastman House Museum of Photography (Rochester), and the British National Film Library in Berkhamsted.

A number of archives have acquired manuscript materials, including studio archives reposing in the University of Southern California, University of Wisconsin, and UCLA among others, as well as personal papers such as those of D. W. Griffith (in the Museum of Modern Art), the George Kleine Collection (in the Library of Congress), the Stanley Kramer Papers (in UCLA), and the Edison Papers (in the Edison Archive in New Jersey), among others—almost all of them compiled in *The National Union List of Manuscripts* (1966, *et seq.*). Not the least of these repositories are the records of various federal and state agencies, such as censor boards and the U. S. Department of Commerce. A good example is the Office of War Information, an instrument of propaganda during World War II, the records of which repose in the National Archives Center in Suitland, Maryland.

Essential to any inquiry into movie history are the tradepapers: early on, *Billboard, New York Dramatic Mirror,* and *The Morning Telegraph* (horseracing paper that covered show business) and later, *Variety, Motion Picture Herald,* and other exhibitors' serials, along with their ancillary yearbooks. A thorough list of them by pedigree appears in Allen and Gomery's *Film History.* Other profitable paper trails include the clipping files of almost all of the libraries. Moreover, within less than a generation most of these data sources, as well as movie stills, will be stored on laser discs and CD-ROM systems to be used as an inventory for a sort of intellectual home-shopping. In addition to the archives specifically dedicated to movies, others such as the Performing Arts branch of the New York Public Library and the Schomburg Center for the Study of African American Culture also house movie clippings.

It should go without saying that a dutiful reader will have combed the usual guides to serial literature, such as *The Reader's Guide to Periodical Literature, The Public Affairs Information Service Bulletin, The Social Sciences and Humanities Index* (in its various guises), *The Essay and General Literature Index,* and of course *The New York Times Index,* and their routes of access into electronic databases. Less familiar but even more necessary to basic research are the specialized film indexes, such as the WPA project, *The Film Index* (1941), its sequel by Richard Dyer MacCann and Ted Perry, *The New Film Index . . . 1930-1970* (1975), John C. and Lana Gerlach's *The Critical Index: A Bibliography of Articles on Film in English, 1946-1973* (1974), and the two annuals, Vincent Aceto, *et al., Film Literature Index* (1973, *et seq.*), and *The International Index to Film Periodicals* (1974, and annually).

Having set forth this guide to the literature, were I to choose one research tool above all others, it would be Robert C. Allen and Doug Gomery's *Film History: Theory and Practice* (1985). At once a theoretical primer, how-to-do-it manual, brief history (rooted in localism), and bibliographical essay, it allows the reader to "do" history.

Their essay on sources captures the pell-mell tumbling forward of the canon of movie history literature. Yet they say "the best place to begin reading" is among the older, anecdotal, inside-dopester-historians who wrote of Hollywood from within: Terry Ramsaye, *A Million and One Nights* (1926); Ben Hampton, *A History of the Movies* (1931); and, anticipatory of later scholars, Lewis Jacobs, *The Rise of the America Film: A Critical History* (1968).

The pace of writing slowed during World War II, resulting in only a few oddments such as *Look* magazine's compendium, *From Movielot to Beachhead* (1945), then resumed in a rush when the study of movies revived by feeding off the many wartime retrospectives induced by a raw stock shortage (and thus a diminution in the number of new movies). And by the coming of foreign movies—first, Eisenstein's Russian movies, because they were "classics," then the

British patriotic movies such as Noel Coward's *In Which We Serve,* followed by a rivulet drawn from literature, Shakespeare's *Henry V* to *The Mill on the Floss.*

For me the *Ur-jahr* was 1957, when I was a young college teacher founding my first "film society" in the rural coastal plain of North Carolina: Arthur Knight's *The Liveliest Art,* Richard Griffith and Arthur Mayer's *The Movies,* and James Agee's reviews bound as *Agee on Film* all appeared in the same year. Agee's wiseguy essays, in which he could feint with damned praise by calling a movie "superb trash," were soon followed by Pauline Kael's own wry pieces that had begun to slouch eastward from their roots in her Bay Area theater program notes.

Lurking below the surface, one imagines a gam of academic historians, perhaps inspired by Siegfried Kracauer's *From Caligari to Hitler: A Psychological History of the German Film* (1947), which Princeton University Press brought out in English. Perhaps in Kracauer they saw a means of imposing an analytical order on a subject that television and suburbanization had threatened to render archaic, therefore classic, therefore worthy of study. Led by A. R. Fulton's *Motion Pictures: The Development of An Art* (1960), easily a baker's dozen or more histories appeared, each one propped by the scaffolding of academic apparatus and festooned with garlands of *ibid*s. At first more focused on getting their story straight and only later bent upon a scholarly analytical "discourse," they aimed at an "art" and its "development," seen in a "long view," emanating from a "reel plastic magic," and only later growing into histories that were "short," "concise," and "interpretive." Meanwhile, in a parallel movement in Europe, particularly based first in France in the circles connected to the serials *Cahiers du Cinema* and then *Tel Quel,* then in Cambridge and the journal *Screen,* the academics reached for more precise analytical tools drawn from the fields of anthropology, feminism, Marxism, Freudian psychology, semiology, and others.

It is this headlong rush of historical and critical writing by a single driven generation that marks the field of film study. Whether the "new historicism" of recent literati whose writing appears in *New Literary History* or the broadening field of social history that, for now, has become "cultural studies," the body of work grows exponentially, rendering the task of writing a brief bibliography daunting. Nonetheless, what follows is an essay on the sources that have guided my chapters. If there is an angle or slant, it is probably in my reluctance to plunge headlong into the new, my wish to cling to documents rather than to sort them into theoretical slots, and in the notion that history itself is a force that alters whoever participates in it as much or more than rigidly teleological or deterministic or ahistorical theories would have us believe.

Following A. R. Fulton's example, Gerald Mast's *A Short History of the Movies*

(1971) began a cycle that, while not bound by theory, asserted a point of view—mainly, that of movie history as a long narrative of the evolution of a movie aesthetic that "reflected" the society that made and consumed the movies. In turn these movies reflected a response to major crises—particularly war, depression, and systemic changes. A few of the writers of this period offered various social, economic, and institutional data at the expense of the anecdotal story. Kenneth MacGowan (who entered academia from Hollywood) wrote a sophisticated insider's book, *Behind the Screen: The History and Techniques of the Motion Picture* (1965), while Robert Sklar (*Movie-Made America: A Social History of American Movies* [1975]) and Garth Jowett (*Film: The Democratic Art* [1976]) culled their data from regulatory, judicial, and industrial publications in their fashioning of more incisive tools of analysis. While clearly social history, their work as yet avoided the sort of self-conscious theoretical modes that were to come. In some ways the most useful of the general works is Robert C. Allen and Douglas Gomery's *Film History: Theory and Practice* (1985) by virtue of its creating a distance between itself and the narrativists, much as Sklar and Jowett had done, while also analyzing without actually embracing the ahistorical theorists. In this way, they managed a skeletal, conventional history, a long bibliographical essay, a how-to-do-it primer, and a modest argument for their own theory that the heart of much movie history resides in studies of local realty trends as evidence of the underlying economic history of movies.

A systematic analysis of the theoretical literature of movies is a time-consuming and daunting prospect. Historians have only just brought themselves to consciously examine sources in the light of theoretical constructions drawn from outside of their own guild. Moreover, those who have done so often have merely formalized their usual attention to language and its fragile meanings. Any reader of Carl Becker's venerable *The Declaration of Independence* (1922) will know that, long before semiology became a tool of analysis, historians took into account the ambiguity of language. Dominick LaCapra in a recent essay pointed out how, a century ago, William M. Sloane, a typical historian in search of the abstract standard of "objectivity," claimed that "history is a science," while in more recent times the historian's duty was not to attain some impossible goal of truth but only to grant "a recognition of the problematic nature of language." See LaCapra's "History, Language, and Reading: Waiting for Crillon," *American Historical Review* 100 (June 1995): 799–828. In yet another instance of a recent exchange over the elusive nature of language, P. N. Furbank in a review chided Robert Darnton for putting too fine a point on the notion of a "reader-response" form of critical reading. In order to "get" the drift of some older essay, Furbank merely argued for careful attention rather than some esoteric tool of analysis. We are not "some eighteenth century reader," he wrote. "He is, rather, ourselves." See Furbank's "Nothing Sacred," *New York Review of Books* (June 8, 1995): 51–55.

Like Furbank's reader, I wish to be attentive to meaning without resorting to extraordinary tools and without consuming every line written by cited authors. Perhaps as an instinctive resistance to too neat forms of causation or explanation, particularly those that neglect to take into account the place of chance, error, and happenstance (and, of course, calculation and design), I have allowed this book to be informed by (though not to say guided by) a sense of the past as a force. As C. Vann Woodward, in his *The Burden of Southern History* (1968), quotes one of William Faulkner's characters in *Intruder in the Dust*: "The past is never dead. It's not even past." In this spirit, I found sympathetic vibrations of John Kenneth Galbraith's *American Capitalism: The Concept of Countervailing Power* (1952) echoing through my thoughts. In it he argues that, apart from ideologies that drive history, the past has also been driven by conflict as surely as Aristotle's dramaturgy, except that, unlike a well-made play, the conflict seemed more like a running firefight between resourceful if not equal adversaries. No beginning, middle, climax, and denouement here: only struggle in perpetuity between "countervailing" powers.

From his own angle in Marxism, the founder of the Italian Communist Party, Antonio Gramsci, who spent much of his life in Mussolini's jails, worked toward a position similar to Galbraith's, thereby softening Marx's teleology. Rather than Marx's certain (but despairingly distant) proletarian revolution—led by, predicted the Leninists, professional revolutionaries—Gramsci anticipated a formulation that echoed Galbraith in its presumption of ongoing combat that resulted more in renegotiated status for the working class. Instead of Lenin's cadres biding their time in Zurich, each crisis of the social order would provide opportunities for organic leaders to contend for improved fortunes for their compatriots. Such enhanced lives seemed particularly capable of attainment during national crises, such as wars during which the aims of workers and bosses coalesced around the flag. In this way, nations might reallocate gains as though war prizes rather than admissions of past inequities. Possibly, neither Galbraith nor Gramsci would recognize their thoughts scattered like lint through these ruminations. In any case, their ideas have provided a prism though which to regard the adversarial relationships in Hollywood between studios and clientele, bosses and workers, censors and free thinkers.

Claiming only passing familiarity with these authors, I commend to the reader—in addition to Galbraith's *American Capitalism*—Albert Maria Cerese,

"Gramsci's Observations on Folklore," in Anne Showstack Sassoon, *Approaches to Gramsci* (1982); and Stuart Hall, "Gramsci's Relevance for the Study of Race and Ethnicity" in *Journal of Communications Inquiry* 10 (Summer 1986), 5–27.

For other essays (culled from hundreds) that link politics and popular culture, see particularly two wry-voiced surveys of criticism: Norman F. Cantor, *Twentieth Century Culture: Modernism to Deconstruction* (1972), and Noel Carroll, *Mystifying Movies: Fads and Fallacies in Contemporary Film Theory* (1988). In the latter book, see particularly the chapter on "Marxism and Psychoanalysis: The Althusserian-Lacanian Paradigm." For more on Louis Althusser, yet another extensor of Marx, see Stuart Hall, "Signification, Representations, Ideology: Althusser and Post-Structuralist Debates," *Critical Studies in Communication* 2 (June 1985); and Robert Sklar's "Oh! Althusser! Historiography and the Rise of Cinema Studies," *Radical History Review* 41 (1988): 10–35.

Regarding the political burdens carried by popular media, either subversively or dimly seen through alien times and cultures, the range of writing is broad. See, for example, Robert Stam, *Subversive Pleasures: [Mikhail] Bakhtin, Cultural Criticism, and Film* (1989). On popular culture in the service of the nation, see Daniel R. Headrick, *The Tools of Empire: Technology and European Imperialism in the Nineteenth Century* (1981), and, on behalf of a specific class, see Susan G. Davis, *Parades and Power: Street Theatre in Nineteenth-Century Philadelphia* (1986, 1988). For "other" meanings that, as Barbara Deming wrote, "flare through the fabric" of the medium, see John Fiske, "Television: Polysemy and Popularity," *Critical Studies in Mass Communication* 3 (Dec. 1986): 391–407, on the possibilities embedded in or drawn from *Hart to Hart*. For this "reader-response" criticism in another century, see Robert Darnton, *The Great Cat Massacre and Other Episodes in French Cultural History* (1984, 1985), on, for example, the political burdens of "Mother Goose" tales.

Along with many other theories of culture, those of Jürgen Habermas have found their way into movie criticism. See Miriam Hansen, *Babel & Babylon: Spectatorship in American Silent Film* (1985) for a careful working of it. For a similar line of argument set in a larger study, see Lizabeth Cohen, *Making a New Deal: Industrial Workers in Chicago, 1919-1939* (1990), and Roy Rosenzweig, *Eight Hours for What We Will: Workers and Leisure in an Industrial City, 1870-1920* (1983). Habermas himself may be read in English in the form of an encyclopedia piece reprinted in *New German Critique* 3 (Fall 1974): 49–55.

Other than Stuart Hall's adaptation of Gramsci to minorities, theoretical modeling as it applies to ethnicity and movies remains inside the covers of scholarly esoterica. Valuable for its attempt at a broadly catholic theoretical scaffolding is James Snead's "Recoding Blackness: The Visual Rhetoric of Black Independent Film," in *Whitney Museum of American Art: The New American Filmmakers Series,* program no. 23 (n.d.): 1–2. Colin MacCabe and Cornel West have edited Snead's posthumous book, *White Screens, Black Images: Hollywood from the Dark Side* (1994), which also anticipates an eventual "independent" black cinema.

The standard narrative histories include Donald Bogle, *Toms, Coons, Mulattoes, Mammies, and Bucks: An Interpretive History of Blacks in American Films* (1974); Daniel J. Leab, *From Sambo to Superspade: The Black Experience in Motion Pictures* (1975); Thomas Cripps, *Slow Fade to Black: The Negro in American Film, 1900-1942* (1977); and Cripps, *Making Movies Black: The Hollywood Message Movie from World War II to the Civil Rights Era* (1993). For an actual viewing of the documents, the reader should consult three videotapes: *Black Shadows on a Silver Screen* (*Post/Newsweek* TV, 1976); *Movies: The Popular Art of the Harlem Renaissance* (Smithsonian, 1984); and *Midnight Ramble* (Northern Lights, 1994).

The study of black audiences has only just begun. Gregory A. Waller's "Another Audience: Black Moviegoing, 1907–1916 [in Lexington]," *Cinema Journal* 31 (Winter 1992): 3–44; Mary Carbine's "The Finest Outside the Loop: Motion Picture Exhibition in Chicago's Black Metropolis, 1905–1928," *Camera Obscura,* no. 23 [May 1990]), 9–42; and Dan Streible's "The Harlem Theatre: Black Film Exhibition in Austin, Texas, 1920–1973," in Manthia Diawara, ed., *Black American Cinema* (1993), 221-36 anticipate a genre of such inquiry grounded in the localism called for in Allen and Gomery's *Film History.*

Almost every ethnic group is represented by a study of its treatment by Hollywood moviemakers, a genre that extends also to other groups—either self-described, such as homosexuals, or those described by a condition, such as deafness. African American images, however, have undergone a more profound scrutiny in the journal literature and one open to ongoing debate. For example, see the two essays on a 1926 black movie: Thomas Cripps, "'Race Movies' as Voices of the Black Bourgeoisie: *The Scar of Shame,*" in John E. O'Connor and Martin A. Jackson, eds., *American History/American Film: Interpreting the Hollywood Image* (1979); and Jane Gaines, "*The Scar of Shame*: Skin Color and Caste in Black Silent Melodrama," *Cinema Journal* 26 (Summer 1987): 3–21. This focus on individual films rather than on a canon extended to other disciplines as well, as in the case of Barbara A. Greadington's dissertation at Miami, *The Effect of Black Films on the Self-Esteem of Black Adolescents* (1977).

But the systematic inquiry into the aesthetics of ethnicity extended mainly to hopeful book titles—James P. Murray's *To Find an Image* (1973), for example—

that at their best analyzed only the more independently made black movies. The most recent dealing with Hollywood is Mark Reid's *Redefining Black Film* (1993).

The situation has been similar in the scholarly treatment of other ethnic group images. Generally, the literature has paid attention mainly to a descriptive mode of inquiry set in a decade-by-decade narrative. The few exceptions to this custom have been directed at the social history of American Indians and Jews. Two useful social histories of Jewish roles in Hollywood movies are Patricia Erens, *The Jew in American Cinema* (1984), and Lester D. Friedman, *Hollywood's Image of the Jew* (1982), both of which offer a sidebar inquiry into Yiddish movies. J. Hoberman's *Bridge of Light: Yiddish Film Between Two Worlds* (1991) broadened the research into those movies made for Yiddish-speaking audiences in Eastern Europe and in America while at the same time seeking a theoretical grounding in a proletarian version of Jürgen Habermas's "bürgerische Öffentlichkeit"—Oskar Negt and Alexander Kluge's sense of a proletarian public life that emerged during "rifts" such as war and revolution in the flow of history.

Indians were served by a more polemical literature that began with Gretchen M. Bataille and Charles L. P. Silet, *The Pretend Indians: Images of Native Americans in the Movies* (1980), and Ralph and Natasha Friar, *The Only Good Indian* (1972). Not until John O'Connor's catalog of a movie series at the New Jersey State Museum, *The Hollywood Indian: Stereotypes of Native Americans in Film* (1981), did scholarship override politics, a trend that continued in the emerging work of Angela Aleiss—for example, her "Native American: The Surprising Silents," *Cineaste*, 21, 3 (1995): 34–35.

If we may follow current practice and regard women as a minority, the literature that has come to the defense of women's interests has been considerable. With respect to movies, the literature followed the splash made by Betty Friedan's *Feminist Mystique* (1963) and the journalism of Gloria Steinem in the magazine *Ms*. In rapid succession came Marjorie Rosen's *The Popcorn Venus* (1973), Molly Haskell's *From Reverence to Rape: The Treatment of Women in the Movies* (1974), and the ur-tract by Laura Mulvey, "Visual Pleasure and the Narrative Cinema," *Screen* (autumn 1975). Rosen and Haskell played the role of discoverers of a heretofore inchoate history. "Gee whiz, look at this!" they seemed to say. To which Mulvey seemed to reply that histories they told were systemic in form and substance and that movies were driven by a "male gaze" that pointed the camera in ways that defined women as objects, perhaps even props, rather than characters.

The stream of literature that ensued was sporadic and often derivative but marked by occasional brilliance. Marsha McCreadie's *The Women Who Wrote the Movies: From Frances Marion to Nora Ephron* (1994) wrote of women as part of the genius of the system, a point taken also by Sharon Smith in her *Women Who Make Movies* (1975). But both were limited to revelations provided by interviews and published autobiographies. Brandon French's largely ahistorical *On the Verge of Revolt: Women in American Films of the Fifties* (1978) was similarly thin, but it at least focused on a narrow era. Compendia of essays filled the interstices: Karyn Kay and Gerald Peary's *Women and Their Cinema* (1979); Patricia Erens's *Sexual Stratagems* (1977); and E. Ann Kaplan's *Women in Film Noir* (1980, rev. ed.). The most scholarly of these was Mary Ann Doane, et al., *Re-Vision: Essays in Feminist Film Criticism* (1980), an AFI monograph. The most rigorous work so far is Michael Renov's *Hollywood's Wartime Woman: Representation and Ideology* (1988).

Inquiry into homosexuality in movies began with Parker Tyler's *Screening the Sexes* (1973), to be followed by Vito Russo's *The Celluloid Closet: Homosexuality in the Movies* (1981) and Richard Dyer's BFI pamphlet, *Gays and Film* (1980).

As for history itself, we begin with venerable books on the transition from stage to screen. C. W. Ceram's *Archaeology of the Cinema* (1965) and A. Nicholas Vardac's *Stage to Screen: Theatrical Method from Garrick to Griffith* (1949), the former about the physics of creating the illusion of motion, the latter about cross-pollination from stage to screen, remain useful. Two other books emphasize the place of the moving image on the cusp between eras of manual and dynamic energy usage: Erik Barnouw's *The Magician and the Cinema* (1981) and G. A. Household's graphic *To Catch a Sunbeam* (1979). For an institutional corporate history of the changeover; see Charles Musser's exhaustive *Before the Nickelodeon: Edwin S. Porter and the Edison Manufacturing Company* (1991). See also Robert C. Allen, *Vaudeville and Film, 1895-1915: A Study in Media Interaction* (1980), and Timothy Lyons, *The Silent Partner: The History of the American Film Manufacturing Company 1910-1921* (1974).

There is also a growing collection of essay literature, much of it anthologized. On the various preclassic narrative and spectacle forms, see for example Tom Gunning's piece on two versions of *The Life of an American Fireman* in John E. O'Connor's pathbreaking anthology/video, *Image as Artifact* (1990). In John L. Fell, ed., *Film before Griffith* (1983), see Raymond Fielding, "Hale's Tours: Ultrarealism in the Pre-1910 Motion Picture"; Edward Lowry, "Edwin J. Hadley: Traveling Film Exhibitor"; and Burnes St. Patrick Hollyman, "The First Picture Shows: Austin, Texas, 1894-1913." In Thomas Elsaesser, ed., *Early Cinema: Space, Frame, Narrative* (1990), see Gunning's "The Cinema of Attractions: Early Films, Its Spectator and the Avant-Garde" and contrast with Musser's aesthetic of early narrative movies. Also see Roger Holman, ed., *Cinema 1900-1906: An Analytical Study* (1982). And on the law read Ralph Cassady Jr., "Monopoly in Motion Picture Production and Distribution, 1908–1915," *Southern California Law Review* XXXII (1959).

Much of the literature I have cited as bearing on the neolithic era I have called "incunabula" has been mined by Eileen Bowser in *The Transformation of Cinema 1907-1915* (1990): Vol. Two in "History of American Cinema." Yet her book also reaches into the earliest days of the movies' migration to California—and to institutionalization. The richest testimony to this transformation is her decision to ground her research in a massive reading and citation of the emerging tradepapers, allowing the reader to gain the greatest sense possible of the growing normativeness of moviemaking practice in every aspect from script to screen.

Yet, because of the way I have organized this book, I would add a brief bibliography on international circumstances such as world war, diplomacy, trade rivalries, and nationalistic fears of Hollywood's threatening cultural hegemony. During the Great War, Hollywood's preeminent position in the world was assured both by the atrophying of the movie production of European belligerents and by government policies in America, first by the Department of State and later by the newly formed Department of Commerce. See, for example, Margaret Dickinson and Sarah Street's *Cinema and State: The Film Industry and the Government 1927-1984* (1985), chapters 1 through 3; Ian Jarvie's *Commerce versus Culture: International Film Trade in the North Atlantic Triangle, 1920-1950* (1994); and David W. Ellwood and Rob Kroes, eds., *Hollywood in Europe: Experiences of a Cultural Hegemony* (1994), from which I have drawn upon Richard Maltby and Ruth Vasey, "The International Language Problem: European Reactions to Hollywood's Conversions to Sound," who in turn used a quotation which I borrowed from David Morley and Kevin Roberts, "Spaces of Identity: Communications Technologies and the Reconfiguration of Europe," *Screen* 30 (Autumn 1989), 21.

For specifically American policies arising out of the commercial dysfunction brought on by the war, first see the studies of propaganda: Larry Wayne Ward, *The Motion Picture Goes to War: The U.S. Government Film Effort during World War I* (1985); Craig W. Campbell, *Reel America and World War I: A Comprehensive Filmography . . .* (1985); Stephen Vaughn, *Holding Fast the Inner Lines: Democracy, Nationalism, and the Committee on Public Information* (1980), particularly pp. 23–24 for CPI's apparent pitting of domestic progressivism against "Prussianism."

For extensions of the link between federal policy and commercialism, including movies, see Kristin Thompson, *Exporting Entertainment: America in the World Film Market, 1907-34* (1985), on the economics of UFA as well as the Germanification of the "Western" genre. For connections of movies to a general American cultural diplomacy, see Emily S. Rosenberg, *Spreading the American Dream: Economic and Cultural Expansion, 1890-1945* (1982). For a curious reference to George Creel, Chair to the CPI, boasting that "we can control world opinion," see Reinhold Wagnleiter, "American Cultural Diplomacy, the Cinema, and the Cold War in Central Europe," in Ellwood and Kroes, *Hollywood in Europe,* 199-210, in which Creel is cited as a character in Gore Vidal's novel *Hollywood.* A good piece on the thin article literature is Timothy J. Lyons, "Hollywood and World War I, 1914-1918" *Journal of Popular Film* 1 (1972): 25-27.

David Bordwell, Janet Staiger, and Kristin Thompson, *The Classical Hollywood Cinema: Film Style and Mode of Production to 1960* (1985), among others, argue that the maturing of an institutional "right way" of studio practice derived in part from published manuals and "how-to" books. For evidence, see Arthur S. Meloy, *Theatres and Motion Picture Houses* (1916); E. G. Lutz, *The Motion Picture Cameraman* (1927); Marguerite Bertsch, *How to Write for Moving Pictures* (1917); Victor Oscar Freeburg, *The Art of Photoplay Making* (1918); John Emerson and Anita Loos, *How to Write for Photoplays* (1921); Eustace Hale Ball, *Photoplay Scenarios* (1917); and Louella O. Parsons, *How to Write for the "Movies"* (1915).

For the beginnings of Hollywood economics and the judiciary, see Janet Staiger, "Combination and Litigation Structures of U.S. Film Distribution, 1896-1917," in Elsaesser, *Early Cinema,* 189-201. See also Cassady, "Monopoly in Motion Picture Production . . . "; and Bowser lists *A Compilation of Legal Agreements between the Motion Picture Patents Company and the Major Film Companies, 1898-1913* (1913), copy no. 7 in MOMA.

Perhaps the best introduction to Hollywood as a producer of popular art is Edward Wagenknecht's adoring treatment of *The Movies in the Age of Innocence* (1962). "Because its silence set it apart from the real world," he wrote, "the film was a created thing, integral and self-sufficient." (8)

In addition to the general works already cited, many general works take up the history of silent Hollywood. See, for example, the early essays in Tino Balio, ed., *The American Film Industry* (1976, 1984); Bordwell, et al., *The Classical Hollywood Cinema;* Thomas Schatz, *The Genius of the System: Hollywood Filmmaking in the Studio Era* (1988); Douglas Gomery, *The Hollywood Studio System* (1986); Thomas W. Bohn and Richard L. Stromgren, *Light and Shadows: A History of Motion Pictures* (1975); Douglas Gomery, *Movie History: A Survey* (1991); and Gerald Mast, *A Short History of the Movies* (1971). Although wider-ranging in style and substance, together they constitute a canon of the history of the Hollywood corporate medium.

Four approaches to the silent Hollywood era that range from the socio-political to the dramaturgical aspects of movies are William K. Everson, *American Silent Film* (1978), less personal than Wagenknecht yet equally driven by a deeply running fondness for movies; Kevin Brownlow's three volumes that represent an acutely intelligent adult's wise summation of a lifetime's love of movies, *The Parade's Gone By* (1968), *The War, the West, and the Wilderness* (1979), and *Behind the Mask of Innocence* (1990); Kay Sloan's *The Loud Silents: Origins of the Social Problem Film* (1988); and Miriam Hansen's *Babel & Babylon: Spectatorship in American Silent Film* (1991), challenging application of Habermas's notion of the politics of "public space."

Two useful collections of documents are Gerald Mast's survey, *The Movies in Our Midst: Documents in the Cultural History of Film in America* (1982), and, more pointedly focused on the silent era, George C. Pratt's *Spellbound in Darkness: Readings in the History and Criticism of the Silent Film* (1973).

The era of silent film has long deserved a synthesis of the emerging literature, much of which had been lost in a fugitive canon of serial essays. The richly researched volume that has earned a place as its era's definitive historical synthesis is Richard Koszarski's *An Evening's Entertainment: The Age of the Silent Feature Picture, 1915-1928* (1990), vol. III in Charles Harpole's *History of the American Cinema*. He has reached not only into the exhibitors' tradepapers that Eileen Bowser learned from in her *The Transformation of Cinema* but also into the emerging trades of the technical guilds, the fan magazines when at the height of their vogue, and the published biographical literature, as well as the studio archives that suddenly opened in the past twenty years (and, in some cases, as quickly closed again). The result was a book in the analytical *gestalt* style of Bordwell, Staiger, and Thompson's *Classical Hollywood Cinema,* yet with greater attention given to the aesthetic merits of the resulting films.

As we have seen, a smidgen of research has begun on the phenomenon of audience behavior—"spectatorship," in current cant—led by the inquiries into ghetto audiences by Gregory Waller, Mary Carbine, and Dan Streible. The general American audience has been the target of a similar scholarly inquiry. Indeed, in the form of quantitative studies of audience responses in the years between the world wars, psychologists at Iowa State and Ohio State Universities directed a number of graduate dissertations. Variations on their methods surfaced in such studies as Samuel Stouffer's *What the Soldier Thinks* during Would War II and in civilian studies such as Leo Handel's *Hollywood Looks at Its Audi-*

ence: A Report of Film Audience Research (1950); Henry James Forman's *Our Movie Made Children* (1935); and Edgar Dale, *Children's Attendance at Motion Pictures* (1933), volumes in the famous "Payne Fund" studies.

Since that time, scholars have treated audiences less empirically and more as atoms of psyche and society. A considerable body of writing has emerged from a group loosely bound by training or residence in the University of Wisconsin, which has correlated audiences with urban demography. Among these analyses are Russell Merritt's "Nickelodeon Theatres 1904–1914: Building an Audience for Movies," in Balio, *The American Film Industry;* Robert C. Allen's "Motion Picture Exhibition in Manhattan, 1906–1912: Beyond the Nickelodeon," in John Fell, ed., *Film before Griffith* (1983); Douglas Gomery's "Movie Audiences, Urban Geography, and the History of the American Film," *Velvet Light Trap* no. 19 (1982): 23–29; and Gomery's "Saxe Amusement Enterprises: The Movies Come to Milwaukee," *Milwaukee History* 2, 2 (Spring 1979): 18–28. Similar studies of many locales may be found in Bruce Austin's two compendia, "Film Audience Research, 1960–1980: An Annotated Bibliography," *Journal of Popular Film and Television* 8, 2 (Spring 1980): 53–80, and " . . . An Update," *JPFT* 8, 4 (Winter 1980–81): 57–59; and in his *Immediate Seating: A Look at Movie Audiences* (1989). See also John Izod's *Hollywood and the Box Office, 1895-1986* (1988).

In addition to these studies based upon the demographics of urban history, another line of inquiry into audiences has a psychological angle. The two most socially analytical works on silent film audiences emerge from entirely different angles. Hansen's *Babel & Babylon* is self-consciously theory-driven, most particularly by Habermas, while Lary L. May's *Screening Out the Past: The Birth of Mass Culture and the Motion Picture Industry* (1980) takes up the institutional, even magisterial, role of movies in everyday life as seen, for example, in the impact on stores of both magazines and books that taught a sort of secular hedonism espoused by movie stars.

Soundfilm audiences continued to be the subject of social inquiry into the effects of movies in such works as the "Payne Fund" studies. But also there were fewer accusatory works that emphasized market research (such as the work of Leo Handel in his *Hollywood Looks at Its Audience*), the purer, academic forms of the genre (such as Margaret Farrand Thorp's *America at the Movies* [1946]), or the psychology of reception (such as Martha Wolfenstein and Nathan Leites's *Movies: A Psychological Study* [1950]).

More recently, the serial literature allows us to anticipate a spate of books on the audience as linked to other popular culture media and the specific impact of these media on the moviegoer as consumer in a "commodified culture." See, for example, Gaylyn Studlar, "The Perils of Pleasure? Fan Magazine Discourse as Women's Commodified Culture in the 1920s," *Wide Angle* 13 (Jan. 1991), 6–33; and Jeanne Allen, "The Film Viewer as Consumer," *Quarterly Review of Film Studies* 5 (Fall 1980), 481–97. Many of the surveys of movie history—Jowett's *Film* and Sklar's *Movie-Made America*, for example—include tabular data on the incidence of moviegoing, the proportion of disposable income spent on it, and other social data.

Another thread of new inquiry follows a course taken in a literature that studies moviegoing as a trait of a certain class or group, much as Waller has done for African Americans in Lexington, Kentucky. See, for example, Roy Rosenzweig, *Eight Hours for What We Will: Workers and Leisure in an Industrial City, 1870–1920* (1983); and Lizabeth Cohen, *Making a New Deal: Industrial Workers in Chicago, 1919–1939* (1990). In each case, the life that workers made for themselves off the job is a dimension of a rounded image. Less central and less political, the Depression-era audience in Andrew Bergman's *We're in the Money: Depression America and Its Films* (1971) is portrayed seeking both "escapist" and success-driven movies.

The literature on movie censorship has been enriched by generations of witty journalism, memoirs, and polemics—all of it so persuasive that serious scholars for years borrowed from it and quoted it as reliable. Every student of the social history of movies has at least skimmed Raymond Moley's *The Hays Office* (1945); Morris L. Ernst and Pare Lorentz's *Censored: The Private Life of the Movie* (1930); Ruth Inglis's *Freedom of the Movies: A Report on Self-Regulation* (1947); Murray Schumach's *The Face on the Cutting Room Floor: The Story of Movie and Television Censorship* (1964); and Jack Vizzard's *See No Evil: Life Inside a Hollywood Censor* (1970).

The first generation of scholarly attention to censorship took up its legal aspects, particularly constitutionality. See the two best: Ira Carmen, *Movies, Censorship, and the Law* (1966); and Richard S. Randall, *Censorship of the Movies* (1968). Thereafter, even up to the present time, the censoring of sexual depictions that were often taken as synonymous with pornography consumed the attention of most scholars, not only from a legal angle but from the point of view of activists such as the Roman Catholic Legion of Decency. See, for example, Paul W. Facey's *The Legion of Decency: A Sociological Analysis of the Emergence and Development of a Social Pressure Group* (1974).

Gradually, the literature shifted to a social angle, sometimes still rooted in erotica and the law, but gradually shifting, as well, to more recent leftist concerns such as feminism. See, for example, Edward de Grazia and Roger K. Newman's

Banned Films: Movies, Censors, and the First Amendment (1982); Robert Fisher's "Film Censorship and Progressive Reform: The National Board of Censorship of Motion Pictures, 1909–1922," *Journal of Popular Film* 4 (1975); Annette Kuhn's *Cinema, Censorship, and Sexuality, 1909-1925* (1988); Leonard J. Leff and Jerold L. Simmons's *The Dame in the Kimono: Hollywood, Censorship, and the Production Code from the 1920s to the 1960s* (1990); and Lea Jacobs's *The Wages of Sin: Censorship and the Fallen Woman Film, 1928-1942* (1991).

More recently—indeed, currently—still other scholars have been working on an integrated inquiry into censorship and society. The original works are Gregory D. Black, *Hollywood Censored: Morality Codes, Catholics, and Movies* (1994); and Richard Maltby, "The Production Code and the Hays Office," in Tino Balio, *Grand Design: Hollywood as a Modern Business Enterprise, 1930-1939* (1993), 37–72. In addition to these monographs, Gerald C. Gardner has drawn letters from the Will Hays papers into a compendium of primary sources, *The Censorship Papers: Movie Censorship Letters from the Hays Office, 1934 to 1968* (1987). The serial literature includes Garth Jowett, "A Capacity for Evil: The 1915 Supreme Court Mutual Decision," *Historical Journal of Film, Radio, and Television* 10 (1990): 3–31; and Stephen Vaughn, "Morality and Entertainment: The Origins of the Motion Picture Production Code," *Journal of American History* 77 (June 1990): 39–65.

The historiography of the advent of sound falls short of the productivity generated by the history of censorship. In the beginning, the journalistic literature appeared promising, what with Frederic Thrasher's celebratory *Okay for Sound* (1946) and Fitzhugh Green's *The Film Finds Its Tongue* (1929). But not until Harry M. Geduld's *The Birth of the Talkies: From Edison to Jolson* (1975) did a reputed scholar take up the topic, and not until Alexander Walker's *The Shattered Silents* (1979) did a popular writer join in.

Thereafter, the literature reposed in essay format in a dedicated issue of *Yale French Studies* (1980); Rick Altman's anthology, *Sound Theory, Sound Practice* (1992); and a clutch of essays by Douglas Gomery, written in a characteristic style in which economic practices set a sociotechnical agenda. In *Film and History*, he cites his own "Economic Struggle and Hollywood Imperialism: Europe Converts to Sound" in the cited *Yale French Studies;* "Tri-Ergon, Tobis Klangfilm, and the Coming of Sound," *Cinema Journal* 16 (Fall 1976): 51–61; and "Problems in Film History: How Fox Innovated Sound," *Quarterly Review of Film Studies* 1 (August 1976): 315–30; and his "The Coming of Talkies: Invention, Innovation, and Diffusion," in Tino Balio, ed., *The American Film Industry* (1976).

I should mention that I have neglected other technologies because their eventual fruition occurred after the end of the scope of this book. A significant body of work on widescreen, faster film, three-dimensional imagery, sound of higher fidelity, and color film has paralleled the writings on the history of sound, but much of the impact of these innovations was not felt until after World War II— that is, after the era of high classical Hollywood. Few general works exist and fewer still approach a quality that might merit a title such as that of Raymond Fielding's anthology of tradepaper pieces, *A Technological History of Motion Pictures and Television* (1967).

Save for a single issue of the Pool Films' magazine, *Close Up*, in the summer of 1929 and Peter Noble's *The Negro in Films* (1948), scholars and critics were all but silent on the subject of the films of "others." For more recent studies, the reader may return to the beginning of this essay, where I have take up the "other" under the rubric of "theories." Current writing on the subject of otherness, particularly with respect to race and ethnicity, has taken another tack. Rather than focusing mainly on Hollywood as a monopolist creator of imagery whose products have shoved ethnicity to the margins of the marketplace, students have taken up "independent" films. This division, at least in the literature if not the movies themselves, has been most evident in the treatment of African American imagery.

Almost every attempt at some genuine, sympathetic, and most importantly, untrammeled, treatment of homosexuals, for example, has arisen from a small circle of independents who aimed at titillating in-group sexual desires. If it ever crossed their minds to reach further toward some other in-group sensibility, the teetering on the edge of pornography that many of their clientele preferred precluded it. As for Hollywood, the mincing style of Franklin Pangborn or Eric Blore, the "buddy" relationships that bonded pairs of women or men, and other slivers of covert meaning provided Hollywood's only fare. Similarly, the stream of "women's pictures," or "weepies" as *Variety* called them, constituted Hollywood's offering to feminism. *Miss Lulu Bett, Stella Dallas, So Proudly We Hail, Magnificent Obsession*—the bringing to bear of excess melodrama to appeal to women's presumed tastes was so formulated as to constitute a genre. A few B-movies by Ida Lupino and Dorothy Arzner, along with a handful of biopics such as *Madame Curie*, filled out the inventory. Thus the literature, until recent times, also remained thin.

On the other hand, African American film for almost a quarter of a century has benefitted from literature that recognized a clearly *separate* audience.

A much debated issue among the critics is the extent of this apartness. In 1978, in *Black Film as Genre*, I argued that to study black film as a thing apart required a looseness of definition. Not to do so risked creating such "a fine pinpoint

[that] we should argue forever over who has the right to dance on the head of the pin." Rather, I preferred to begin with "those motion pictures made for theatre distribution that have a black producer, director, and writer, or black performers; that speak to black audiences or, incidentally, to white audiences possessed of preternatural curiosity, attentiveness, or sensibility toward racial matters; and that emerge from self-conscious intentions, whether artistic or political, to illuminate the Afro-American experience."

The search ensued for some aesthetic formulation that either challenged this assertion or reframed it in a way that broke with Hollywood convention. The least persuasive efforts have argued that necessity was the mother of invention. That is to say, the shoestring adversity of black filmmaking, rather than the creative genius of the filmmaker, defined the aesthetic quality of the medium.

Other voices, such as Teshome Gabriel and Clyde Taylor in their essays in Mbye B. Cham and Claire Andrade-Watkins's *Blackframes: Critical Perspectives on Black Independent Cinema* (1988), propose a historical metaphor, an echo of Jewish collective history—the sense of nomadic diaspora that defined a group character that was caught in movies. A tentative, yet booklength, analysis, Mark A. Reid's *Redefining Black Film* (1993) argues not so much from the nature of movies but rather from their place in a multiracial society that locates creative power "within the polyphonic nature of reception and which permits dialogue within any genre, between genres, and among the viewers of African-American film." Speaking mainly of "black womanist film reception," by which he means something like "feminist," Reid suggests possible outcomes of the dialogue between audience and maker: "assimilation, resistance, and accommodation," each mode an attitude taken by the viewer toward the authority, vision, and the aesthetics of a movie—reader-response definition of value, if you will. Two other books, both as analytical but less "high-church" on the subject of the separateness of black film, set forth a wider range of readings of African Americans in movies: Manthia Diawara, ed., *Black American Cinema* (1993); and Ed Guerrero, *Framing Blackness: The African American Image in Film* (1993), the former an anthology, the latter focused on so-called "blaxploitation" films but also extending to the present.

As we have seen, the shaping of Hollywood into an institutionalized studio system continued through the 1920s, peaking in the ensuing decade. Surely in that era, the outward signs of such establishmentarianism could be seen in the trappings of publicity and stardom. See the literature of the ancillary aspects of movie-making: George Eells, *Hedda and Louella: A Dual Biography of Hedda Hopper and Louella Parsons* (1972); Martin Levin, ed., *Hollywood and the Great*

Fan Magazines (1971); Richard Dyer, *Stars* (1979); Edgar Morin, *The Stars* (1960); and such serial literature as Maria LaPlace, "Bette Davis and the Ideal of Consumption: A Look at *Now Voyager,*" *Wide Angle* 6 (1985): 34-43. More recent scholarship presses the notion of "system" still further, as in Richard DeCordova's *Picture Personalities: The Emergence of the Star System in America* (1990).

At the same time the postwar literature grew more specialized and more tightly focused and was no longer rooted in the journalists' sweeping surveys of "the liveliest art." Instead, scholars of all disciplines followed the leads of a handful of prewar and wartime researchers, such as the editors of *Fortune,* who devoted several issues from 1935-37 to individual analyses of studios, and the editors of *The Annals of the American Academy of Political and Social Sciences,* who gave two full issues in 1926 and 1947 to essays on the industry. On the eve of World War II, investigations were taken up by the Congress and the Department of Justice as part of an eventual antitrust suit, a happenstance that provided hundreds of pages of data for future scholars—for example, Mae Dena Heuttig, *Economic Control of the Motion Picture Industry* (1944); and Michael Conant, *Antitrust in the Motion Picture Industry* (1960).

The drive toward ever more scholarly specialization may be seen in the recent crop of new works. Balio's *Grand Design* (1993) enriched an earlier popular genre of decade studies of the entire industry. Ben M. Hall's *The Best Remaining Seats: The Golden Age of the Movie Palace* (1988) reopened interest in moviehouses themselves, anticipating Douglas Gomery's *Shared Pleasures: A History of Movie Presentation in the United States* (1992). Michele Hilmes's *Hollywood and Broadcasting: From Radio to Cable* (1990) looked into a neglected intramedia history. The breadth of inquiry seemed endless: there were books on movie acting, technology, the place of writers in the system, film music as an aspect of creativity, and an ever-flowing fount of how-to-make-it-in-Hollywood books, astrologies of the stars, and various genres of scandal-mongering that might have drawn a blush from Kenneth Anger, the author of the first of the form, *Hollywood Babylon* (1975). Beginning this latter rage for inside dope were two venerable books by recognized authors: Hortense Powdermaker, *Hollywood, the Dream Factory: An Anthropologist Looks at the Movie-Makers* (1950), and Leo C. Rosten, *Hollywood: The Movie Colony, the Movie-Makers* (1941).

Note, also, that the literature reflects a persistent scholarly concern for the interaction between screen and society, art and life. One of the most imaginative such books is Robert B. Ray's *A Certain Tendency of the Hollywood Cinema, 1930-1980* (1985). Dozens of critics have found ideologies covertly or unconsciously embedded in Hollywood movies, but Ray has shown a cozy, lineal relationship between movies and society over three crucial decades. Moreover, he finds endless reassertions of themes he traces back to such colonial genres as Pilgrim captivity tales.

Nick Roddick has taken up a similar thread in his *A New Deal in Entertainment: Warner Brothers in the 1930s* (1983), but one grounded more in the studio archives where conventional historical documentation reasserts its authority after a generation of challenges to the semiological, ephemeral flimsiness of documents by Wittgenstein, Eco, and other scholars. Here we might list scores of ably done, if less rigorously searched, studio biographies, and for that matter biographies of "the moguls" who ran the studios as fiefs. But the standard bibliographies in Allen and Gomery's *Film History,* Bordwell's *The Classical Hollywood Cinema,* and a new work, just out by Richard Maltby and Ian Craven, entitled *Hollywood Cinema: An Introduction* (1995), contain entries that cite all such literature in redundant detail. Thus, every bibliography, however "selected," will include the many useful standards ranging from compendia of memoranda, such as Rudy Behlmer, ed., *Memo from: David O. Selznick* (1972), through studio histories by Behlmer, Bernard F. Dick, Bob Thomas, Richard Schickel, and scores of others.

If a reader wished to pursue the history of a particular film, director, or writer, the list of relevant books and essays is daunting. A curious reader would be best served by consulting the fuller bibliographies in the major works as well as the annual compendia of serial literature. For instance, for generalized research on a given director, three handy works are Andrew Sarris, *The American Cinema: Directors and Directions, 1929-1968* (1968), and Richard Koszarski, *Hollywood Directors 1914-1940* (1976), and his *Hollywood Directors 1941-1976* (1977).

Genre films, a historical form that has been codified by usage over time, not only supplied the formulas of the B movies that earned the studio's weekly bread and butter but gave texture, historicity, and creative energy to many major movies. Every book worth its salt includes a chapter on the phenomenon of the movie that earns its grosses by imitating its forebears yet taking some new turn of imagination—"the same only different," in Hollywood cant. Some monographs focus their entire attention on the genre and its place in both the art and the system of Hollywood. See, for example, Stuart M. Kaminsky, *American Film Genres: Approaches to a Critical Theory of Popular Film* (1974), and Thomas Schatz, *Hollywood Genres: Formulas, Filmmaking, and the Studio System* (1981). The best assemblage of theoretical essays is Barry Keith Grant's *Film Genre Reader* (1986), a compendium of a dozen-and-a-half of the most thoughtful critics. A more *outre* collection is Todd McCarthy and Charles Flynn's *Kings of the Bs: Working within the Hollywood System* (1975). And a *sui generis* personal view of the films of an era, which sheds light on the place of genre films in the Hollywood canon, is Barbara Deming's *Running Away from Myself: A Dream Portrait of America Drawn from the Films of the Forties* (1969). While not concerned exclusively with genre film, Ray's *A Certain Tendency of the Hollywood Cinema* takes up ritual, redundant worrying of themes such as the savagery-versus-civilization thread running through westerns.

Almost every genre—the action and adventure yarn, the western, the musical, the screwball comedy, the melodrama, the musical, the urban forms of film noir and gangster movies—has acquired its own canon of criticism. Among the most useful works are Rick Altman's book, *The American Film Musical* (1987); Jane Feuer's *The Hollywood Musical* (1982); Will Wright's *Six Guns and Society: A Structural Study of the Western* (1975); John L. Lenihan's *Showdown: Confronting Modern America in the Western Film* (1980); Stanley Cavell's *Pursuits of Happiness: The Hollywood Comedy of Remarriage* (1981); James Harvey's *Romantic Comedy in Hollywood* (1987); Mary Ann Doane's *The Desire to Desire: The Woman's Films of the 1940s* (1987); James B. Twitchell's *Dreadful Pleasures: An Anatomy of Modern Horror* (1988); Andrew Tudor's *Monsters and Mad Scientists: A Cultural History of the Horror Movie* (1989); Richard Maltby's "Film Noir: The Politics of the Maladjusted Text," *Journal of American Studies* XVII (1984): 49-71; George F. Custen's *Bio/Pics: How Hollywood Constructed Public History* (1992); and Thomas Patrick Doherty's *Teenagers and Teenpics* (1988). In addition to such analytical works as these, every genre has drawn the attention of listmakers and compilers, and sometimes practitioners such as John Ford and Alfred Hitchcock have been scrutinized as authors of a personal genre. Finally, some authors have treated recurring thematic material, often narrow in scope or brief in timespan, as though the films in question constituted a genre. See, for example, John E. O'Connor's *The Hollywood Indian* (1980); Thomas Cripps's *Black Film as Genre* (1979); and Jeanine Basinger's *The World War II Combat Film: Anatomy of a Genre* (1986).

The definitive work, so far, on World War II and the process of American moviemaking remains Clayton R. Koppes and Gregory D. Black, *Hollywood Goes to War: How Politics, Profits, and Propaganda Shaped World War II Movies* (1987). While less focused on movies, George H. Roeder Jr.'s *The Censored War: American Visual Experience during World War II* (1993) also rigorously studies the place of visual imagery in wartime. For a view of an ethnic group as affected by wartime on film, see Cripps, *Making Movies Black*. For a broader sweep, see Thomas Patrick Doherty, *Projections of War: Hollywood, American Culture, and World War II* (1993).

Bibliographical Essay

Bibliographies seem almost redundant in their dutiful recording of the many books on Hollywood and World War II. Many of them are little more than picture books or compendia of plot outlines. After Koppes and Black, and Doherty, the best books tend to analyze war movies as a genre. See, for example, Basinger, *The World War II Combat Film*; Bernard F. Dick, *The Star-Spangled Screen: The American World War II Film* (1985); Richard A. Maynard, ed., *Propaganda on Film: A Nation at War* (1975); Michael Renov, *Hollywood's Wartime Woman: Representation and Ideology* (1988); Lawrence H. Suid, *Guts and Glory: Great American War Movies* (1978); and Allen L. Woll, *The Hollywood Musical Goes to War* (1983). The periodical literature may be found cited in Koppes and Black, *Hollywood Goes to War,* and in Robert Fyne, *The Hollywood Propaganda of World War II* (1994). Film as seen from the angle of a government agency may be found in a briefer form in Allan M. Winkler, *The Politics of Propaganda: The Office of War Information, 1942-1945* (1978).

The decline of the old Hollywood was accompanied by a wrenching political struggle that extended not only through the ranks of Hollywood but into the committee rooms of the U.S. Congress. See, for example, Nancy Lynn Schwartz, *The Hollywood Writers' Wars* (1982); Edward L. Barrett Jr., *The Tenney Committee: Legislative Investigation of Subversive Activities in California* (1951), a rather soft look at the era; Robert Vaughn, *Only Victims: A Study of Show Business Blacklisting* (1972), a curiously spineless view by an actor; and two leftist angles in Victor S. Navasky, *Naming Names* (1981); and Larry Ceplair and Steven Englund, *The Inquisition in Hollywood: Politics in the Film Community, 1930-1960* (1983).

On the Paramount "divorcement" case, see the durable Michael Conant, *Antitrust in the Motion Picture Industry: Economic and Legal Analysis* (1960). Events in Hollywood institutional and artistic history thereafter are scattered among a broad, often uneven, terrain of literature. Among the better entries are Ethan Mordden's *Medium Cool: The Movies of the 1960s* (1990); Tino Balio's collection, *Hollywood in the Age of Television* (1990); Jackie Byars's *All That Hollywood Allows: Re-reading Gender in 1950s Melodrama* (1991); Timothy Corrigan's *A Cinema without Walls: Movies and Culture after Vietnam* (1991); Brandon French's treatment of tentative change in women's roles, *On the Verge of Revolt: Women in American Films of the Fifties* (1978); and an inquiry into postwar shifts in black roles, Mark A. Reid's *Redefining Black Film* (1993).

A literature on technological history is emerging. See, for example, Richard Hincha, "Selling CinemaScope: 1953–1956," *Velvet Light Trap* xxi (Summer 1985):

44–53; Hilmes's *Hollywood and Broadcasting*; and John Belton's work on CinemaScope, culminating in his *Widescreen Cinema* (1992).

Finally, the biographies and career chronicles of the creators of movies—writers, directors, producers, and performers—genres that require extreme caution in their use, are handily accessible by consulting more detailed bibliographies as well as the indexes of serials. "Biographies" of classical movies, such as *Casablanca* and *Gone with the Wind*, may be readily found in the extant lists and indexes, as may the volumes of journalism, reviews, and such, which are frequently cited.

Index

Index

Index

OTHER TITLES IN THE SERIES:

LIBRARY OF CONGRESS CATALOGING-IN-PUBLICATION DATA
Cripps, Thomas.
  Hollywood's high noon : moviemaking and society before television / Thomas
Cripps.
     p.   cm.—(The American moment)
  Includes bibliographical references and index.
  ISBN 0-8018-5315-X (hc : alk. paper).—ISBN 0-8018-5316-8 (pbk. : alk. paper)
  1. Motion pictures—Social aspects—United States.   2. Motion pictures—United
States—History.   I. Title.   II. Series.
PN1995.9.S6C73   1997
302.23'43.0973—dc20   96-18689